P9-DEN-469

THE
COSMIC
DANCERS

Also by Amit Goswami:

THE CONCEPTS OF PHYSICS

THE

COSMIC

DANCERS

Exploring
the Physics of
Science Fiction

by AMIT GOSWAMI

with MAGGIE GOSWAMI

1817

HARPER & ROW, PUBLISHERS, New York

Cambridge, Philadelphia, San Francisco
London, Mexico City, São Paulo, Sydney

UNION COLLEGE LIBRARY
BARBOURVILLE, KY. 40906

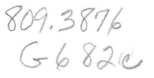

809.3876
G682c

To Kate Wilhelm and Damon Knight
and to the memory of John W. Campbell

Permissions acknowledgments appear on p. 291.

THE COSMIC DANCERS. Copyright © 1983 by Amit Goswami. All rights reserved. Printed in the United States of America. No part of this book may be used or reproduced in any manner whatsoever without written permission except in the case of brief quotations embodied in critical articles and reviews. For information address Harper & Row, Publishers, Inc., 10 East 53rd Street, New York, N.Y. 10022. Published simultaneously in Canada by Fitzhenry & Whiteside Limited, Toronto.

FIRST EDITION

Designed by Ruth Bornschlegel

Library of Congress Cataloging in Publication Data

Goswami, Amit.
  The cosmic dancers.

  Bibliography: p.
  Includes index.
  1. Science fiction—History and criticism.
2. Literature and science.   I. Goswami, Maggie.
II. Title.
PN3433.8.G67   1983   809.3'876   82-48118
ISBN 0-06-015083-1

83 84 85 86 87 10 9 8 7 6 5 4 3 2 1

UNION COLLEGE LIBRARY
BARBOURVILLE, KY 40906

Acknowledgments

We are grateful to many people. At best, this is only a partial list.

First and foremost, thanks to Kate Wilhelm and Damon Knight, who have been instrumental in many different ways in the writing of this book. We won't count the ways.

Thanks to Michael Coan, whose enthusiasm for science fiction has rubbed off on us over the years. The rubbing must have been good to produce this effect.

Thanks to our wonderful friends, who by their comments and love have made this project worthwhile, especially Fleetwood Bernstein, Ed Black, Gery Marino-Black, Rosemarie Hazen, Mary Ann Francis, Nicholas Chrones, Larry Brown . . .

Thanks to our colleague, Carolin Keutzer, whose patience with our beginner's psychology has been phenomenal, and to our biologist collaborator, David Clark. Some of our ideas on brain-mind germinated during my collaboration with these two people. We are immensely grateful.

Thanks to Gordon Aubrecht and Nilendra Deshpande, our physicist friends, for a careful reading of the manuscript. Of course, if any mistakes remain, they do not share in the responsibility.

Thanks to Ram Dass, John Lilly, and Ian Stuart for helping us understand some of the very difficult areas of experience reported here.

Thanks to Carol Brandt for her efforts on our behalf. Thanks to artist Dan Steffan for his faithful and enthusiastic artwork, which often was even better than we asked. Thanks to Buz Wyeth, Terry Karten, and all the others at Harper & Row without whose help this production would not have materialized.

Finally, thanks to all the dancers—the physicists and the science fiction students, the science fiction writers and the enthusiasts, and all the other participants in the dance. That includes practically everybody on earth, doesn't it? We might as well end these acknowledgments by thanking our unitive consciousness.

Amit Goswami
Maggie Goswami

Contents

Foreword

by Kate Wilhelm

I met Amit and Maggie over six years ago. My ignorance was so transparent about Amit's world of physics that I knew it would take only moments for him to gauge it, and no doubt dismiss me. But strangely, for months, although we spent many evenings together, we did not talk about physics at all. Our conversations ranged over all of science fiction, which he knew better than I, to parapsychology, the mysteries of consciousness, eastern mysticism, the collective unconscious. We talked about world events and local elections, finance, war, the women's rights movement. In short, we talked about everything that people everywhere are interested in.

Amit and Maggie are vitally involved in the world and everything in it. They like this world, take joy in exploring its many avenues.

Eventually it came out, of course, that in my mind physics was firmly linked to trying to move objects up inclined planes, trying to stop movement already started, or trying to start an object that did not want to move. The very name of the new physics, quantum mechanics, made my eyes glaze over, made me think instantly of three other things I had to do right now.

I had tried, sometimes even conscientiously, to follow articles about physics, but always, at the first page filled with mathematics that dazed me, I had put it aside for later when I would have more time.

Over the years, with patience and good humor, Amit has answered my questions about physics, not with math that I cannot follow, but in language that is accessible and lucid.

I would not pretend to know physics now, but at least I know why it is exciting. Amit's eyes gleam and his accent becomes more pronounced as he rushes through the words that are both a barrier and a threshold to the sharing of the speculations his field is investigating. The main ideas of human thought are converging. Physics, psychology, philosophy, religion—they form a web, each strand of which leads to a center where they fuse into one another and no one of them can be considered separately.

It is stimulating to talk to Amit about these weighty matters, but, more, it is fun. He and Maggie have brought this same stimulation and fun together in this book. If you already know physics, you will like following their meanders through the stories to show where the science could work and where it could not. If you don't know physics, I can think of no better way, no way more enjoyable, than following the reasoning here to grasp the basics of physics. The stories range from robotics to black holes to alterations in consciousness, but, as Amit would say, "Never mind. Look, it's really very simple." It is. And great fun.

chapter one

What the Dance Is

Perhaps you can recall, no doubt easily and with pleasure, moments reading science fiction when you felt swept into the action, dipping and leaping into the cosmic music. In those moments (regardless of whether in general you are most intrigued by its science, scenarios, or futurology), you resonate to the rhythm of the dance science fiction choreographs between science and reality. Not all fiction is so captivating, or gives us the entire universe for a stage. What is special about science fiction?

With occasional exceptions, readers of science fiction intuitively have no problem distinguishing a science fiction work from other forms of literature. But when it comes to a formal definition, they would give many answers, few of them in consonance. If you think that writers of science fiction would do better (after all, they create the stuff), or critics (since they make a living defining it), reconsider. Here is a sample of their disparate wisdom:

A handy short definition of almost all science fiction might read: realistic speculation about possible future events, based solely on adequate knowledge of the real world, past and present, and on a thorough understanding of the scientific method. To make this definition cover all science fiction, it is necessary only to strike out the word 'future.' [Robert A. Heinlein, author]

Science fiction is a branch of fantasy identifiable by the fact that it eases the 'willing suspension of disbelief' on the part of its readers by utilizing an atmosphere of scientific credibility for its imaginative speculations in physical science, space, time, social science, and philosophy. [Sam Moskowitz, anthologist]

Science fiction is that class of prose narrative treating of a situation that could not arise in the world we know, but which is hypothesized on the basis of some innovations in science and technology, or pseudoscience and pseudotechnology, whether human or extraterrestrial in origin. [Kingsley Amis, critic]

These are all fine definitions, except of course that (a) they don't agree with each other and (b) if we demanded all these criteria from writers, then only author Brian Aldiss' definition would be correct: "science fiction doesn't exist."

Damon Knight, who is both a writer and a critic of science fiction, understands this situation perfectly. Since he also possesses a thorough, analytical sort of mind, he makes a list (all encompassing?) of promising definitional components; according to Knight, science fiction is about:

1. Science
2. Technology and invention
3. The future and the remote past, including all time travel stories
4. Extrapolation
5. Scientific method
6. Other places—planets, dimensions, etc.—including visitors from such places
7. Catastrophes, natural and man-made

Knight proposes that if a story contains three or more of the above elements, we call it science fiction, otherwise not.

Knight's definition is a perfect example of how far a logical reductionistic approach can take you. But fiction isn't logical, not even science fiction; thus you can go only so far with logic and classification. So, after all that, even Knight hasn't told us what science fiction is really about, what its dance is.

Let me say what I think the dance is. Science, especially today's science, is a very big affair in which individual imagination soon ceases to find suitable vents. Thus most practitioners of science become like bricklayers, laying brick upon brick atop this mammoth structure that we call science, but very few have any idea where (if anywhere) it is going. In short, everybody becomes so busy laying bricks that they forget why they are doing it. They become so content with the evolution of the structure that nobody remembers that sometimes what is necessary is not *evolution* but *revolution*, a genuine shift from the currently accepted supertheory (or paradigm—to use philosopher Thomas Kuhn's word). Science fiction reminds us of these revolutions that science is also about. Although science fiction does not itself produce a paradigm shift, it keeps telling us when one is needed. Thus I will add one more definition to the already large list:

Science fiction is that class of fiction which contains the currents of change in science and society. It concerns itself with the critique, extension, revision, and conspiracy of revolution, all directed against static scientific paradigms. Its goal is to prompt a paradigm shift to a new view that will be more responsive and true to nature.

Obviously its job never ends.

This book is about science fiction and the possibilities for change that science fiction promotes. Mostly these possibilities revolve about two noble frontiers of human activity: space travel and adventures in consciousness. Traditionally, when speaking of the physics of science fiction, the former has received the lion's share of attention. However, recent advances in physics, notably quantum mechanics, the theoretical framework for the motion of sub-microscopic particles, have suggested a framework for science fiction's portrayals of such paranormal phenomena as telepathy. These advances, along with current developments in the area of consciousness research, may very well contribute to a paradigm shift. Thus, happily, I can give a full measure of attention to the scientific basis not only of tales of space travel, but also of those involving expanded consciousness capabilities as well.

SCENARIO STORIES

One recurrent practice in this book is to use scenarios from various science fiction stories to reveal the basic discipline of the dance, the physical laws. In order to extend the rules successfully, you first must know them. To expand your view of reality beyond what is known, you must begin with the known.

Science fiction writers are often at their best in introducing the rules of the game. Witness the following quotation from Jules Verne's *Twenty Thousand Leagues Under the Sea;* the narrator and his assistant, Ned, are talking about an undersea object they are investigating (which turns out to be the *Nautilus,* the submarine that is the real hero of this book):

". . . it must be built in some incredibly powerful way."

"Why?" Ned asked.

"Because incalculable strength is needed to stay at great depths and withstand the pressure there."

"Really?" said Ned, blinking.

"Yes, and I could give you some figures to prove it easily."

"Oh, figures!" answered Ned. "You can make figures do whatever you want."

"Perhaps in business, Ned, but not in mathematics. Now listen. The pressure of one atmosphere is represented by a column of water thirty two feet* high. In actual fact, the column of water would not be that high, because here we're dealing with sea water which has a greater density than fresh water. Well, now, Ned, when you dive down into the sea, for every thirty two feet of water between you and the surface, your body is supporting an additional pressure of one atmosphere, or in other words of 14.7 pounds per square inch of surface. It follows that at 320 feet this pressure is equal to ten atmospheres, a hundred atmospheres at 3200 feet, and a thousand atmospheres at 32,000 feet or about six miles. This is the same as saying that if you could reach such a depth in the ocean, your body would undergo a pressure of 14,700 pounds per square inch. Now, Ned, do you know how many square inches there are on the surface of your body?"

"I have no idea, Monsieur Aronnax."

"About two thousand six hundred."

"That many?" [*Science Fiction,* p. 198]

Most stories of this kind (including this one, of course) use the science just

---

*A slight mistake here; it should be thirty-four feet.

to provide a setting, a background for an intense human interest story; the writers are not simply being altruistic to physics teachers. However, this is not to say that the human interest is essential or used universally. Many authors write their stories primarily for the setting. Perhaps they are sympathetic to William B. Yeats' words:

> Players and painted stage took all my love
> And not those things that they were emblems of.

A popular example of a novel in which the setting *is* the story is Arthur Clarke's *Rendezvous with Rama. Rama* is an alien spaceship which intrudes into the solar system and is investigated by a team of scientists. The investigation reveals one innovation after another of alien technology which the scientists work to explain, in the process introducing a variety of everyday physical principles. Only at the very end are there some genuine surprises.

Authenticity and accuracy in the portrayal of science are key features of scenario stories. Hal Clement, whose *Mission of Gravity* is another outstanding example of a setting-centered story, says in the appendix to this novel:

> The fun . . . lies in treating the whole thing as a game. I've been playing the game since I was a child, so the rules must be quite simple. They are; for the reader of a science fiction story, they consist of finding as many as possible of the author's statements and implications which conflict with the facts as science currently understands them. For the author, the rule is to make as few such slips as he possibly can. [p. 216]

In the following example Frank Herbert proves himself an excellent player of this game. One of the popular "magic wands" of science fiction is a body shield made up of a force field that repels all high-speed objects; only slow objects can get in. Unfortunately, a shield which would keep out bullets would also prevent air molecules from penetrating, because air molecules at ordinary temperatures move at about the same speed as bullets, some 500 meters per second. When I encountered such a shield on page 34 of Herbert's epic novel, *Dune,* I said to myself, "Aha, how is the wearer going to breathe? Caught you, Herbert!" But I lost my advantage on the next page when these lines convinced me that Herbert was quite aware of the problem:

The air within their shield bubbles grew stale from the demands on it that the slow interchange along barrier edges could not replenish. [p. 35]

FUTUROLOGY

Most science fiction introduces ground rules only as part of a setting which is dominated by some sort of futurology. Jules Verne's *Twenty Thousand*

Leagues Under the Sea is an excellent example; the idea of water pressure is put forth in the excerpt quoted previously only to introduce a futuristic innovation (for Verne's time): the submarine Nautilus. Many people consider the Nautilus to be the precursor of today's atomic submarines. Verne was lucky in this idea; not all futuristic innovations portrayed in science fiction turn out so well, but they don't have to; they merely have to seem plausible by contemporary standards. Jules Verne knew this and was not too concerned with accuracy in his futuristic innovations, as amply demonstrated in his novel Journey to the Moon. In this story, a cannon launches a vehicle with such great speed that it overcomes earth's gravity and travels all the way to the moon. Such a feat is not possible, not then and not now, not in the way Verne described, yet it made an excellent futuristic setting for science fiction. So rockets are very different from Verne's cannonball; to demand absolute fidelity between imaginative projection and eventual fact is to miss the point of futurology.

The importance of futurology lies in the fact that it provides the incentive to examine the present more carefully. Holocaust stories, for example, are written with this idea very specifically in mind. And it is provocative that a science fiction writer, Lester del Rey, in a story entitled "Nerves," described an accident in a nuclear power plant long before the Three Mile Island incident and even before talk about the peaceful use of atomic energy became common. It is also no coincidence that many science fiction writers venture into futurology even outside the arena of science fiction. H. G. Wells proposed as early as 1934 that universities establish a new branch of study to be called human ecology; this was decades ahead of the ecology movement of the sixties. Science fiction writers deal with science and technology in an intimate way, but from an outsider's point of view. Thus they often are able to see the ugly side of science better than the practitioners themselves.

But don't get the impression that this kind of futurology about the dangers of science and technology is pessimistic; it is simply realistic. Wells explained this while talking about a lecture that he gave in 1902 before the Royal Institution in London:

I called this lecture "The Discovery of the Future" and I drew a hard distinction between what I called the legal (past regarding) and the creative (future regarding) minds. I insisted that we overrated the darkness of the future, that by adequate analysis of contemporary processes its conditions could be brought within the range of our knowledge and its form controlled, and that mankind was at the dawn of a great changeover from life regarded as a system of consequences to life regarded as a system of constructive effort. I did not say that future could be foretold. We should be less and less bounded by the engagements of the past and more and more ruled by a realization of the creative effects of our acts. [Experiment in Autobiography, pp. 553–554]

Scenarios, settings based on science and technology, and futurology, speculations about the future, form the rhythm and tempo of the science fiction dance. But in its defiance of often arbitrarily narrow boundaries sometimes imposed by scientists, science fiction demands serious attention. Einstein's theory of relativity, for example, insists that material objects can never achieve, let alone surpass, the speed of light. Scientists live quite docilely with such restrictions, but tell that to science fiction writers! They are tenacious in their attempts to figure out ways to bypass the speed-of-light limit of relativity. Since the theory of relativity is well established experimentally, many scientists consider this matter a closed subject and tend to discredit science fiction writers' attempts as wishful thinking. Perhaps they are. Yet physicists themselves have raised the possibility of faster-than-light travel through the development of the theory of tachyons, faster-than-light particles. Although tachyons have yet to be found experimentally, the fact that the idea of tachyons has been conceived and is consistent with relativity encourages us to pay more attention to Clarke's law, a principle formulated by science fiction writer Arthur C. Clarke:

When a distinguished but elderly scientist states that something is possible, he is almost certainly right. When he states that something is impossible, he is very probably wrong. [*Profiles of the Future*, p. 14]

Nevertheless, some attempts of science fiction writers to overrule scientific laws are reminiscent of science fiction's rich heritage of sword and sorcery, and magic. We must distinguish between serious thinking and what H. G. Wells used to call "scientific patter." When a writer waves an interesting idea at the reader but backs it up only with meaningless patter, he or she is using the idea as a magic wand. Such "science" may be acceptable, though gratuitous, in fantasy literature, but readers should retain their freedom to be disdainful of such approaches in science fiction.

An example is called for. Wells' classic *The Time Machine* (which will be discussed later in detail) is about traveling back and forth in the time dimension, in violation of well-known physical principles. But Wells does it with credibility in this address by his time traveler to a group of skeptical listeners:

"Are you so sure we can move freely in Space? Right and left we can go, forward and backward freely enough, and men have always done so. I admit we move freely in two dimensions. But how about up and down? Gravitation limits us there."

"Not exactly," said the medical man, "there are balloons."

"But before the balloons, man had no freedom of vertical movement. He can go up against gravitation in a balloon, and why should he not hope that ultimately he may be able to stop or accelerate his drift along the time dimension, or even turn about and travel the other way?" [pp. 16–17]

Now compare this with the following excerpt from another science fiction story about time travel that Damon Knight cites in his book *In Search of Wonder:*

"How did you come to travel through time?"
"By dimensional quadrature," Macklin replied. [p. 98]

Knight comments: "Beautiful: 'By dimensional quadrature,' i.e., by the fourth dimension, i.e., time—or, 'How did you travel through time?' 'By time travel.'" In other words, this is an example of pure scientific patter, a magic-wand use of a scientific idea.

Somewhat similar in approach to scientific patter is what is called imaginary science, science completely cooked up by the author which has very little to do with the real world and physical principles and laws. The author never makes any connection. These writings too belong to fantasy literature and not to science fiction, and I shall have very little to say about them.

We must, however, distinguish imaginary science from paranormal science or what Kingsley Amis, in his previously quoted definition of SF, calls pseudoscience. "Paranormal" means beyond normal; the phenomena under this label include telepathy (mind-to-mind information transfer) and psychokinesis (the ability to move an object with psychic power) among others. In contrast to imaginary science, these phenomena are backed by some scientific investigations that seem to indicate credibility.

The label *pseudoscience,* however, is a misnomer, as is *paranormal.* In science, there is no normal, there are only accepted supertheories or *paradigms,* to use Kuhn's term again. Any new theory is received with a lot of healthy skepticism (physicist Freeman Dyson noted in 1958 that the first theories of internal structure of the atom were greeted as mysticism), but this is hardly enough reason to label the theory or the phenomena it pertains to as paranormal. Such labeling may originate from a deep distrust by the scientific establishment of the ways of some psychics. While some distrust may be justified, should it preclude the scientist from having an open mind? Psychologist Abraham Maslow wrote:

If there is any primary rule of science, it is, in my opinion, acceptance of the obligation to acknowledge and describe all of reality, all that exists, everything that is the case. Before all else science must be comprehensive and all-inclusive. It must accept within its jurisdiction even that which it cannot understand or explain, that for which no theory exists, that which cannot be measured, predicted, controlled, or ordered. It must accept even contradictions and illogicalities and mysteries, the vague, the ambiguous, the archaic, the unconscious, and all other aspects of existence that are difficult to communicate. At its best it's completely open and excludes nothing. [*The Psychology of Science,* p. 72]

Increasingly, today's science has imposed entrance requirements in terms of approved subjects of investigation. Although parapsychologists, investigators who study the paranormal, have been admitted to membership in the prestigious American Association for the Advancement of Science, every once in a while reputable scientists improperly attempt to discredit their work without proper scrutiny. In contrast, partly thanks to the efforts of the late editor of *Analog,* John W. Campbell, and partly due to that same fire of defiance that drives science fiction writers against scientific dogma, the paranormal has become an integral part of futuristic science portrayed in science fiction. Unfortunately, much of the portrayal is fashioned in a magic wand sort of way. But some writers—notably Ian Watson, Kate Wilhelm, and Ursula Le Guin—have delved into theoretical frameworks, such as those of psychologist Carl Jung and of quantum mechanics, in dealing with the paranormal. The efforts of such writers leave me free to remark that the dance between science fiction and science has become one of a mutually contributing partnership.

It may very well be that future experimentation will disprove the existence of the paranormal to everybody's satisfaction, but chances are that it will be the other way around, and thus the time has come for a serious look at these phenomena. Ultimately, of course, the issues will have to be settled in the arena of science, but science fiction helps to keep the issues alive through childhood and adolescence.

Quantum mechanics, the twentieth-century marvel of modern physics, has implications that have convinced many serious physicists that what we are dealing with here is no less than a union of metapsychology (science of the origin and structure of the mind) and metaphysics (theories attempting to explain reality itself from first principles). Carl Jung (1951) predicted many years ago that "sooner or later nuclear physics and the psychology of the unconscious will draw closer together as both of them, independently of one another and from opposite directions, push forward into transcendental territory." And it is delightfully satisfying to see science fiction movies such as *Star Trek* and *The Empire Strikes Back* (sequel to *Star Wars*) increasingly use Jung's ideas in their futurology.

Ultimately, the most common bond between science fiction and physics, the one that makes them such good partners in the dance of reality, is imagination. Both physicists and science fiction authors know the following lines from Lewis Carroll's *Through the Looking-Glass* all too well:

Alice laughed. "There's no use trying," she said: "one *can't* believe impossible things."

"I daresay you haven't had much practice," said the Queen. "When I was your age, I always did it for half-an-hour a day. Why, sometimes I've believed as many as six impossible things before breakfast."

And nowhere is imagination more essential than when you explore the nature, structure, and destiny of reality itself. Both physicists and science fiction writers truly are cosmic dancers, shaping and expressing our vision of reality. In their exploration of strange entities such as black holes, they often lose themselves completely in the dance of reality. It is this dance that I have tried to capture in this book.

HOW TO READ THIS BOOK

While a book is linear, usually read from front to back, a dance is more like a hologram: to see any part of it is to get some idea of the meaning of the whole dance. If you have seen or heard about a hologram, you know that it is a special sort of photograph in which any small part gives the whole picture. If you look at "coherent" light (light waves dancing in step) through any piece of it, you still see the whole picture. So I wanted to write a book in which you would always get the message of the whole book from whatever page you read. But I don't think I have quite succeeded.

However, I have (I think) succeeded to the following extent: the book consists of four informal parts, each about one of the major paradigms of science fiction literature—exploration of the solar system (Chapters 2–5); star dreams, about travel to the stars (Chapters 7–11); hyperspace and related concepts (Chapters 12–14); and, finally, mind and its connection to reality as a whole (Chapters 15–19). Except for Chapter 6 on waves, which is prerequisite for subsequent chapters, one can read each of these parts separately without chronological dependence.

Fiction is basically nonlinear. However, physics, which forms a large part of the book (necessarily, since science fiction is so intertwined with physics as to be really physics fiction), is best talked about in a chronological fashion, and so it has been. Accordingly, especially for the science initiate, there is some advantage in reading the book from beginning to end.

The book is written for the nonscientist who shares with the author an interest in and enthusiasm for science fiction and/or space, time, mind, reality, and so forth. All the science is explained in simple but meaningful terms. Since I strongly believe that a book is first of all communication, that is what I have attempted to achieve.

chapter two

Newton's Principia: *Some Science Fiction Writers Don't Like It!*

Newton's celebrated *Principia* has been recognized as the beginning of modern science. I first looked at it as a curious college student, but I didn't like it: the language was obscure, the proofs of formulas were not the same ones I was familiar with from my physics courses. So one evening I gave up reading *Principia* in favor of a science fiction paperback. It was *Fahrenheit 451*, Ray Bradbury's haunting story about a society of bookburners. But, tired, I soon fell asleep with the book on my chest. And I dreamed.

Suddenly I was a character in Bradbury's novel, running away from the city of the bookburners. Soon I found myself among the renegade band of people working to salvage books by memorizing them. When I was taken to their leader for his assignment of the book I was to memorize, he asked what I did. Without thinking, I replied that I was a student of physics. "Good," he responded. "We finally have a physicist among us. You, my young friend, will memorize Newton's *Principia*." I protested, but he was already talking to the next person. So utterly horrified was I with the prospect of having to memorize *Principia* that, even after waking, the feeling persisted.

Yet, if a real catastrophe today threatened to destroy all our books, and there was an opportunity to save only one, many people would want that book to be *Principia*. The ideas Newton expressed in this book basically generated most of the future progress in science and technology. Thus, saving this one book would quite likely revive the present scientific era of civilization.

In *Principia,* Newton gave us a set of laws governing the motion of terrestrial and celestial bodies. To many science fiction writers, these laws are anathema because of the barrier they erect to imaginative storytelling. Most SF writers like to write about interplanetary or interstellar, if not intergalactic, intrigue; such story lines usually involve quite a bit of space travel across vast regions of space. According to Newton's laws such space voyages, if manageable at all, would be very elaborate affairs, demanding huge amounts of human and material resources, gigantic quantities of energy and, of course, immensely long travel times. Such elaborate requirements dwarf the idea of a hero, and make hero-based adventure stories kind of obsolete. You cannot manufacture a rocket ship in your backyard, not if you go by Newton's book—it's as simple as that. Since adventure stories continue to dominate science fiction—with the hero carrying all the action instead of relegating some of his tasks to scientists and technologists (he would need quite a gang of them)—there is good reason for writers to consider Newton's laws to be tyrannical limits which they would love to circumvent.

Yet this is only part of the story. Behind this revolt against scientific limits, there remains among SF writers the genuine concern about unnecessarily narrow limits that scientists often impose on themselves due to a lack of imagination. One of the best functions of science fiction is that it is permissive to new ideas, even when those ideas go against the grain of prevalent scientific thought and established physical laws. The science fiction writer seems to know that laws aren't nature but only our all-too-human ways to describe nature. Thus no law or laws, and Newton's are no exception, should be regarded as infallible.

And limits can be expanded if nature allows it, although it may take a genius actually to break through in concept. Einstein proved it! In Newton's framework, a space hero who leaves for a distant star and returns to earth-time after twenty years will himself have aged twenty years also. But Einstein, with his relativity theory, has extended our hero's life. According to Einstein, if the hero's spaceship is fast enough, he will age very little during the trip; he won't have to face a very difficult middle-age transition when he comes back.

Having presented the science fiction writers' side, let's sound a precautionary note. The laws to be discussed in this chapter (along with science fiction writers' attempts to circumvent them) have passed the test of time. It is extremely unlikely that they can be broken, especially in the domain in which they are applied. What we can hope for is that the domain can be extended and that a revolution of physics may take place that, while accommodating some science-fictiony ideas, will still bear out Newton's laws as a special case in the old domain. Indeed, one of the major thrusts of this book is to examine the extent to which we can find the tenets of such a "paradigm shift" within science fiction and today's science. The word *paradigm* was adopted by philosopher Kuhn precisely to describe such revolutionary new supertheories.

If, as presented in the following pages, some of the SF writers' attempts to rewrite Newton's laws seem naive, be kind. First, the episodes will introduce you to the Newtonian framework on which stands most of macroscopic physics. Second, you will get some idea of how science fiction writers operate, what kind of thin line between triviality and greatness they tread. Finally, the chapter will set the stage for a more realistic discussion of space travel to be presented in future chapters.

THE TRAVEL PLAN OF CYRANO DE BERGERAC AND NEWTON'S FIRST LAW OF MOTION

French writer Cyrano de Bergerac, who lived in the seventeenth century, is regarded by many SF historians as one of the precursors of today's science fiction writers. Cyrano enjoyed toying with scientific ideas, often in mock seriousness. Here is one of Cyrano's ideas.

Everybody knows, and knew even in Cyrano's time, that the earth moves; one of its motions is to rotate about an axis through the poles with a twenty-four-hour cycle. Cyrano's idea was to put the earth's spin to good use. Suppose you go up in a balloon and hover overhead for a while. (With today's technology, you may prefer a helicopter.) As the earth moves away from under you, different places come into your view. After a while you may wish to land at one of these places. What a cheap way to travel!

Does the idea make sense? Only the kind of sense that makes it a good joke. All objects, according to Newton's first law of motion, have a property called inertia. This is the tendency to remain in a state of rest or of constant speed in a straight line unless acted on by an external force. Because the hovering balloon too must have inertia, it will continue to move with the earth below. Thus a beautiful, cheap method of traveling is thwarted by one of Newton's laws. You still think science fiction should be in love with Mr. Newton?

Actually, inertia is not much of a deterrent to our travel plans—in fact, it can be a boon! Thus, when a rocket leaves for a trip to the outer rim of the solar system from the Florida coast, it will continue to move with earth's rotational speed as it leaves, and so we don't have to push it as hard as we would have to otherwise. Of course, the rocket must leave in the same direction as the earth rotates, but that's easy to arrange.

With today's space platforms orbiting the earth every now and then, you may already have had the opportunity to watch inertia in action: an object thrown from a space platform continues on its way without change in its speed and direction, strictly in accordance with Newton's first law. However, inertia is far from obvious in earthbound phenomena. If you roll a ball on a floor, it soon comes to rest. In order to keep your car moving, you have to apply force by continuing to press the gas pedal. So where is the evidence for inertia in such examples? Now we come to the rest of Newton's first law: in these examples there are external forces, adverse ones of friction, that change the motion and bring it to a stop. There is a story of two robots (*Star Wars* style) who were visiting Niagara Falls. One of them mused to the other, "I wonder what keeps all that water going?" The other looked surprised, "What's there to stop it?" So when an object does not continue its motion under inertia, always ask, what's doing the stopping?

Coming back to science fiction writers, I have a young friend who sometimes brings samples of his writing to me, no doubt to check out his science. This is an excerpt from one of his UFO stories:

I saw a UFO approaching us at tremendous speed. When it was directly overhead, something dropped from it, and the next moment the UFO was gone. Very soon we saw the object the UFO left behind. It was an alien being in a parasuit. The alien landed within ten feet of us, and as we approached, it spoke to us in plain English, "Hello, where's the nearest bathroom?"

Unfortunately, my friend makes the same mistake as Cyrano (but perhaps not deliberately); he leaves out the inertia of the alien being as it jumped from the UFO: its inertia would have carried it very far away before it could land.

WHICH WAY COMETH THE BLACK CLOUD?

Few scientists ever manage to write science fiction, although a much larger number think about it. Of those who write, only a few become successful. And among this rare breed of successful writers, once in a while there will be a writer whose first book makes a splash. Astrophysicist Fred Hoyle is such a scientist.

Because Hoyle is a scientist, he has a delightful tendency to create a scenario in which scientists confer with each other using a language that is pretty close to being authentic. This is great because it more easily draws the reader into intimacy with the story line.

Let me give you an example from Hoyle's first novel, *The Black Cloud*. An astronomer working at California's Mount Palomar observatory has just discovered that a huge black cloud is traveling toward the solar system. How could he tell? By comparing photographs taken earlier with ones taken later, he noted that the cloud appeared bigger in the later photos, showing that it was moving closer to the earth. But now the important question arises, what is the cloud's path? Will it avoid the solar system or collide with it? A group of astronomers and physicists find the answers in this scene:

. . . Dave Weichart spoke up for the first time.
"I've two questions that I'd like to ask. The first is about the position of the cloud. . . . what I'd like to know is whether the center of the cloud is staying in the same position, or does it seem to be moving against the background of the stars?"
"A very good question. The centre seems, over the last twenty years, to have moved very little relative to the star field," answered Herrick.
"Then that means the cloud is coming dead at the solar system. . . . I can make it clear with a picture. [Figure 1a] Here's the Earth. Let's suppose first that the cloud is moving dead towards us, like this, from **A** to **B**. Then at **B** the cloud will look bigger but its centre will be in the same direction. This is the case that apparently corresponds pretty well to the observed situation. . . . Now let's suppose that the cloud is moving sideways, as well as towards us, and let's suppose that the motion sideways is about as fast as the motion towards us. Then the cloud will move about like this. [Figure 1b] Now if you consider the motion from **A** to **B** you'll see that there are two effects—the cloud will seem bigger at **B** than it was at **A**, exactly as in the previous case,

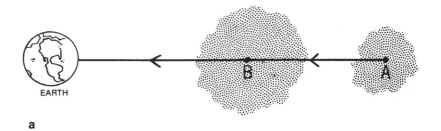

a

Figure 1. **(a)** Black cloud coming straight at earth. *A* and *B* are two subsequent positions of the cloud. **(b)** In this case the path of the cloud does not intersect the earth.

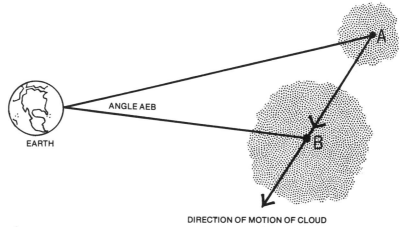

b

but now the centre will have moved. And it will move through the angle **AEB** which must be something of the order of thirty degrees."

"I don't think the centre has moved through an angle of more than a quarter of a degree," remarked Marlowe.

"Then the sideways motion can't be more than about one per cent of the motion towards us. It looks as though . . . On the facts as they've been given to us that cloud is going to score a bull's eye, plumb in the middle of the target. Remember that it's already two and a half degrees in diameter. The transverse velocity would have to be as much as ten per cent or so of the radial velocity if it were to miss us." [p. 20]

As you can see, the main argument showing that the cloud is coming toward the solar system is quite clear, especially if you look at the figures. Yet there are some words and sentences here and there that may be slightly perplexing, such as: "Then the sideways motion can't be more than about one per cent of the motion towards us." Or how about this sentence: "The transverse velocity would have to be as much as ten per cent or so of the radial velocity if it were to miss us." If these sentences puzzle you, you are ready for the rest of this section about quantities designated as vectors. If you understand them, you are aware already of the vector nature of velocity.

So far in the chapter, I have spoken of speed, the rate at which distance is covered in motion. But speed alone is not enough to specify motion; we must in addition call attention to the direction of motion. The word *velocity* is used in physics to designate both speed and the direction of motion. Quantities such as this, with both magnitude and direction, are called vectors in mathematics. Another example of a vector quantity is force, the agency that pulls or pushes an object. In contrast, quantities without any connotation of direction go by the name of scalars. Temperature (the degree of hotness or coldness of a body) and mass (the amount of matter in a body) are examples of scalar quantities.

The advantage of introducing mathematical concepts such as vectors to describe physical quantities is that we can make use of mathematical theorems and rules when dealing with such ideas. Suppose you shoot an arrow with a speed of 4 m/sec (meters per second) in the northerly direction, but there is a wind blowing due east at a rate of 3 m/sec. Obviously the arrow will be blown sideways, but we can figure out exactly to what extent by using the mathematical addition rule for vectors.

To combine the velocity vector of the arrow with that of the wind, represent each vector by an arrow of proportionate length with the arrowhead pointed in the appropriate direction, drawing them foot to foot (Figure 2a). The resultant vector, the sum of the two, is given by the long diagonal of the completed parallelogram as shown. The length of the diagonal gives the magnitude of the resultant velocity, and the angle it makes with any of the sides gives the direction.

We can reverse this argument to realize that any vector can be thought of as the sum of two perpendicular vectors, called its components. To find the component of a vector in any given direction and its perpendicular, we can proceed as follows. Drop a perpendicular from the tip of the arrowhead representing the vector onto the given direction; then complete the parallelogram as shown (Figure 2b). In the figure, vector **OA** is called the parallel component, and the vector represented by **OB** is called the perpendicular or transverse component of the vector **OR**.

Finally, you can understand Hoyle's jargon. When he uses the phrase "radial velocity," he is talking about the component of the velocity vector of the cloud in the radial direction, parallel to the direction toward the earth. And the transverse component is the component in the perpendicular direction, the sideways direction. Clearly, if you add a very large radial component with

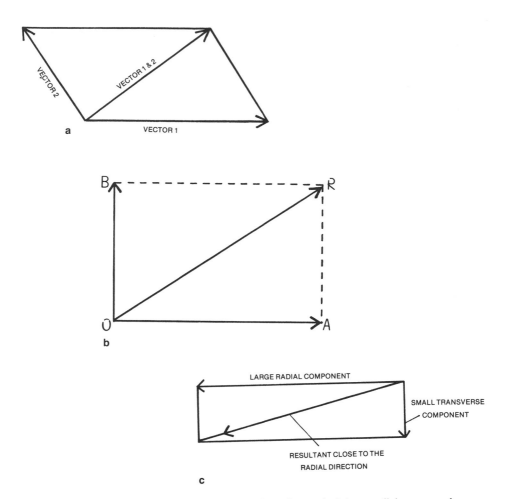

Figure 2. (a) Addition of two vectors; the short diagonal of the parallelogram as drawn is the sum vector. (b) The vector **OR** can be resolved into two vectors along and perpendicular to a given direction **OA**. The vector **OA** is called the parallel component; **OB**, the transverse component. (c) See text if you need further explanation.

a small transverse component, the total or resultant will be pointed rather close to the larger component (Figure 2c).

IS REALITY DETERMINISTIC AND CAUSAL?

The novel *Tau Zero,* by Poul Anderson, is one of the most ambitious space travel ventures in science fiction. Its crew members traveled to the "edge" of the universe in the course of their voyage. How is this possible? Well, the ship just continued to speed up during its journey, as observed by one of the crew:

. . . "we have reached the marches of the Solar System. Every day—no, every twenty-four hours; 'day' and 'night' mean nothing any longer—each twenty-four hours we gain 845 kilometers per second in speed." [p. 29]

Such motion, in which the speed changes, is called accelerated motion. In contrast, motion at constant speed in a straight line (constant velocity) is called natural motion. To be precise, acceleration is the rate of change of velocity. It's the measure of the change in motion that, according to Newton's first law, is brought about by an external force acting on a body. The quantitative statement of the relationship of the external force and the acceleration it produces is provided by Newton's second law of motion: the external force needed to produce a given amount of acceleration is the product of the mass of the body (the quantity of matter contained in it) and the required acceleration.

Conversely, Newton's second law also tells us this: if the forces acting on objects are known, we can calculate their acceleration. Once we know the acceleration, it is only a matter of mathematics, or computer power, to solve (predict) the motion of the objects, namely to find out where the objects will be at all times. However, to start up the computer, we have to provide it with some added information in the form of the objects' positions and velocities at some initial instant of time. Once we have these initial data, or initial conditions as we call them, and we know all the forces that act on the bodies along with their masses, Newton's second law and mathematics can do the rest.

This idea—that given a few initial data about the objects in the universe and the forces acting on them, we can determine the destiny of these objects—has given us the philosophy of determinism. The man who first glimpsed the possibility that the universe may very well be deterministic was philosopher René Descartes. The story is that while Descartes was visiting the Versailles palace in France, he took special notice of the huge assemblage of automata in the garden there: water began to flow, music started to play from nowhere, sea nymphs came into action, and the statue of mighty Neptune rose from under the water. And this went on and on in a fantastic display of machine power. This panorama presumably gave Descartes the idea that the universe is like this automatic machinery.

With the power of Newton's laws before us, we can see the substance behind Descartes's idea. French mathematicians of the eighteenth century who solved the motion of many celestial bodies with the help of Newton's laws were quite verbal proponents of the potency of the deterministic philosophy. Said Pierre Simon de Laplace, the leader of the French school:

An intelligence that, at a given instant, was acquainted with all the forces by which nature is animated and with the state of the bodies of which it is composed, would—if it were vast enough to submit this data to analysis—embrace in the same formula the movements of the largest bodies of the universe and those of the lightest atoms: nothing would be uncertain to such an intelligence, and the future, like the past, would be present to its eyes.

In short, according to Laplace, the universe is a machine on a grand scale, a world machine; just as Descartes suspected, the universe operates on the same principles as an automaton.

Science fiction writers also, following the lead of scientists and futurologists, have been profoundly influenced by the deterministic philosophy. Robert A. Heinlein, the dean of American science fiction in the fifties and sixties, gave us his own version of the world machine, a conscious computer, in his novel *The Moon Is a Harsh Mistress*. In this story, the lunar colony is trying to escape earth's tyranny. The colonists start a revolution (modeled after the American Revolution, of course), and the computer naturally is the leader. Initially, it calculates the probability of success of the revolution to be minuscule, but the odds pick up as the revolution progresses because the computer has more and more data to play with. It never claimed to have all the data for a completely deterministic prediction, but the final success of the revolution leaves the reader with a sense of pleasurable reinforcement of his or her belief in the deterministic philosophy.

But modern physics, as we shall see later, has discovered that strict determinism does not hold, at least not in the submicroscopic particle world of atoms and such. Instead, only probabilities of the behavior can be calculated. This is quite satisfactory for large assemblies of such particles and events; but for a small number, the outcome of a given situation cannot be predicted with accuracy.

And science fiction writers are well aware of this dent that modern physics has made in the perfection of a deterministic reality. Isaac Asimov, in his masterpiece, *Foundation Trilogy*, imagines that even the evolution of an entire galactic civilization can be predicted through the logical analysis of what he calls the science of psychohistory. However, as the plot unfolds, Asimov allows the predictions of the analysis to fail occasionally as a reminder that physical reality is not deterministic in the strict sense.

Closely related to determinism is the idea that all phenomena can be analyzed in terms of cause and effect, as when a force produces an acceleration. Whereas reality is strictly causal according to Newtonian physics, in the modern theory of quantum mechanics strict causality does not hold. We are unable, for example, to ascribe a strict cause-effect sequence to the behavior of a single atom. One of science fiction writers' biggest battles with Mr. Newton centers around causality—the principle of cause-effect sequence. And again, modern physics seems to have come to their rescue, at least to some extent.

Let's consider an example. In his novel *The Stars My Destination*, Alfred Bester suggests a phenomenon that would certainly be objected to from a strict Newtonian viewpoint:

A researcher named Jaunte set fire to his bench and himself (accidentally) and let out a yell for help with particular reference to a fire extinguisher. Who so surprised as Jaunte and his colleagues when he found himself standing alongside said extinguisher, seventy feet removed from his lab bench. [p. 3]

Bester labels this phenomenon teleportation: "Teleportation of oneself through space by the effect of mind alone." But teleportation is seen as a clear violation of the Newtonian paradigm because of the traditional belief that the mind itself is governed by Newton's laws. If teleportation were a mental phenomenon, we should be able to analyze it with the Newtonian concept of forces and acceleration. The problem then is that few scientists are convinced of the existence of a "mental" force capable of acting on external objects. With modern physics, the scientist's reaction is somewhat different. In quantum mechanics, physical reality has gaps—tiny intervals of time during which the fate of causality is uncertain. And an open-minded physicist can wonder if phenomena such as teleportation could occur in these gaps. Modern physics has not "proved" teleportation, not yet anyway, but it legitimizes an investigation into it.

Is reality deterministic and causal? Reality at large, the macroscopic universe that we generally interact with, indeed seems to be deterministic and causal, strictly according to Newton's laws. What then are the chances of the fruition of the science fiction writers' dream of bypassing causality in the universe at large? The physics of submicroscopic particles reveals at least one domain of reality, the submicroscopic world, where strict determinism and causality do not hold. Now a fascinating question is: to which domain does the mind belong? If the mind is a quantum mechanical phenomenon, then it may very well be a different ball game. Watch out, Newton!

Let's return once more to *Tau Zero*. In the excerpt quoted above, the acceleration of the spaceship is expressed in the very unusual units of 845 kilometers per second per day. In the currently accepted scientific system of units, acceleration is expressed in terms of meters per second per second (abbreviated m/sec^2 and pronounced meters per second squared). When we convert units we find that the spaceship in *Tau Zero* accelerates at a rate of 9.8 m/sec^2, the same acceleration with which all falling bodies on earth rush to the ground. Incidentally, it was the Italian scientist Galileo who discovered that all falling bodies on earth fall at the same rate, independent of the bodies' weights. (Strictly speaking, this is true only in vacuum—the total absence of air.) It has become customary, especially in science fiction, to express acceleration in units of this 9.8 m/sec^2, which is referred to as 1 g (g for Galileo, of course). Thus, for reference:

$$1 \ g = 9.8 \ \text{m/sec}^2 = 32.2 \ \text{feet/sec}^2$$

Here feet/sec^2 is the unit used in the engineering system for acceleration.

19 Newton's Principia: *Some Science Fiction Writers Don't Like It!*

Now back again to *Tau Zero:* at 1 *g,* how long does it take the spaceship to achieve nature's speed limit, the speed of light? Since light speed is given by the enormous number 3×10^8 m/sec (recall that a positive power of ten is just the number of zeroes put after 1: $10^8 = 100,000,000$), the answer is: about a year. (One year is 3.2×10^7 seconds; at 1 *g,* the speed changes at a rate of 9.8 m/sec each second—9.8 m.sec^2—so in a year the change in speed is $9.8 \times 3.2 \times 10^7$ or roughly 3×10^8 m/sec.) However, the size of the universe is so huge, about 10^{26} meters, that, even at light speed, it takes some 10^{10} years to reach its end. So, does the story in *Tau Zero* make sense?

It does. Einstein's theory of relativity, which recognizes nature's speed limit, predicts stranger-than-fiction phenomena once a spaceship approaches the limit, the speed of light. Somehow, time slows down on board the ship; all clocks, including the biological ones of the human body, run at a slower pace compared to their pace on earth. Thus, in shiptime, it does not take the crew of *Tau Zero* 10^{10} years to reach the edge of space, but only an incredible 24 years or so. Such is the magic of relativity!

ACTION AND REACTION: THE THIRD LAW

Suppose you were in a rocket ship and were somehow thrown off the rocket. If you don't think you'd have a problem, perhaps the following excerpt from one of Robert A. Heinlein's novels, *Space Cadet,* will help you reevaluate your position.

Matt took a couple of trial steps. It was like walking in mud; his feet would cling stickily to the ship, then pull away suddenly. It took getting used to.

. . . A cadet near the end of the chain tried to break both magnetized boots free from the ship at the same time. He accomplished it, by jumping—and then had no way to get back. He moved out until his static line tugged at the two boys on each side of him.

One of them, caught with one foot free of the ship in walking, was broken loose also, though he reached wildly for the steel and missed. The cadet next to him, last in line, came loose in turn.

No more separated, as the successive tugs on the line had used up the energy of the first cadet's not-so-violent jump. But three cadets now dangled on the line, floating and twisting grotesquely.

The instructor caught the movement out of the corner of his eye, and squatted down. He found what he sought, a steel ring recessed in the ship's side, and snapped his static line to it. When he was certain that the entire party was not going to be dragged loose, he ordered, "Number nine—haul them in, gently—very gently. Don't pull yourself loose doing it."

A few moments later the vagrants were back and sticking to the ship. "Now," said the instructor, "who was responsible for that piece of groundhog stupidity?" [p. 84]

In space it really is impossible to stop your motion—kicking, crawling, cursing, nothing helps. This is because nothing is there to react back to your attempt to generate an action force. Without a reaction, you can't generate an action. Forces come in equal and opposite pairs. This is Newton's third law. All forces are interactions—it takes two to make a force.

You don't ordinarily realize it, but a simple maneuver like walking is not accomplished because *you pull yourself* forward, but because you push the ground backward with your feet, and in response the *ground pushes you* forward. That's why walking on ice is difficult; ice does not react back too well, and the action force is limited by how much reaction you can stimulate.

But now maybe you are asking the same question as Heinlein's hero following the scene just quoted. Suppose everybody in the group managed to get loose from the ship, how would they return?

Presently, Matt said, "Sergeant Hanako—"
"Yes? Who is it?"
"Dodson. Number three. Suppose we had all pulled loose?"
"We'd have to work our way back on our rocket units." [p. 86]

The sergeant is right, of course. In space the only way to change your motion, that is, generate a force, is through rocket action. When a part of the body is discarded with high speed, the discarded part reacts back on the main body. That's why you see debris coming out of the tail of rockets. It's the backward-heaving debris that gives a rocket a forward push.

Another interesting, and slightly confusing, feature of the action-reaction nature of forces occurs in the firing of a bullet by a gun. Everybody knows that the gun recoils, demonstrating the effect of the reaction of the bullet on the gun. The confusion arises because somehow the reaction seems to be of less magnitude; the bullet leaves the gun with great speed, but the gun recoils only a bit. The puzzle is resolved if you remember the second law of motion; the acceleration due to a force depends on the mass. Since the gun has a greater mass, its acceleration is much less than that of the bullet. If a cannon fired an equally huge cannonball, then its recoil would be as great as the forward velocity of the cannonball. Jules Verne used this idea in his novel *Upside Down;* the story's heroes wanted to straighten out earth's rotation axis by means of the recoil from such a huge cannon firing a huge cannonball.

We have mentioned Cyrano de Bergerac before. This fun-filled author thought of an interesting idea to defy gravity.

Finally—seated on an iron plate,
To hurl a magnet in the air—the iron
Follows—I catch the magnet—throw again
And so proceed indefinitely.

Not surprisingly, this method doesn't work. For one thing, it ignores the third law. Every time the rider of this antigravity vehicle throws the magnet up, he and the plate not only do not follow the magnet, but must recoil downward as the magnet's reaction force acts on them.

REACTIONLESS DRIVE, OR THE DEAN DRIVE

Lance Leatherhide, boy graduate, stood in dismay before his angry thesis advisor, Prof. MacBlast. Stern in his frock coat and pince-nez, MacBlast thundered his disapproval, "Of all the idiotic fantasies I have ever seen, *this* one takes the cake for sloppy experiments, moronic calculations, sophomoric ideas, and sheer imbecility! No scientist worthy of the name would give serious consideration to any childish theories that ignore *every* law of physics in the book." He paused to take a deep breath, while waving the offending sheaf of papers under Lance's nose. "And don't imagine," he continued, "that I am going to permit my daughter to marry an imitation scientist like *you*. There hasn't been any insanity in my family so far, and I intend to keep it that way."

Sadly, Lance took the manuscript, with all its revolutionary discoveries, under his arm and left the professor's office. "But it still moves," he muttered under his breath, "and someday I'm going to prove it to you, and to all the other mossbacks of the scientific 'establishment!'" [Philip R. Geffe in Knight, 1977, p. 175]

Any physical law is a limit on the human potential. But of Newton's laws, perhaps the most restrictive is the third law, because it makes acceleration in space very difficult. Sure, we have built rockets, but rockets have to carry a large mass of fuel which must be discarded in an orderly fashion so that the payload can carry on. This costs efficiency. Therefore, many science fiction writers would like to have a reactionless drive, although scientists would typically react like Professor MacBlast to the idea.

The idea of reactionless drive is deceptively simple. Arthur Clarke puts it this way: "You pull on your bootstrap, and away you go." If you try pulling on your bootstraps while sitting on the floor, you will find that you do indeed go somewhere. But does the idea work in space?

You can even use the "bootstrap effect" to propel yourself in a boat on a river in an emergency. Tie a rope to the front end of the boat and pull on it toward yourself. The boat will respond. But is this technique worth anything in space? Unfortunately, no. Neither of the above cases is an example of a true reactionless drive, because there is a reaction. In the first case, it is the friction of the floor, a reaction force, which moves you, and in the second it is the friction of the water. (Notice the dual role of friction here as a force that accelerates motion instead of opposing it as in its previously discussed role.) In space there is no friction, so pulling on your bootstraps cannot help.

Yet people keep trying. In 1963 there was an article in the SF magazine

Analog about a machine constructed by a fellow named Dean who claimed to have demonstrated a reactionless drive. Dean's machine made such a splash with readers of science fiction that it is now customary in SF circles to refer to a reactionless drive as a Dean drive. But does the Dean machine really work where it counts—in space?

Russell Adams, inspired by his own research, recently wrote an entertaining article (also published in *Analog*) on the Dean machine that should cool the enthusiasm many science fiction readers may still feel for it. Interestingly, Adams discovered in a search of the US Patent Office at least fifty patent applications claiming to have perfected one form or another of a reactionless drive. In each case he found, as a result of careful experimentation, that the working of the machine was utterly dependent on the existence of the friction force of the ground or table supporting the machine. Without friction, that is, under conditions of space, these machines haven't the slightest hope of success.

Let's consider an example following Adams. Figure 3 shows a simple "Dean drive." Suppose the clown lifts the hammer, slowly enough so that it doesn't disturb the plank, then suddenly slams the hammer down. This can be expected to produce motion, and it does, but only in the presence of friction with the floor. To prove this contention, put the plank on wheels. Wheels possess tremendously reduced friction. And with wheels the model oscillates back and forth, but never travels anywhere.

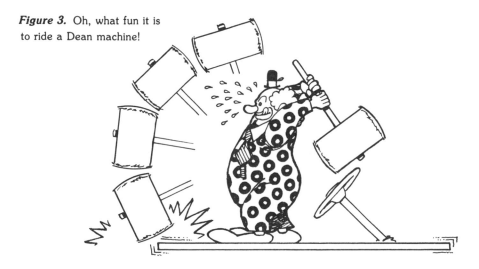

Figure 3. Oh, what fun it is to ride a Dean machine!

You see, the reason the machine works in the presence of friction is that the device can hold still while you pull the hammer in the first phase of the experiment. With wheels the device moves in one direction while you lift the hammer, and in the other when the hammer delivers its blow. But there is never any net motion in one direction.

We can lament with the science fiction writer that the reactionless drive does not work. What this means for rockets is that they have to carry huge reaction masses on board only to discard them en route. This works fine if you're thinking of "short" trips within the solar system, but for long trips to the stars this is almost a hopeless constraint; too much reaction mass is needed. As we shall see in a later chapter, even assuming optimal operation, a one-hundred-ton rocket would need to carry some billion tons of "trash" for a journey to the stars, and still it would take a long time to complete the trip.

Finally, the following excerpt from Arthur C. Clarke's *Rendezvous With Rama* gives an example of reactionless drive from one of science fiction's best craftsmen. *Rama*, an alien vessel that has moved temporarily into the solar system, is making its departure in this scene as the crew aboard the earth spaceship *Endeavour* watches.

Hour after hour that acceleration held constant. *Rama* was falling away from *Endeavour* at steadily increasing speed. As the distance grew, the anomalous behavior of the ship slowly ceased; the normal laws of inertia started to operate again. They could only guess at the energies in whose backlash they had been briefly caught, and Norton was thankful that he had stationed *Endeavour* at a safe distance before *Rama* had switched on its drive.

As to the nature of that drive, one thing was now certain, even though all else was mystery. There were no jets of gas . . . thrusting *Rama* into its new orbit . . . No one put it better than Sergeant Professor Myron, " . . . there goes Newton's third law." [p. 266]

But such an incident remains unlikely outside of science fiction for the same reason as the Dean drive doesn't work.

THE CONSERVATIVE REALITY

In Buddha's philosophy, the wheel has a strongly symbolic meaning. There is a lot of movement at the rim of a wheel, but the center of the hub remains motionless. Likewise, to Buddhists, there may be a lot of activity at the periphery of an enlightened human's psyche, but his/her inner self remains still, entirely unaffected by the humdrum or bustle of everyday life.

Physicists too, in dealing with motion, have seen an analogy to the wheel since the time of the renowned Descartes. As Descartes first noted, motion concerns change, but there are several motion-related quantities which do not change when considered in their totality: reality is conservative. Just as the inner self of the Buddhists represents the permanent aspect of personal reality, these quantities—energy, momentum, and angular momentum—must be regarded as permanent aspects of physical reality.

Let's talk first about energy. Intuitively, everyone knows what energy is. It is the one entity without which all our space dreams come to naught in a hurry, right? But a scientific definition of energy is cumbersome at best. Try this: energy is the capacity for doing the product of force times displacement.

Actually, the definition is not all that obscure. The product of a force and the displacement of the object on which the force acts comprises the scientist's definition of work. Thus, energy is the capacity for doing work. Notice that this definition of work excludes physiological work that produces no physical displacement of an object. For example, King Kong could hold a mature sequoia tree on his palm for an hour, and that still would not count as work.

When an object moves, it obviously has the capacity for doing work, and hence, energy. Energy of motion is called kinetic energy. The kinetic energy of an object is equal to half the product of its mass and the square of its velocity:

$$\text{kinetic energy} = \tfrac{1}{2} \text{ mass} \times (\text{velocity})^2$$

Be relaxed about the formula—you encounter such formulas even in science fiction. In *Lucifer's Hammer*, Larry Niven and Jerry Pournelle's masterpiece, the hammer is a comet directed at the earth. How much energy will it deliver? Scientists compute the answer in this scene:

"Now, she's coming at cometary speeds. *Fast.* . . . Shall we say fifty kilometers a second as a reasonable closing velocity?"

"Sounds good," Forrester said. "Meteors go from twenty to maybe seventy. It's reasonable."

"Right. Call it fifty. Square that, times a half. Times mass in grams. Bit over two times ten to the twenty-eight ergs . . ." [p. 93]

One little detail is omitted. In order to calculate the energy in the unit of ergs using the above formula, you must express the velocity in centimeters/sec before squaring. If you use standard metric units, m/sec for velocity and kg for mass, the kinetic energy is given in the unit of joules. For reference, 1 joule = 10^7 ergs.

It takes work to lift an object to a height because you have to overcome the force of gravity acting on the object. Where does the work go? It goes into storage in the object that you lifted; the object now has a potential capacity for doing work, potential energy. We say that an object at a height relative to the ground has a potential energy equal to its weight times its height.

When an object falls from a height, the object accelerates. Thus, its kinetic energy continually increases, and its potential energy continually decreases. Nevertheless, it is a fact that at each and every stage of the object's fall, the sum of its kinetic and potential energies remains the same, equal to the original starting value. This is the principle of conservation of energy: when energy is converted from one form to another, such as from potential to kinetic, the total energy—the sum of the two forms—always remains the same. Peo-

UNION COLLEGE LIBRARY

ple who build roller coasters respect this law; they never make any subsequent rises of the roller coaster higher than the initial height of the car.

Energy exists in many other forms, such as heat, electricity, waves, nuclear energy, and so forth. The energy conservation law holds for all these energy forms. Energy can be converted from one form to another but always with the constraint of the conservation law: the sum of all the forms always remains constant. Energy can be neither created nor destroyed.

Poet William Blake wrote the following beautiful lines about energy:

> Man has no Body distinct from his Soul!
> for that called Body is a portion of Soul
> discerned by the five Senses,
> the chief inlets of Soul in this age.
> Energy is the only life and is from the Body;
> and Reason is the bound or outward
> circumference of energy.
> Energy is eternal delight.

You can argue with Blake about the delightfulness of energy. But the conservation law denies any argument about whether energy is eternal.

Like energy, momentum is an *everyday* word. When something is hard to stop, we say it has a lot of momentum. Somewhat obscure is the fact that under suitable circumstances even a pinhead-size particle can be hard to stop because of its great momentum. Passengers on fast-moving spaceships have to worry about this, as in the following conversation from Isaac Asimov's *The Stars, Like Dust*:

> Gilbret held up a hand. "I know quite well it's an unlikely accident. The incidence of meteors in space—especially in interstellar space—is low enough to make the chances of collision with a ship completely insignificant, but it does happen, as you know. And it did happen in this case. Of course any meteor that does hit, even when it is the size of a pinhead, as most of them are, can penetrate the hull of any but the most heavily armored ship."
> "I know," said Biron. "It's a question of their momentum, which is a product of their mass and velocity. The velocity more than makes up for the lack of mass." [p. 423]

Thus, momentum is the product of mass and velocity; they both count. Also, since motion is relative, it is the relative velocity that is relevant in figuring the momentum. Since spaceships move with very high velocity, intruder particles must have a large relative velocity with respect to a spaceship and thus a large momentum.

The conservation law for momentum is simply this: for a closed system of bodies, a system without any interaction with the world external to that system, momentum is conserved. As a corollary, momentum is conserved for the system that is the universe.

Although Newton himself did not discover the law of conservation of momentum, it follows from his second and third laws of motion. Thus, this law is part and parcel of the Newtonian framework. Most important is its connection with the third law which is this: since internal forces in a body are action-reaction pairs, the two components of an interacting pair internal to a body gain equal and opposite momentum, but the total momentum of the body remains the same.

We can now gain additional insight into rocket motion. A rocket is accelerated forward by the reaction on its main body due to the debris that's thrown out of its rear. The main body and the debris gain equal and opposite momentum in the process.

Let's deal again with the question of reactionless drive. You can see that reactionless drive would imply violation of the law of momentum conservation. To many physicists this is even more unthinkable than the fallibility of Newton's third law. Physicists have been able to connect the law of conservation of momentum to a fundamental symmetry principle of space, homogeneity, the idea that space is similar everywhere. Physicists adore symmetry and beauty; they would be very dismayed if they found out that nature was willing to forfeit homogeneity of space for reactionless drive.

Let's discuss an idea that science fiction writer Isaac Asimov has used intelligently in his novel *The Gods Themselves*. You see, momentum conservation (and other conservation laws as well) applies only to closed systems. But suppose the universe isn't closed, but coupled to a parallel universe! Then momentum conservation would not have to hold, and we could have reactionless drive—acceleration without the discard of reaction mass. Listen to the possibilities from one of Asimov's characters:

If the moon were to be driven out of its orbit and sent out of the solar system, the conservation of momentum would make it a colossal undertaking, and probably a thoroughly impractical one. If, however, momentum could be transferred to . . . another universe, the moon could accelerate at any convenient rate without loss of mass at all. [p. 283]

Of course, you realize that such a parallel universe coupled to ours would be tantamount to saying that the universe is inhomogeneous, again arousing the aesthetic objections of physicists. Parallel universes are not exactly a novel idea, either, since they often are used as a magic wand when a science fiction writer is devoid of other solutions to a problem. Yet it is an idea which doesn't fade away; every now and then it is revived even by serious physicists to deal with some paradoxes, as we shall see later.

Anyhow, the important point in the present context is that such ideas as reactionless drive, which sound simple, may not be *really* so simple at all. If reactionless drive were realized, as many SF writers believe it will be some day, we might very well find that we do not live in an isolated universe, but that we have extra-cosmic connections.

Unlike energy and momentum, the concept of angular momentum, which applies to rotational motion, is less familiar. But the concept and its conservation are easily grasped with the help of the following example. Imagine an ice skater spotlighted on the ice. With her arms extended, she slowly spins round and round. Suddenly she pulls in her hands and lo! she speeds up. This commonplace miracle is something we all have seen. What's the secret? A conservation law, that of angular momentum, has come into play. Angular momentum is the rotational counterpart of the concept of momentum.

Let's be more specific. Imagine on object rotating about a center in a circle of radius r. If the velocity of the object is v and its mass m, then the angular momentum of the object is given as the product mvr, the product of its mass, its velocity and its distance from the center.

Coming back to our slowly revolving ice skater, we can imagine that each component mass of her body describes a circle about a center. Since her arms are extended, their masses on the average are going around in circles of large radii. But when she contracts her arms, the radii become smaller on the average. Since the product mvr must remain the same by the demands of angular momentum conservation, and since the mass m of course doesn't change, we see that the velocity v must increase. And, unavoidably, our ice skater speeds up.

You never know where angular momentum conservation may show up. The closing scene of Arthur Clarke's *Childhood's End* is one of the most dramatic ever created in science fiction. This is the story of humankind's graduation en masse from its psychic childhood. An entire generation of humans prepares to join the cosmos, the force that Clarke calls the "Overmind." The only surviving member of their bereft parent generation witnesses this grand finale:

He glanced up at the Moon, seeking some familiar sight on which his thoughts could rest. . . . The face that her satellite now turned towards the earth was not the one that had looked down on the world since the dawn of life. The Moon had begun to turn [faster] on its axis.

This could mean only one thing. On the other side of the Earth, in the land that they had stripped so suddenly of life, *they* were emerging from their long trance. As a waking child may stretch its arms to greet the day, they too were flexing their muscles and playing with their new-found powers. . . .

Very gently, the ground trembled underfoot.

"I was expecting that . . . if they alter the Moon's spin, the angular momentum must go somewhere. So the Earth is slowing down. . . ." [italics in the original, pp. 210-212]

The earth-moon is a coupled system; if one gains angular momentum from a source within the system, it can only be at the expense of the other's. Even the actions of the children of the "Overmind" are in accordance with at least one of the conservation laws of mechanics.

chapter three

Gravity Scenarios

I suggest you try my favorite demonstration to see how fast 1 *g* of acceleration is. First, challenge a friend to catch a falling dollar bill which you hold so that its midpoint is between his open thumb and forefinger. When you release the dollar bill, it falls so fast that the time of fall is shorter than the time it takes his brain to react; he won't be able to catch it. But suppose you are on the moon and getting bored. As a diversion, remembering this demonstration, you challenge a friend to catch a dollar bill. She accepts the challenge, you release the bill, she catches it! There are three possible explanations: (a) she has "woman's intuition"; (b) she is telepathic; or (c) a dollar bill falls slower on the moon than on the earth. Which explanation is correct?

Of course, this is not too much of a puzzle for science fiction or space aficionados; they know that the acceleration of fall on the moon is about one sixth that on earth, because the moon's gravity force is only one sixth as strong as that of the earth on any given object. H. G. Wells, who wrote one of the most famous lunar stories, *The First Men in the Moon,* used this weak gravity on the moon to account for many unusual scenarios. At one point the main character of this book exclaims: "I leaped with all my might. I seemed to shoot up in the air as if I should never come down." And although Wells was quite mistaken in thinking there might be plants and insectlike creatures on the moon, we have to give him credit for making his lunar creatures enormous in size, reflecting the small gravity of the lunar landscape.

But why is gravity weaker on the moon? To answer this, we have to know something about the nature of the gravity force, and who but Isaac Newton himself comes to our aid. In his *Principia,* Newton not only gave his laws of motion but also told the world about the nature of the gravity force which exists between all objects and acts along the line joining them. The magnitude of the force is proportional to the masses of each of the objects, and inversely to the square of the distance between them. This is Newton's law of universal gravitation.

Let's now investigate the factor six which is how much stronger earth's gravity is compared to the moon's on their respective surfaces. Earth is 81 times more massive than the moon, which should make earth's gravity force 81 times greater than the moon's. But the distances are different, too. For large spherical objects we have to count distance from the center, since the mass can be thought of as concentrated at the center; accordingly, the distance of an object on the surface of a planetary body is equal to the radius of the body. Now earth's radius is about 3.7 times the lunar radius; but the dependence on distance squared is one of inverse proportionality. Thus, the gravity of the earth is *less* by the factor of 13.7 (square of 3.7) on account of its greater radius. And now the total factor is 81/13.7 which is about 6.

The revolutionary fact about Newton's gravity law is not that it enables us to perform such calculations, but the suggestion that gravity is universal. At the time of Newton, when heavenly motion was regarded as something totally different from terrestrial motion, to suggest universality of physical law required extreme boldness and imagination, qualities Newton obviously had in abundance. Before Newton's law of gravity, human beings were earthlings, separated from the cosmos by superstitious beliefs they themselves invented. After Newton's laws, the human spirit could fly with no bounds, knowing that the universe had to reckon with it. And nowhere has this spirit more richly expressed itself than in science fiction's application of the gravity law to various fictional scenarios.

However, before we go into any of these adventures in gravity, I ask you to remember one thing. Gravity force between two ordinary mass objects, although nonzero, is minuscule compared to other forces that act on them. For example, take a 50 kg person, and one of 70 kg, standing a meter apart. The gravity force between them is something less than a billionth of the earth's gravity force on them (which is their weight). So you can be sure that, if one of them says to the other, "I am attracted to you," she is not talking about gravity.

A TUNNEL THROUGH THE EARTH

In Damon Knight's novel *Beyond the Barrier*, the hero was caught in more than one predicament. But he always managed to keep his cool. Why? Because he remembered his basic physics, as in the following episode:

The thought of the gulf below him was hideous. What, actually, was happening to him at this moment? The answer came at once. He was acting out one of the oldest physics problems in the book, something that *every freshman* was familiar with—the imaginary tunnel drilled through the Earth. . . . In fact, his body was a harmonic oscillator. [p. 128]

In case, unlike Knight's hero, you have never been a physics freshperson in college, some explanation is called for. To avoid complications due to the rotation of the earth, let's imagine a pole-to-pole tunnel through the earth's center. Now, let's study the gravity force on a body in this tunnel. It is unusual; your intuitive expectation from the inverse square law is that the gravity force on the body should increase as the square of the distance from the center decreases as the body falls. However, this is not so, because if a body is inside the volume of the earth, then as far as the outer shell (surface) of the earth's sphere is concerned, one side of it pulls the body outward or "up,"

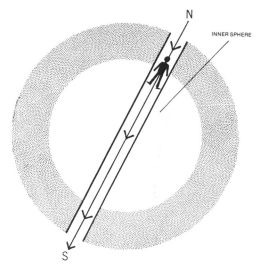

Figure 4. Down the tunnel through earth I fall. My attracting sphere of gravity shrinks as I fall deeper and deeper in the hole, and my acceleration decreases, reaching zero at the center; but there my velocity reaches its peak, decreasing on the other side of the center.

and the opposite side downward or "in." These opposite effects cancel out, so that all the gravity force on the body comes from the instantaneous inner sphere (Figure 4). If we assume uniform density, the mass of this inner sphere continually decreases as the body falls. Since mass = volume × density, and the density is constant, mass decreases as the volume. And if you recall that volume is proportional to the cube of the radius, the distance from the center, you can see that the mass of the inner sphere decreases as the cube of the distance from the center, as the body falls through the tunnel. Thus, there are two effects on the force: an inverse square law increase as the radius decreases, and a cubic law decrease. When we combine the two, the net effect is that the attraction decreases as the distance from the center does, in direct proportion.

Thus, an object entering such a tunnel would fall toward the center with less and less acceleration. At the center, there would be no force at all on the body, and therefore its acceleration would cease. Would the body stop? No, it has by then piled up a tremendous speed and would continue to move through the tunnel toward the other end under its own inertia. However, as soon as it is on the other side of the center, the force of gravity due to the instantaneous "inner sphere" of the earth would start acting up again, but this time with a role reversal. The force would now be opposite to the direction of motion, thus it would slow the body down. By the symmetry of the problem, you can guess that the object would reach the other side of the earth before it momentarily came to rest again. As Knight's hero puts it, "unless friction retarded him too much, he would rise at the antipodal point to exactly the same level he started from!"

What happens after the body reaches the other side? It starts the journey back, unless somebody snares it just as it comes out. The pattern of oscillation continues indefinitely in the absence of friction. Such an oscillating body is called a harmonic oscillator.

For a harmonic oscillator, the period of the oscillation is always the same. How do we figure out the period? Knight's hero carries out the cutest little calculation in his head as he falls (and all this without even a pocket calculator!):

Call the radius of the Earth four thousand miles—about twenty million feet, for convenience. Gravity at the surface of the Earth, thirty-two feet per second per second. The square root of twenty million over thirty-two would be two hundred and fifty times the square root of ten . . . times *pi* . . . about twenty-five-hundred seconds. Call it forty-two minutes. He ran through the calculation once more, found no error.

Very well, in forty-two minutes, if he was right, he would be emerging from the far side of the planet. [pp. 128–129]

As it turned out in the story, the hero had some surprises coming to him yet. But the calculation is quite accurate for the earth as is. What's more, if we send a train underground along a chord of the earth's spherical body (Figure 5), the train also falls like a harmonic oscillator, practically free of any

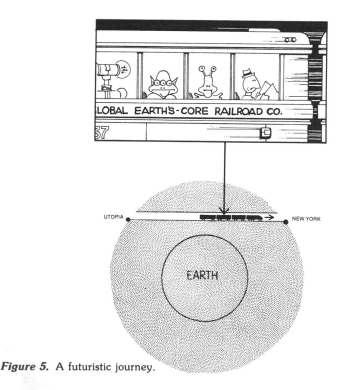

Figure 5. A futuristic journey.

energy cost, taking exactly 42 minutes for the journey, neglecting friction. Many futurists are really excited about trains like this. In science fiction, such trains are old hat, of course. You can find an example of such trains in Robert A. Heinlein's novel *The Moon Is a Harsh Mistress.*

A VOYAGE NEAR A NEUTRON STAR

Larry Niven is a science fiction writer with the very special talent of creating novel SF perspectives from fertile ideas he picks up from the forefront of physics. And nowhere is this ability better exemplified than in the title story of his collection named *Neutron Star.*

What is a neutron star? A neutron star is a very compact star built almost entirely from elementary particles called neutrons, which are the neutral components of atomic nuclei. Neutron stars are so compact that in their asteroid-size bodies of only a few tens of kilometers radius is packed two or three times the mass of our sun. In quantitative terms, the density of neutronium (neutron-star matter) is a hundred trillion times greater than that of solar matter or of earthly water. Neutron stars are the final result of the evolution of stars that start out as three or more solar masses, spew out some of their mass in gigantic explosions called supernovae, and then collapse under their own gravity. Neutron stars have been observed in quite large numbers since 1965, and now there is a whole catalogue of them. What makes a neutron star quite readily observable is that it rotates fast, with a period of one second or less (compare this with the sun's rotational period of about thirty days), and emits pulses of radiation with this characteristic period. For this reason, neutron stars are also known as pulsars.

Now to Niven's story. The hero of the story has a contract with a "puppeteer" of a nonhuman race to explore a neutron star, BVS-1. The puppeteers had developed a spaceship with an impregnable hull; yet when they sent a couple of explorers in an orbit within a mile of BVS-1, an unknown force (force-X) somehow penetrated their "General Products hull" and killed the pilots. The puppeteers want the hero of the story to find out more about this unknown force.

As our hero approaches BVS-1, he too starts to feel the presence of the unknown force.

Something gripped the ship through a General Products hull. A psychokinetic life form stranded on a sun twelve miles in diameter? But how could anything alive stand such gravity? Something might be stranded in orbit. There is life in space: outsiders and sailseeds, maybe others we haven't found yet. For all I knew or cared, BVS-1 itself might be alive. It didn't matter. I knew what the X-force was trying to do. It was trying to pull the ship apart. . . .

Gravity was changing faster than I liked. The X-force was growing as zero hour approached, while the compensating rocket thrust dropped. The X-force tended to pull the ship apart; it was two gee forward at the nose, two gee backward at the tail, and diminished to zero at the center of mass. Or so I hoped. . . .

The back wall was fifteen feet away. I had to jump it with gravity changing in midair. I hit on my hands, bounced away. I'd jumped too late. . . . It [the center of mass] had left me behind. . . .

Under something less than half a gee, I jumped for the access tube. For one long moment I stared into the three-foot tunnel, stopped in midair and already beginning to fall back, as I realized that there was nothing to hang on to. Then I stuck my hands in the tube and spread them against the sides. It was all I needed. I levered myself up and started to crawl. . . .

I knew what force was trying to tear the ship apart.

It was the tide. [p. 25]

Niven has an almost plausible explanation of why the puppeteers would be ignorant of such a common phenomenon as tides. The puppeteer's mother planet doesn't have a moon. And without a moon, the tidal effects on a planet would be rather inconspicuous. Yet the explanation isn't perfect; every planet has to have a life-supporting sun. And the sun too creates a tide, although often a less prominent one than does a moon.

Perhaps now you are inquisitive about why the tidal effects are so devastating in the vicinity of a neutron star. Curiously, the answer lies in the examination of the commonly acknowledged fact mentioned above: the tidal effect of a moon is greater than that of the sun of a planetary system. And ultimately, the answer also relates to the more fundamental question: what causes tides?

WHAT CAUSES TIDES?

If an earthling is asked "What causes tides?" he probably will say without much thinking, "The gravity pull of the moon, of course." And of course he will be wrong. Tides are not caused by lunar gravity per se, but by the fact that the force of lunar gravity is different at different points on earth. That is to say, some parts of the earth are more strongly attracted than others. The moon is 240,000 miles away from the earth's center, but the radius of the earth is 4000 miles. Thus, the near side of the earth is only 236,000 miles from the moon, while the far side is 244,000 miles away. Since gravity force decreases with distance, clearly the force of lunar gravity is stronger on the near side than at the center, and it is weaker yet on the far side.

We can think of the force of lunar gravity at the center of the earth as the average of the moon's gravity pull. Compared to this average, the near side has an excess pull, what we term a positive gravity gradient, which creates a

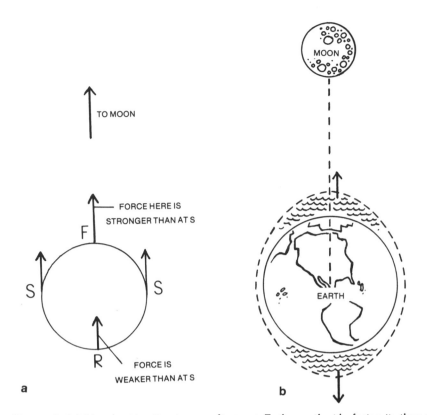

Figure 6. (a) Moon's attraction is more fierce at *F*, the earth side facing it, than the average force at *S*. Au contraire, the attraction at the rear side *R* is less than the average. (b) Two tides during a twenty-four-hour day explained. The ocean water facing the moon bulges because of a positive gravity gradient; this is obvious. The water on the other side must also show a bulge, because of a negative gravity gradient: the earth underneath is attracted away from it.

positive tidal force toward the moon. Likewise, on the far side, there is a deficit, a negative gravity gradient, or negative tidal force away from the moon (Figure 6a). It is these gravity gradients that cause simultaneous tides at the near side and the far side, but there is no tidal force at the center. This is the reason that Niven's hero in "Neutron Star" tries to find the center of mass of his ship. The net effect of the positive and negative gradients is to stretch the object ("The *X*-force tended to pull the ship apart").

Now you can understand why there are two tides during a twenty-four-hour period. When the moon is overhead at a certain place on earth it pulls the near side of the earth away from the center, thus causing a tide. But there is a similar effect on the opposite side as the earth's center is pulled away from that side, and there is a tidal bulge there as well (Figure 6b). As the earth continues to rotate, the situation will be reversed twelve hours later;

but clearly, every place on earth will experience two high tides during a twenty-four-hour period.

Thus, it is the gravity gradient, the variation of gravity force on a large body from one point to another, that is responsible for tides; in order for the tidal effect to be large, the variation of the force has to be large. And here, the most important consideration is how close you are to the gravitating object. Therefore, although the sun's gravity force on the earth as a whole is obviously much greater than the moon's, the sun is much, much farther away, so the *variation* of this gravity force over the earth's body is much less spectacular than the variation of the moon's. As a result, the moon's tidal effect is greater than that of the sun by more than a factor of two. This is not to say that the effect of solar tide is negligible. In fact, twice in a month the sun, the moon, and the earth line up, during periods of the full and the new moon. The tidal force of the sun and the moon now act in unison, and the bulge is certainly greater. The greater tidal bulge is called the spring tide. Likewise, when the sun and the moon pull at right angles, also twice in a month, the tidal bulge is at a minimum, giving us the neap tide.

Now you can appreciate the greatness of Niven's story. Because of the compactness of a neutron star and because a neutron star does not emit as much radiation as an ordinary star, it is entirely plausible to approach very close to it, particularly in a spaceship with an "impenetrable" hull. The gravity gradient or the tidal force *that* close to a neutron star will be considerable over the length of a spaceship, and even over the length of a human body.

Another tide-related phenomenon, Roche's limit, is sometimes mentioned in science fiction. If a small planet or satellite approaches too near a sun or larger planet, the tidal force tends to rip it apart. The planet's own gravity counteracts this tendency, but Roche's limit is reached when the tidal force overcomes the planet's self-gravity.

One final question may be bothering you. We spoke so much of the tidal force, the gradient of gravity, but how about the effect of the gravity force itself on an approaching body? This is a funny thing about gravity: when we are in free fall under gravity alone, we feel no adverse effect. Sure, we feel weightless, but that's because we customarily stand on a planet's surface which, acting on us with a reaction force, gives us the feeling of weight. The absence of this reaction force is responsible for the feeling of weightlessness. Otherwise, there really is no effect of the gravity force, however large it may be, in free fall. We shall discuss more about this in a later chapter.

Isn't it reassuring to know that even if you fell toward a black hole (the hypothesized supermassive, invisible stars from which even light cannot escape), the black hole's gravity would cause you no more discomfort than when your car coasts down a long, steep hill? But watch out for that tidal force! Not only would it hurt, but it would change your shape quite conspicuously (Figure 6c).

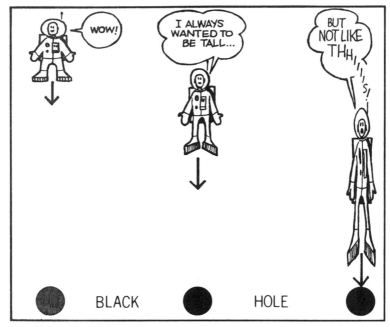

Figure 6(c).

GRAVITY AND ANTIGRAVITY

Imagine yourself sitting restfully in your backyard under the shade of an apple tree when an apple detaches itself from the tree. But instead of falling downward like other apples, this one "falls" upward. You would be witnessing an antigravitating apple; such a discovery would indeed make your name as immortal as Newton's, who hit upon the idea of universal gravity by observing a normal, downward-falling apple.

You're right, your chance of seeing an upward-falling apple is feeble, but as a reader of science fiction you will recognize that the idea of antigravity is quite common in SF literature. However, the scenario in which antigravity is discovered is purposefully more sophisticated than upward-falling apples; there may be complicated machines at work in a laboratory, perhaps mention of a new kind of material, and so forth. The SF writer tries to create the impression that, although antigravitating objects are not commonplace in nature, there nevertheless may be such objects, and—with intelligence, luck, or both—we might discover one in laboratory experimentation.

One related concept frequently encountered in science fiction is the idea of a gravity shield, a shield made of material that can screen off gravity. H. G. Wells was among the first to use this idea powerfully in his novel *The First Men in the Moon;* its hero, Cavor, conceived of the gravity shield in analogy to "screens of various sorts to shut off light or heat, or electrical influence of the sun, or the warmth of the earth." Wells wrote:

You can screen things by sheets of metal from Marconi's rays [radio waves], but nothing will cut off the gravitational attraction of the sun or the gravitational attraction of the earth. Yet why there would be nothing is hard to say. Cavor did not see why such a substance should not exist, and he believed he might be able to manufacture this possible substance opaque to gravitation . . .

Anyone with the merest germ of imagination will understand the extraordinary possibilities of such a substance . . . For example, if one wanted to lift a weight, however enormous, one had only to get a sheet of this substance beneath it and one might lift it with a straw. [p. 23]

But Cavor's ambition for "Cavorite" goes far beyond lifting heavy objects. With a friend's help he constructed the spaceship described below for their journey to the moon.

"Imagine a sphere, large enough to hold two people and their luggage. It will be made of steel and thick glass; it will contain a proper store of solidified air, concentrated food, water distilling apparatus, and so forth, and enamelled, as it were, on the outer steel—Cavorite. The inner glass sphere can be airtight, and except for the manhole, continuous, and the steel sphere can be made in sections, each section capable of rolling up after the fashion of a roller blind. These can be easily worked by springs, and released and checked by electricity conveyed by platinum wires fused through the glass. . . . Except for the thickness of the blind rollers, the Cavorite exterior of the sphere will consist of windows or blinds, whichever you like to call them. Well, when all these windows or blinds are shut, no light, no heat, no gravitation, no radiant energy of any sort will get at the inside of the sphere, it will fly on through space in straight lines, as you say. But open a window, imagine one of the windows open. Then at once any heavy body that chances to be in that direction will attract us. . . ." [p. 42]

How does this marvelous spaceship lift off from earth? The Cavorite shield makes it completely weightless and such a weightless object is buoyed up to the top of the ocean of air, just as a cork released at the bottom of a swimming pool rises to the top of the water. It then continues by inertia, retaining the motion of earth's rotation. Once in space, Cavor and his friend navigate by manipulating the shutters to draw on the gravitational attraction of the sun, the moon, or the earth, whichever is appropriate, until they reach the moon, their destination.

Well done. But, so many years after Wells wrote this, we still don't have a gravity shield, and for very profound reasons. Wells' Cavorite is modeled after an electrical shield. The latter is possible because of the existence of two kinds of charges, positive and negative. Between charges of the same kind—for example, positive and positive—the electrical force is repulsive. For unlike charges, positive and negative, the electrical force is attractive. It is this existence of both attractive and repulsive forces in electrical phenomena that makes shielding possible. Moreover, we now know that material properties such as shielding that metals possess (for example, an automobile body is virtually impenetrable to the electrical forces of lightning) are really a manifestation of the electrical interactions within matter in the submicroscopic, the atomic, scale.

On the other hand, with gravitation as Newton saw it (and Newton's theory explains most gravitational phenomena), there is only one kind of mass, positive, and only an attractive force. All masses attract each other gravitationally, according to Newton; there is never any repulsion. This is the fundamental problem in creating antigravity.

There is also a second, technical problem. Gravity is inconsequential at the atomic level. Newton's law of universal gravitation states that the magnitude of the gravity force is proportional to the two masses involved, and inversely proportional to the square of the distance between the two masses. If we use the minuscule masses of atomic particles and the appropriate distances between them, we find that the gravity force between subatomic particles, even at subatomic distances, is minuscule compared to other forces acting upon them. Thus, even if there existed negative masses and hence—theoretically— gravitational repulsion, it would still be unlikely for any manifestation of it at the atomic level to give us a special material like Cavorite that could shield gravity; the masses have to be quite sizable to produce an effect such as shielding.

Actually, there is a third, very serious theoretical objection. A close look at the idea of the negative mass object reveals that it would possess some strange properties. Newton's second law tells us that the acceleration of an object due to a force is given by the equation $F = ma$, or

$$\text{force} = \text{mass} \times \text{acceleration}$$

If mass is negative in this equation, the direction of acceleration is opposite to the direction of force. So if you push a negative mass one way, it accelerates the opposite way.

Suppose we analyze the mutual effects of a positive mass and a negative mass, keeping the above perverse behavior of the latter in mind. Look at Figure 7. The gravitational repulsion of the negative mass accelerates the positive mass to the right. The force on the negative mass is to the left, but since it accelerates in a direction opposite to the force acting on it, the acceleration of the negative mass is also to the right. So instead of moving away from the positive mass, the negative mass actually chases it. This is very different from the behavior of two charges that repel each other; in that case we see actual repelling motion.

If we look at the concept of mass as the quantity of matter in a body, as Newton did, then we don't see any hole in the above argument. But people after Newton have wanted to understand the concept of mass better through

Figure 7. The negative mass always chases the positive mass.

the laws that introduce mass to us. When we think of it, mass enters physics through two independent laws. First, the second law of motion, in which the role of mass is seen as connected with an object's inertia, introduces "inertial mass." But mass also appears in the law of gravitation, which mass we naturally can think of as "gravitational mass." But now we ask, Suppose the mass of an object that appears in Newton's gravity law, gravitational mass, is not identical with its inertial mass that appears in Newton's second law? Could it be that the object's gravitational mass is negative, but its inertial mass remains positive? Unfortunately, Einstein would object to that. After very careful study of the gravity phenomenon, Einstein gave us a powerful principle named the principle of equivalence according to which the gravitational and inertial masses of all objects must be strictly equal—no exception. This has since been verified experimentally. Moreover, Einstein's theory of gravitation, the general theory of relativity that encompasses Newton's gravity law as a special case and that has spectacular ingredients such as curved space, is based on this equivalence principle. It would be a very turbulent situation indeed if this theory were so seriously compromised.

We may as well accept that it is impossible to construct a gravity shield, especially since the existence of negative masses would not lead to gravitational repulsion. So, do we give up on antigravity devices? Maybe not. There is yet another curious aspect of the chasing of a positive mass by a negative one. It seems that by putting a negative mass behind a regular positive mass spaceship, we can accelerate the latter indefinitely. Recalling the concept of conservation of energy, you may object to this on the ground that this would mean the creation of energy from nothing. But this objection can be overruled by noting that a negative mass has negative energy, and therefore the energy of the negative mass becomes more and more negative as it accelerates, thus becoming less and less. So the energy that the positive mass keeps gaining is actually at the expense of the decreasing energy of the negative mass.

The above suggestion for a space-drive is from a respected physicist, Banesh Hoffman. The idea has found its way into science fiction in Ian Watson's novel *Miracle Visitors*, in which you can see his "circuit diagram" of a space-craft propelled by a "bipolar gravity field" generated by such a positive mass–negative mass pair.

But here comes the flaw. In quantum theory (its ideas will be expounded later), the existence of negative mass and negative energy states causes a deep theoretical problem. The energy-emitting transmission of normal matter to such states (strange as it sounds, this is allowed in quantum theory) will fill even a small region of space with infinite energy. This is impossible, and signals the breakdown of the entire theoretical picture involving the negative mass. Thus, the idea of a space vehicle being accelerated by a negative mass which keeps chasing it may not be valid after all, since it leads to the collapse of the underlying physics.

As you may suspect from these arguments, most physicists today do not believe in the idea of negative mass or antigravity. Nevertheless, experimental physicists have a compelling motive for looking, so far fruitlessly, for a negative mass. The perverse behavior of the negative mass depicted in Figure 7 is due to our tacit assumption of the validity of the equivalence principle: that the gravitational and inertial masses of objects are equal. Suppose this is not the case. Suppose that somehow a negative mass did not obey the equivalence principle and its inertial mass was positive although its gravitational mass was negative. Such a negative mass object would truly be repelled by a body of positive mass and would be a genuine antigravity object. Arthur C. Clarke is correct, of course, when he says: "There is nothing inherently absurd in the idea that there may be substances which possess negative gravity." But if these particles were found, we might have to discard the equivalence principle as universal.

chapter four

How Large Is Our Spaceship?

Inventor Buckminster Fuller coined the phrase "Spaceship Earth" to remind us that earth, like a spaceship sailing through the vast, practically empty ocean of space, is a finite ecosystem with a finite amount of resources. What makes Fuller's metaphor perfect is that it is literally true. Earth indeed moves through space, taking two hundred million or so years to complete its journey around the center of our galaxy. In its slow journey, our position in space changes hardly at all in the span of a single human lifetime; an entire civilization can rise and fall while the earth advances just a bit in its cosmic journey. Only the astronomer's measuring instruments verify the truth of earth being a spaceship.

But we, the inhabitants of earth, don't much behave as if we lived in the finite environment of a spaceship. Consider. The technological advancement of the last century, of which we are justly proud, has been possible only because of the plentiful availability of energy in the form of cheap fossil fuels. But fossil fuel consumption has a price tag—air pollution. Air pollution is already a problem of worldwide proportion. Now suppose the energy consumption continues to double every twenty years, as it has for the past few decades, and suppose that we continue to depend on fossil fuel for our energy. Then the nightmare of some of John Brunner's SF novels could soon become a reality. The following is an excerpt from Brunner's novel *The Sheep Look Up*. You won't like it.

In spite of the few cars, the air stank. She had taken off her mask, not wanting to be conspicuous—at least, no more than was due to being white. In this district people didn't wear them. They seemed inured to the reek. The chests of the children were shallow, as though to discourage overdeep breathing.

She stared at the Santa Clauses. Behind those once white beards, now grimed from an excursion in the open, she could not make out their faces. She did, though, notice that the second man in the line was only moving his lips, not booming out his "Ho-ho-ho!" His eyes were bulging with the effort of repressing a cough. [p. 42]

Now if we really convinced ourselves that we live on a spaceship, we would act differently. Robert A. Heinlein's science fiction novel *Space Cadet* centers around a spaceship. Here's how the crew of the spaceship *Randolf* handles air pollution:

. . . the primary purpose of the "farm" is to take the carbon dioxide out of the air. For this purpose each man in the ship must be balanced by about ten square feet of green plant leaf. [p. 146]

Carbon dioxide is potentially one of the most dangerous air pollutants on our spaceship earth. Carbon dioxide blanketing the earth helps keep the earth warm; however, continually increasing the amount of carbon dioxide in the atmosphere produces an increasing "greenhouse effect" (the trapping of heat using the principle of greenhouses). At some stage, excessive heat trapping could heat the earth to such an extent as to trigger a whole series of devastating climatic changes; it has been calculated that one of the Antarctic glaciers will melt in the next 25–100 years, putting all of our Atlantic seaboard under water. Yet this problem is readily solved by farming, growing extra vegetation *Randolph* style. Farming would not only eliminate excess carbon dioxide from the atmosphere, but would also supply the trees for a future fuel reserve. It would be very much like the dividend of fresh food and flowers that *Randolph*'s crew receives from its harvest.

Perhaps the spaceship metaphor can be extended. Let's ask an intriguing question: how big is our spaceship? The question may seem paradoxical to you if you think that the earth is isolated, but it's not. Most of our energy comes directly or indirectly from the sun, you know—including the fossil fuels. Thus, the sun, as the source of our energy, is very much a part of our spaceship—it is our massive hydrogen fusion reactor.

So on our cosmic journey, we literally take the sun along (or the sun takes us along, there is really no difference since gravity is mutual). Likewise, the whole solar system tags along: the other solar planets and their satellites. They all are a part of our spaceship—Venus and Mars, our closest neighbors; the gas giants, Jupiter and Saturn, and their satellites; even the distant Neptune and Pluto, our sentinels at the door to outer space.

Science fiction writers have always recognized this. In Kurt Vonnegut's *The Sirens of Titan,* a novel of interstellar intrigue involving the Trafalmadorians, the involvement of earthpeople is not confined to earth alone, but spreads all over the spaceship to Mars and to Titan. We must catch on to this new perspective of our cosmic home and catch on fast, because time may be running out for us.

The dangers from pollution, overpopulation and famine, faulty economics, the oil crisis, the arms race, and the continuing limited warfare on our globe are much more serious than we are ready to accept. It is not improbable (nor is it doomsaying to suggest) that a few of these things, synergistically acting, could start off a chain reaction. SF writer Kate Wilhelm's Hugo-winning novel *Where Late the Sweet Birds Sang* is based on such a future holocaust. In the following excerpts Wilhelm describes the sequence of events that culminates in the near destruction of life on our planet.

". . . The pollution's catching up to us faster than anyone knows. There's more radiation in the atmosphere than there's been since Hiroshima—French tests, China's tests. Leaks. God knows where all of it's coming from. The famines are here . . . and there are plagues. . . . We're having shortages no one ever dreamed of. Tin, copper, aluminum, paper. . . ."

Cholera struck in Rome, Los Angeles, Galveston, and Savannah. Saudi Arabia, Kuwait, Jordan, and other Arab-bloc nations issued an ultimatum: the United States must guarantee a yearly ration of wheat to the Arab bloc and discontinue all aid to the state of Israel or there would be no oil for the United States or Europe. They refused to believe that the United States could not meet their demands.

Rationing, black markets, inflation, and looting had turned the cities into battle mounds. . . . With the failure of radio and television communication, there was no way for the government to cope with the rising panic. [pp. 13–15, 21]

You get the picture. However, it is less urgent to realize that such a catastrophe could happen than it is to know that it can almost certainly be avoided. While necessarily learning to live in harmony with our ecosystem, we can begin to explore the entire solar system, expanding our quarters in the rest of our spaceship. It would be more constructively productive to direct our technology away from the arms race and wasteful consumer-oriented pursuits, and toward further exploration of our nearby space. Our present technology is adequate except for some details which can be learned "on the job."

I like science fiction because SF writers are among those pioneers who recognize the urgency of opening the sky. I feel like the hero of one of Kurt Vonnegut's (non-SF) novels, *God Bless You, Mr. Rosewater,* who expressed his gratitude in this emotional outburst:

I love you sons of bitches. . . . You're all I read any more. You're the only ones who'll talk about the *really* terrific changes going on, the only ones crazy enough to know that life is a space voyage, and not a short one, either, but one that'll last for billions of years. You're the only ones with guts enough to *really* care about the future, who *really* notice what machines do to us, what wars do to us, what cities do to us, what big, simple ideas do to us, what tremendous misunderstandings, mistakes, accidents and catastrophes do to us. You're the only ones zany enough to agonize over time and distances without limit, over mysteries that will never die, over the fact that we are right now determining whether the space voyage for the next billion years or so is going to be Heaven or Hell. [p. 18]

EXPLORING THE SOLAR SYSTEM

How do we go about exploring the solar system? The initially popular idea of science fiction was that of colonizing the nearby planets first and then slowly moving out to the outer-rim planetary systems. Early in the game, Mars and Venus were thought to be habitable; when it became apparent as a result of space probe investigations that the environments of these two planets are not especially friendly to life, ideas for making them habitable began to take shape. Nowadays, perhaps as a result of studies in this field by serious scientists, such solutions as terraforming are mentioned frequently in the SF literature. Terraforming (I think James Blish first coined the word) is the idea of engineering the climatic conditions of a planet such as Venus so that it becomes habitable to Terrans.

Another influential change has taken place recently in our view of the rest of the solar system. Early on, the faraway planets were believed to be definitely hostile to life. But thanks to the work of exobiologists, it is now clear that there is nothing inherently impossible about life developing even in the atmosphere of Jupiter, let alone in far more suitable places such as the satellite Titan of Saturn.

A major impetus to the science fiction dream of exploring the solar planets, near and far, has come from the success of our space projects. In a matter of only decades our accomplishments include manned flight to the moon, unmanned landings on Venus and Mars, and close space probe observations of the Jupiter and Saturn systems among other feats such as the space lab. The space age is truly off the ground.

The main problem in exploring nearby space is gravity; it costs energy to overcome gravity, and such science-fictiony ideas as antigravity and the reactionless drive, which would bypass this energy demand, have little chance to materialize. I will first give you some idea of the physics involved in realistic journeys around the solar system. I call these stage I ideas; they are already in practice.

Next comes a series of stage II ideas. These involve such recently publicized ventures as space colonies and solar sails. We can reasonably expect these stage II ideas to be implemented within the next few centuries.

And finally, there are some stage III ideas, which are very long-range and admittedly farfetched. For example, as popular as it is in SF, terraforming is a stage III idea because, by even the most optimistic estimates, it would take about ten thousand years to achieve success in terraforming a planet such as Venus. This time scale is so huge compared to the pace of today's science and technology that all the ideas of this stage are considered for little more than the sheer fun of speculation.

STAGE I: ARTIFICIAL SATELLITES

In a novel depicting the near future, *The Fountains of Paradise,* Arthur Clarke has one of his characters proclaim:

"Go out of doors any clear night . . . and you will see that commonplace wonder of our age—the stars that never rise or set, but are fixed motionless in the sky. We, and our parents, and *their* parents have long taken for granted the synchronous satellites and space stations, which move above the equator at the same speed as the turning earth, and so hang forever above the same spot." [p. 44]

The first such artificial satellites (not synchronous ones) ascended into our sky in the late fifties and early sixties; but already in the eighties, communication satellites—those that are used for radio and video transmission—have become quite common, although space stations have not. The idea of communication satellites was suggested by Arthur C. Clarke, actually, not too long before the first satellites were launched. However, the idea of an artificial satellite is itself very old. It was suggested by Isaac Newton himself.

The principle is quite simple. If you throw a stone horizontally from a mountain top, the stone will fall to the ground following a curved parabolic path (Figure 8a). If you throw the stone harder, the stone will still hit the ground describing another parabola in the air, but the radius of the parabola will increase (Figure 8b). And this is the thing: the harder you throw, the larger is the "radius." Now we can ask, Suppose you throw the stone so hard that the radius of its trajectory is just a bit greater than the radius of the earth itself. What happens? The stone will no longer fall back to earth, but will fall around it in a circle (Figure 8c). The path of the stone will curve at the same rate as the surface of the earth, thus excluding the possibility of any collision between the two. The stone has become a satellite. If there were no atmosphere, it would continue indefinitely in its path.

Question. If the earth attracts the stone toward it with the gravity force, why doesn't the stone fall into the earth? This is the same question as, Why don't the planets fall into the sun? or, Why doesn't earth's moon fall into the earth? The answer is: because of the "horizontal" velocity tangential to the path. The gravity force is responsible for an acceleration, one that is always directed toward the center. Such an acceleration is called a centripetal (center-seeking) acceleration. As the projectile (or planet) moves tangentially in its path, it also falls a little under the centripetal acceleration. The result of these two motions is that the projectile continually orbits (Figure 8d).

The most usual paths of orbiting bodies are ellipses, elongated circles (Figure 8e). German astrophysicist Johannes Kepler, Galileo's contemporary, was the first to discover this (Kepler's first law); before him everybody, following Greek thinking, assumed that all heavenly objects move in circles. (Before the scientific era, people also believed that angels push the planets around and around the sun.) Newton's discovery of the gravity law explained the details of Kepler's observations on the solar planets.

Coming back to the stone thrown around the earth, we know that its

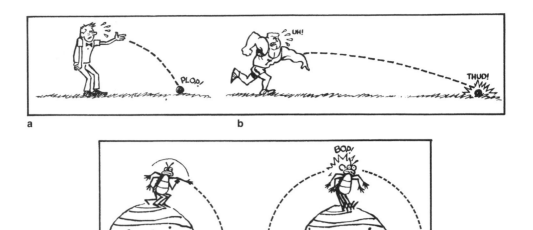

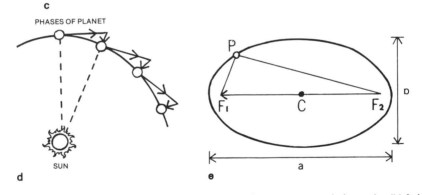

PHASES OF PLANET

SUN

P

F_1 C F_2

D

a

Figure 8. (a) I throw a ball; it falls to the ground, tracing a parabolic path. (b) I throw the ball harder, and the parabola reaches farther out. (c) If the ball is thrown very hard—at a speed of 8 kilometers per second, to be precise—it would make a complete circle around the earth. (d) A planet does fall a little bit from its instantaneous tangential course as it goes around the sun. (e) An ellipse with its major axis a and minor axis b defined as shown. F_1 and F_2 are its two foci. C is the center. To draw an ellipse, make a loop with a piece of cord, anchoring the two ends with thumbtacks at F_1 and F_2 on a drawing board. Put a pencil through the loop and draw. The point P at the pencil will go around and make an ellipse.

horizontal velocity has to be 8 km/sec (5 miles/sec or 18,000 miles/hr) before it can become a satellite. And this is true for all artificial satellites; 8 km/sec is the minimum velocity requirement for them. You can see why there was such a huge time lag between Newton's suggesting the idea and our carrying it out. Rockets had to be invented and developed before the feat could be accomplished.

One important thing about these Kepler orbits is that the period, the time it takes for the satellite to complete an orbit, varies with the average distance from the earth. Kepler's third law gave the exact relationship: the square of the orbital time period is proportional to the cube of the average distance. A satellite in a circular orbit such as that of the first Skylab, just 400 kilometers above the earth's surface, has a period of only one-and-a-half hours; but if we launch a satellite in an orbit farther away from the earth, the period will increase. If we put a satellite at a distance of 35,700 kilometers (or 22,300 miles) from the earth's surface, the satellite's period will be 24 hours (23 hours 56 minutes to be exact; the 4-minute difference takes account of earth's orbital motion around the sun). Such a satellite is synchronized with earth's rotation, and has many uses.

We previously mentioned Heinlein's novel *Space Cadet*. Heinlein makes great use of physics in all his books; *Space Cadet* is especially filled with gravity scenarios. This excerpt describes a spaceship in a synchronous orbit:

Terra space station and the school ship *Randolf* lie in a circular orbit 22,300 miles above the surface of the earth, where they circle the earth in exactly twenty-four hours, the natural period of a body at that distance. Since the earth's rotation exactly matches their period, they face always one side of the earth—the ninetieth western meridian, to be exact. Their orbit lies in the ecliptic, the plane of the earth's orbit around the sun, rather than the plane of the earth's equator. This results in their swinging north and south each day as seen from the earth. When it is noon in the middle west, Terra station and the *Randolph* lie over the Gulf of Mexico; at midnight they lie over the South Pacific. [p. 58]

And of course, there is also an advantage in having satellites with highly elongated elliptical orbits. Spider and Jeanne Robinson have written about a dance troupe in orbit in the novel *Stardance*. The troupe tape their dance repertoires while in free fall, but don't want to change their work habits, acquired while growing up on earth. Here's how things work out for them:

By the second year our studio was taking shape. We settled on a highly elongated orbit. At perigee [the point of the orbit closest to the earth] the studio came as close as 3200 kilometers to Earth (not very close—Skylab was up less than 450 klicks [kilometers]), and at apogee [the point of the orbit farthest away from earth] it swung way out to about 80,000 klicks. The point of this was to keep Earth from hogging half the sky in every tape; at apogee Terra was about fist-sized (subtending a little more than 9° of arc), and we spent most of our time far away from it [Kepler's second law: the closer a satellite is to its primary, the faster it swings around]. Since we made a complete orbit almost twice a day, that gave two possible taping periods of almost eight hours apiece in every twenty-four hours. We simply adjusted our "inner clock," our biological cycle, so that one of these two periods came between "nine" and "five" subjective. [p. 125]

MORE STAGE I: ESCAPING THE EARTH

Science fiction writer Jules Verne was ahead of his time in many products of his imagination. He wrote *Journey to the Moon* in 1860, more than a hundred years ahead of the actual lunar expedition. One of Verne's strengths as an SF writer was his awareness of actual scientific estimates, and his characters used them quite impressively. In the following excerpt Impey Barbicane, the president of the Baltimore Gun Club, is proposing a trip to the moon to fellow members:

"There is no one among you, my brave colleagues, who has not seen the Moon. . . . Enter into my plans, and second me with all your power, and I will lead you to its conquest. . . . I have looked at the question in all its bearings, and I have resolutely attacked it, and by incontrovertible calculations I find that the projectile endowed with an initial velocity of 12,000 yards per second, and aimed at the Moon, must necessarily reach it."

And Mr. Barbicane was quite right, at least in principle. Any projectile launched with a velocity of 12,000 yards per second, or in more conventional units 11.2 kilometers per second, will indeed overcome earth's gravity and be free to travel outward. Accordingly, this velocity is referred to as the escape velocity from the earth.

How do you figure this? Intuitively, we can guess that it is all a matter of energy. If we endow a projectile with sufficient kinetic energy, it will escape the bondage of earth's gravity. The minimum kinetic energy needed can be calculated from considerations of the potential energy of the projectile.

We know that the potential energy of an object at a height above the ground is computed as the product weight times height. But this is the potential energy relative to the ground. To find a value for the potential energy without reference to the ground, we ask, Where is the potential energy zero? Answer: potential energy is due to earth's gravity, therefore it must vanish where the force vanishes—that is, at infinite distance from the earth. But this is also the greatest height of the object that we can think of! Thus, this must be where the object has maximum potential energy. Surprise! The maximum value of gravitational potential energy is zero. What kind of quantity is potential energy, then? A negative quantity, of course.

Thus, the total energy of an object bound to earth—the sum of its kinetic and potential energy—is negative, unless the kinetic energy is large enough to compensate for the negative potential energy. You can think of the negative potential energy as a well; kinetic energy is needed to escape the well, and the amount depends on how deep the well is. On the earth's surface the depth of the well is such that a minimum velocity of 11.2 kilometers per second is needed to get free of the well without dropping back.

This escape velocity crucially depends on the ratio of mass to radius of the planet or the body you are trying to escape. This ratio is smaller for the planet Mars than for earth, and for the moon the ratio is smaller still. Thus, it is easier to escape Mars and the moon than the earth. This is the reason that Mars has a thinner atmosphere and the moon has no atmosphere at all.

One way to concretize the concept of the gravity potential-well is to plot it for any gravitating object to show how the well changes as we move farther and farther away from the object. If we do this for the sun's gravity-well, we get a graph as shown in Figure 9. You see how the well becomes shallower as we get to the outer planets. Thus, launching spaceships out of the solar system is much easier from the outer planets.

Figure 9 has one conceptual trap that you must avoid. It may seem that

Figure 9. The sun's gravity well. The planets' astrological signs are shown not because the planets' courses obey astrology but because astronomers for historical reasons still use these symbols.

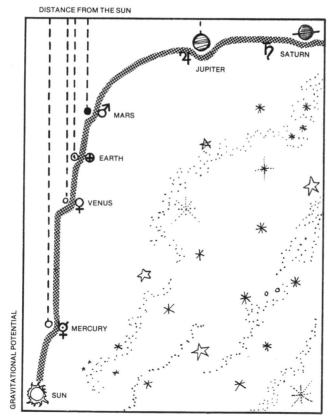

going toward the bottom of the well is free. But this is not necessarily so, because in rocket motion speeding up and slowing down both require that reaction mass be pushed out of the rocket; back or front, the energy cost is the same. Thus, when a rocket escapes earth's gravity (in Figure 9 earth's gravity is indicated by the little kink on the curve), the rocket continues to move with earth's orbital velocity about the sun; it cannot come any closer to the sun unless it is slowed down deliberately. So, to reach Venus from earth we slow down the rocket; to reach Mars, we speed it up: but both maneuvers cost us energy.

Our space program started when Mariner II took a close look at Venus in 1962. And now at the end of 1980, the probe Voyager I has just finished its swirl around Saturn, feeding back an astonishing amount of new data such as the fact that the *F*-ring of Saturn (one of the outer rings) is three-braided. Earlier the Viking mission to Mars disheartened and surprised a few of us with the discovery that there is no trace of life, no biological activity of any kind, on this most nearly earthlike planet in the solar system. Fortunately, now Voyager I has confirmed what we suspected some time ago—that Titan's atmosphere, consisting of nitrogen and hydrocarbons, is very much like earth's primeval atmosphere. Thus, astronomers and exobiologists will continue to look at Titan with interest, as science fiction writers have been doing for some time.

What the space missions of the past twenty years have taught us is this: we have a future in space. Exploration of our spaceship, the solar system, holds the promise not only of knowledge and wonder, but also of usefulness. Time now to ponder the next step: stage II ideas.

STAGE II: WHERE TO PUT UP A SPACE COLONY?

We live today in the middle of an energy crisis. And a related crisis, the dangerously increasing total population of the earth, looms on the horizon. Under these conditions the idea of building colonies in space looks better and better. Once built, the colonies would have an immediate impact on earth's energy scene; through their enhanced ability to collect solar energy, they would be able to divert enough of it in concentrated form onto earth to earn their necessary "trade balance." And after the idea of living and growing up in the colonies was accepted, there would be a substantial impact also on the population scene. So argue the proponents of space colonies, although opponents make a good case against ever getting back enough energy to justify the economics of building these colonies.

However, technologically the idea of space colonies is sound, so let's get on with the question of where to build these colonies. In the immediate future, we can only think of locating the colonies close to the earth-moon planet system. Are there points in space between these two bodies that are stable (meaning that, if we placed our colonies at such points, the colonies would stay there and not move away)? In order not only to include them in earth's energy planning but also to insure their own survival, the colonies' whereabouts must be a matter of certainty.

In principle, solving the motion of a third body under the gravity force of two other bodies (in this case the earth and the moon) sounds simple. Unfortunately, it happens to be impossible to find an exact analytical solution except for a few special cases. These special cases were discovered by the eighteenth-century French mathematician Joseph L. Lagrange, who found that there are indeed two points of stability for the motion of the third body. If placed in either of these points (points L4 and L5 in Figure 10) with just the right velocity, the body should stay there forever with respect to the other two bodies. (Lagrange actually found five points, but three of them are only quasi-stationary; the slightest perturbation, such as from a fourth body—and there are an abundance of bodies in the solar system—will take them away from their positions on a journey of no return.)

The validity of Lagrange's calculation has checked out in a most spectacular fashion. The sun-Jupiter system can be regarded as a two-body system like that of the earth-moon; in the intervening space all the other astronomical bodies in the vicinity have a negligible influence on the motion of a third body under the gravitational forces of the sun-Jupiter system. Thus, there should be two Lagrangian stable points for this system (Figure 10). And we do indeed find two asteroid groups trapped at these points, as shown in the figure. In the leading group, there are nine asteroids altogether, named for famous Greeks of the Trojan War, such as Achilles. In the trailing group, there are five asteroids which are called by Trojan names, such as Hector (except for one that carries a Greek name—a spy?). Because of the naming of these asteroids, the Lagrange points are often referred to as the Trojan points.

These asteroids trapped at the Trojan points have been watched for a long time, and Lagrange's theory is gloriously validated by these observations. According to theory, these points are ones of dynamic stability; if a perturbation from a fourth body does manage to dislodge an object from the Trojan point, the Trojan object will not stray forever, but will return.

Princeton physicist Gerard O'Neill, who did most of the preliminary, nitty-gritty calculations of the feasibility of space colonies, initially suggested the Trojan points of the earth-moon system as the locations of the first colonies (in fact, the trailing point, L5, was suggested specifically; hence, there is now a group of space-colony enthusiasts known as the L5 Society). However, later research has shown that these points for the earth-moon system may not be as stable as those for the sun-Jupiter system. In that case, perhaps a simple synchronous orbit would be a better choice for the first colony. At this time, the situation is somewhat uncertain.

There is a real advantage in building a colony as near to the moon as

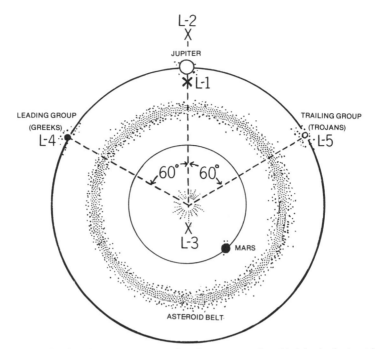

Figure 10. The five Lagrange points for the motion of a third body (asteroid) in the gravity field of the sun and Jupiter. Only L-4 and L-5 are stable.

possible, for example at a Trojan point, because it is considerably cheaper to haul things up from the moon than from the earth. Besides, we would be using some of the moon's resources instead of taking another gouge from earth's already dwindling supply of materials. One of Robert A. Heinlein's tricks, the catapult, used in his novel *The Moon Is a Harsh Mistress,* can be used very profitably here. Read any of the popular books on space colonies, including O'Neill's *The High Frontier,* for details of catapult use and other ideas.

MORE STAGE II: SOLAR SAILS

Not only could we make efficient use of the energy of sunlight through such constructions as the space colonies, but we could also use the momentum of the sunlight to propel "sailboats" from one part of our huge spaceship to another. The idea of solar sailing has been used by Arthur Clarke in the title story of his book *The Wind from the Sun.* As the metaphor suggests, sunlight fills the function of the wind for solar sailboats. Just as wind reflects off a regular sail, giving it a force perpendicular to the plane of the sail, so does light, when reflected from a sail made of special material such as Mylar. And just as we can propel a regular sailboat in any direction using the technique of "tacking," so could we tack with solar sailboats.

Let's look at how tacking works. It may be helpful to refer back to some concepts regarding vector quantities that were discussed in Chapter 2, such as the idea of parallel and transverse components of a vector. The force of solar light on the sail (which is perpendicular to the plane of the sail) can be resolved into a parallel component along the direction of the keel, the direction of motion, and a component perpendicular to this direction (Figure 11). It is this parallel component that propels the boat; and as long as you don't orient your sail perpendicular to the keel line, or parallel to the incident sunlight, there always is a parallel component. For best results, the sail's plane is maintained halfway between the direction of solar light rays and the direction of motion of the boat.

There is, however, the problem of the transverse component—which is very much unwanted, because it tends to sway the boat sideways. In the case of a marine boat in water, the resistance of the water against the keel (which is made heavy and deep for this reason) kills the sideways component. In the case of a solar sailboat, fortunately, the sun's gravity force cancels this unwanted component. Typically, the sailboat would orbit the sun. By fixing the

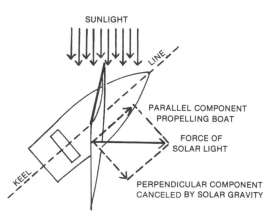

Figure 11. How the solar sail propels a ship with the help of the force of sunlight. The top figure is an artist's conception of a solar sailboat sailing through space. Don't worry about the sailor—he's wearing his space suit.

sail to gather energy, the riders could guide the boat uphill against the sun's gravity, farther away from the sun. The reverse action of backing the sails to act as a brake would edge the boat inward toward the sun. Thus, tacking anywhere in the solar system seems to be possible.

Unfortunately, there are some limitations. First, the size of the sail and its mass. The pressure of sunlight is very feeble; therefore, to collect enough sunlight to obtain a sizable propelling force would necessitate a lot of area (force = pressure × area). However, the mass of the sail must be small at the same time, otherwise we would lose in acceleration. Second, the mass of the ship attached to the sail would be a limiting factor to the acceleration achievable. (This is also a limit for rocket ships.) And finally, since light pressure diminishes inversely as the square of the distance from the sun, the sailboat would not be very efficient near the edge of the solar system.

At present, futurologists see the major problem in manufacturing and safeguarding the flimsy sails—where to make them, how to put them up, and so forth. In spite of these difficulties, enthusiasts anticipate the coming of solar sails as early as the turn of the century.

As for the problem of light pressure decreasing away from the sun, SF writers Larry Niven and Jerry Pournelle, in their book *The Mote in God's Eye,* have posed a novel suggestion: the use of lasers as the light source. Laser intensity does not diminish with distance as rapidly as the intensity of ordinary light. Of course, there are many technical problems with this idea, not to mention the problem of the energy required by the laser.

THE DYSON SPHERE: AN ASTOUNDING STAGE III IDEA

Scientists and futurologists have conceived many plans for the optimal use of solar energy, but the ultimate among such plans is the Dyson sphere. Developed by physicist Freeman J. Dyson, this is an idea whose time might not come for thousands of years; it is the idea of enclosing the sun entirely within a revolving sphere.* The inhabitants of the inside surface of such a sphere would have all the sun's energy to use as they pleased and a land area that could handle any population problem for a long time to come.

Predictably, the Dyson sphere idea has sparked the imagination of many science fiction writers, notably Larry Niven's in his novel *Ringworld*. Unfortunately, Niven does not envision the full glory of the Dyson sphere in his story, but places only a ring around the sun. To give you some idea of the enormity of Dyson's vision, I will quote from a genuine sphere story, *Orbitsville*, by British writer Bob Shaw. The story opens with a space mission led by its renegade hero, who is escaping the wrath of earth's dictatorial ruler. The

*Dyson himself credits this idea to SF writer Olaf Stapledon.

mission ends (and the second half of the story begins) with the discovery of Orbitsville, which is a Dyson sphere; this is how it looked to its discoverer:

He watched as the outer doors of the dock slid aside to reveal a blackness unrelieved by the stars. At a distance of two thousand kilometers the sphere not only filled half the sky; it was half the sky. The observed universe was cut into two hemispheres—one of them glowing with starclouds, the other filled with light-absorbent darkness. There was no sensation of being close to a huge object, rather, all felt poised above infinite deeps. [p. 66]

How does one accumulate the huge quantities of material that surely are necessary to build a Dyson sphere? Dyson, himself an expert in futuristic estimates, suggests that perhaps one or more planets of the solar system—Jupiter alone might suffice—could be broken up via nuclear explosions and reassembled. Obviously, *we* could not do it, but a very advanced civilization might. Anyway, here's how the author of *Orbitsville* envisions the sphere's construction:

There could only be one source for such an inconceivable quantity of shell material, and that was the sun itself. Matter is energy, and energy is matter. Every active star hurls the equivalent of millions of tons a day of its own substance into space in the form of light and other radiations. But in the case of Pengally's star one individual or many had set up a boundary, turned that energy back on itself, manipulating and modifying it, translating it into matter. [italics in original, p. 83]

Shaw's imagination is so far out as to border the impossible. It is doubtful that the sphere, even if material were available, could be built. Such a sphere is unstable against even minor perturbations—a substantial meteor impact might destroy it. Dyson himself is, of course, quite aware of this, as he writes:

A solid shell or ring surrounding a star is mechanically impossible. The form of "biosphere" which I envisaged consists of a loose collection or swarm of objects travelling on independent orbits around the star. The size and shape of the individual objects would be chosen for the convenience of the inhabitants. . . . [*Interstellar Communication*, p. 114]

Thus, Dyson seems to be thinking more in terms of a whole "swarm" of space colonies, placed side by side in such a way as to enclose the entire sun.

TIME IS ON OUR SIDE

In the preceding sections, we have scanned a likely chronology of technological stages in the exploration of the solar system, our extended spaceship. When we become mired in our immediate problems of world hunger and energy shortage, it is important, I think, to remember this alternative scenario of our development. But now an important question arises: can the exploration of space intensify before we solve such problems as poverty? Is it morally right even to consider establishing a space colony, at tremendous expense in resources and human-power, when billions of people on our base planet go hungry? Especially, given the factional condition of humankind today, which maintains the constant threat of war and violence among nations, is it prudent even to speak of exacerbating this division among people? (Who will the fortunate ones be to live in the "celestial cities"?)

Novelist Kate Wilhelm, in a recent unpublished address to a national convention of science fiction writers, observed:

Some writers will look at our world and find it acceptable, even good, the highest achievement homo sap sap [homo sapiens sapiens] can possibly accomplish. . . . Many readers are constantly reassured by this affirmation. But there are other writers who will look at the world and cry out, but it's absurd, tragic, unjust, arbitrary. Why? Who did this to my world? . . . Register for the draft? Why? Whom are we going to fight and why? How good will our cause look in a hundred years? What kind of reality is it that says every generation has to fight a war? Why? Why? Why?

When I spoke with Wilhelm on the subject of the SF writers' dream of space exploration, she was quite emphatic in her belief that we must first put our earth in order, eliminate at least poverty and war, before we take the giant leap to space.

This confronts us with the question of evolution, evolution of homo sapiens, or homo sap sap as Wilhelm terms it. Before we can deal with such concerns as those raised above, we must develop an unprecedented awareness of who we are and what we are. We need to understand not only the nature of human evolution but also where we are in that evolutionary scale.

We have vaulted many rungs in the evolutionary ladder, most recently in the sixteenth and seventeenth centuries as such men of science as Galileo, Descartes, and Newton spurred us to enormous leaps in our understanding of the material world. They played midwife to the age of science and technology that has thrived for the last three hundred years. We must now ask if we have reached the top of the ladder, or is there a next step? If so, are we ready for it?

A look at history shows that every major technological era has been followed by a relative lull while evolution shifted emphasis. Many people will disagree with me on this, but I see signs of a plateau in the growth of technology. Physics, the womb from which this technological era sprang, is encountering some dead ends in its own development. The twentieth century has been crammed with such revolutionary achievements as nuclear energy, transistors, and computers. But now, with the physics of elementary particles in its forefront, physics has become remote from our immediate reality, and only zealots will insist that any major technological fallout will result from this front of physics in the foreseeable future. Of course, in the field of biological technology, a new area called genetic engineering is tampering with the genes, but its emphasis is on modification rather than creation. There is also increasing scientific activity in the area of brain research, and I believe this signifies the trend of the shift.

This shift toward the understanding of our brain and consciousness could not be a coincidence, but is rather a natural step on the evolutionary ladder. For one thing, it comes just at the point of history when we urgently need it. Today more than ever, with the threat of atomic warfare, it is important that we understand ourselves: our goals, our purpose, our aspirations. We can play the old-fashioned political games with the new war machines, but to a fatal end. If we remain the same, if war and superiority over others is in our hearts, arms control talks are futile, and the arms race will continue or accelerate. And to think about bringing poverty to an end is equally meaningless, because from our present competitive perspective, poverty is simply the inevitable plight of "unfit" humans. We need a basic shift in our philosophy, a basic and dramatic change in our regard for our fellow humans—nay, for our very reality.

Research on brain and consciousness can help implement this shift. Consider this. In our entire human history, very little research (in the scientific sense) has been done on consciousness. Not that the field has not had its Einsteins and Newtons (Jesus and Buddha were such figures), but its premises have not significantly determined the nature of growth of the human culture. Although the Buddhists carried out a substantial amount of research (they constructed an entire map of the inner world of our mind), the implication of such research has never been explored. And Jesus' message about the transformation of consciousness has gotten lost in the labyrinth of dogma and Western logic. We now have a chance to escape that labyrinth; perhaps brain research will offer us the needed Ariadne's thread.

Futurist author Thea Alexander, in her novel *2150 A.D.*, sees this next step of consciousness evolution as the development of a new way of living, in what she calls the macrosociety, based on an acknowledgment of the ultimate oneness of all human beings:

". . . the basic metaphysical premise of Macro philosophy is that all is one perfect, macrocosmic, indivisible whole. It's the ancient idealistic concept that all is perfect, all is mind—one universal mind. However, in 2150, . . . they don't just talk about it, they live it, by organizing their society on this premise. . . ." [p. 32]

And anthropologist Pierre Teilhard de Chardin earlier introduced the related concept of the "Noosphere," a planetary web of consciousness. Teilhard

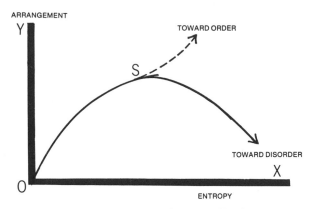

Figure 12. Our evolutionary options according to Teilhard.

illustrates his view of human evolution with a graph (Figure 12). The curve displays the evolution of energy in a graph where information, or orderly arrangement, is plotted against entropy, disorder. The curve bifurcates at the point S. This is the crossroads. From S the energy takes either the dissipative path of increased entropy or the one of increased consciousness (order). Ours is the choice of path.

We shall explore the new consciousness research and the science fiction writers' responses to it later. Now let's return to Kate Wilhelm's concerns—should we undertake space travel before we have dealt with poverty and war? I believe that space travel will not happen, anyway, until we reach a new plateau in an increased level of awareness of the nature of human consciousness. From that raised level, massive war and violence perpetrated by entire human societies will certainly be a thing of the past. And poverty will become a matter of individual choice, not a forced, conditioned one as it is today. Then from the vantage of this plateau, we will see technology take a new surge from which we shall soar into space, in and around our entire spaceship. Time is on our side.

chapter five

Simulation of Gravity

Arthur C. Clarke has a knack for details, and his 1973 Hugo-winning novel, *Rendezvous with Rama,* is rich in descriptions of the kinds of things necessary in a space colony such as *Rama.* For example, a space colony certainly needs a self-sustaining ecological system, including a source of energy, the details of which Clarke very carefully develops. But even before ecology, any space vehicle intended as a prolonged, perhaps lifetime, environment for its inhabit- ants needs a way of generating gravity. If life develops naturally on planets with gravity, living creatures evolving on a planet may have an inherent need for gravity. Can one simulate gravity in a space colony?

Ask Arthur Clarke. Clarke's cylindrically shaped craft has artificial gravity. An investigating team from earth enters the cylinder at one end at its axis. At the axis there is no gravity, no weight of any sort. But as three men from the team start moving (down or up, you figure it out) toward the wall of the cylinder, the situation begins to change.

He [Lieutenant Commander Mercer] grasped the first rung and gently pro- pelled himself along the ladder. Movement was as easy as swimming along the sea bed. . . .

The rungs were spaced a uniform half-meter apart, and for the first portion of the climb Mercer missed the alternate ones. . . . at around [rung] two hun- dred noticed the first distinct sensations of weight. The spin of Rama was starting to make itself felt.

At rung four hundred, he estimated that his apparent weight was about five kilos, or about eleven pounds. . . .

A few minutes later, they were on the first step. It was a strange experi- ence, after months in space, to stand upright on a solid surface, and to feel it pressing against one's feet. Their weight was still less than ten kilograms, but that was enough to give a feeling of stability. [p. 50]

The story continues with the men's continued descent toward the cylinder wall. The farther they descend, the more their apparent weight increases, until, at the wall, it reaches a maximum approximating their earth weight.

You undoubtedly caught the line that gives away the secret of the space- craft's simulation of weight: the spin of the spaceship does it. It is a fact that in a spinning vehicle mysterious forces act on you. Such forces in general are called pseudoforces. Centrifugal force, perhaps the most familiar of pseudo- forces, provides the astronauts their apparent weight while they explore *Rama* (Figure 13).

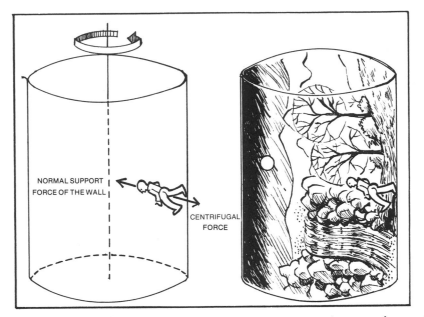

Figure 13. Artificial gravity in a rotating cylinder. The normal support force arises from the reaction of the inner wall of the cylinder in response to the centrifugal force with which an inhabitant presses on the cylinder wall. By the way, the waterfall veers to its right instead of falling straight down. This is the result of another pseudoforce, the Coriolis force (explained later).

At this juncture, you may ask several questions. Perhaps two questions predominate. First, where do pseudoforces come from: what is their nature and origin? Second, what is so special about gravity that it can be simulated by a pseudoforce? Pseudoforces are radically different from real forces. Real forces arise from the interaction of two objects; as far as we can tell, pseudoforces do not. On the other hand, it is possible to do away completely with the notion of pseudoforces; that is, one can analyze any given instance of motion of objects under pseudoforces without the notion of pseudoforces! If this sounds strange, it's because pseudoforces are strange!

Pseudoforces act on objects in accelerating reference frames, such as a car taking off from rest or a spinning spaceship. You are familiar with the mysterious force that tends to push you back into your seat when a car or an airplane takes off. From inside the car or plane, your perception is that of a force that pushes you into the seat. Yet an outside observer can interpret things differently. She can say that as the car accelerates, you continue in the state of rest (or natural motion) because of your inertia, and the accelerating back of the seat presses forward against you. There is no extra force. The force is a mirage; it is your inertia that creates your sensation.

Which view is right? Both views can be considered correct. The view depends on the frame of reference from which one analyzes a situation. From the point of view of an observer stationed in an accelerating reference frame—that is, if the analysis is carried out with respect to three mutually perpendicular rods tied together at an origin moving with the accelerating car—then there is a pseudoforce. But if the analysis is carried out from a reference frame either at rest or in natural motion (such reference frames are called inertial reference frames), there is no pseudoforce.

In any case, pseudoforces clearly have to do with the inertia of objects; hence, they sometimes are referred to as inertial forces. Some people think, following the lead of physicist-philosopher Ernst Mach of Austria, that the inertia of bodies has to do with matter in the faraway parts of the universe. In this view mass, which is a measure of inertia, arises from the action of remote masses in the rest of the universe. If you imagine yourself in an otherwise empty universe, your mass will vanish, according to this view. This philosophy is often referred to as Mach's principle. Although pseudoforces perhaps have something to do with the distribution of masses in the rest of the universe, nobody yet has been able to develop a concrete connection.

THE PLANET OF *MISSION OF GRAVITY*

Hal Clement, whose most famous novel is *Mission of Gravity,* has done his readers a great service. He has appended to his story an account of how he researched the basic science ideas in it. The idea of creating this unusual planet came to him when he read a scientific paper published by an astronomer, K. Aa. Strand, on a binary star system classified as 61 Cygni.

A binary (or double star) system consists of two stars orbiting each other in Kepler orbits following Newton's law of gravity. Astronomer Fredrich Bessel, back in 1934, discovered that the trajectory of the star Sirius was not a straight line, as it had to be if it were following a course of natural motion in space. Bessel argued that the irregularities of the motion of Sirius, the zigzagging of its path, must be due to the gravitational influence of a companion star, perhaps too dim to see with the naked eye. This companion star, Sirius B, was soon discovered, verifying Bessel's hypothesis. Since then millions of binary stars have been discovered and catalogued.

What was special about Strand's binary system was that one of the two partners had to have a planet-size object, about sixteen times the mass of Jupiter, revolving around it, in order that the trajectories could be made to comply fully with Newton's laws. As you may know, there is very little direct astronomical evidence for planets (of other stars) since they have no light of their own. So this kind of evidence, although still somewhat indirect, is quite welcome, and surely provides fertile material for an SF story. At least, Clement thought so. But he had to face some challenging problems.

As noted above, the planet of *Mission of Gravity,* named Mesklin by the author, is sixteen times more massive than our Jupiter. However, Clement argued in his appendix that the planet, composed of matter with density many times greater on the average than Jovian matter, cannot be as bulky as Jupiter. So he chose the size of his planet to be just about that of Neptune, quite reasonable for a planet of this kind.

Now comes the major problem of the story. Mesklin, by the author's choice, has a radius of 24,000 miles at the equator, compared to earth's 4000 miles. In other words, Mesklin's equatorial radius is six times greater than earth's. If you recall the rules of gravity force discussed in Chapter 3, this difference between the radii would make Mesklin's surface gravity 6^2 or 36 times weaker than earth's. But of course, Mesklin's mass more than makes up for it; Mesklin is 16 times heavier than Jupiter, which in its turn is 318 times more massive than earth; this makes its surface gravity, or, which is the same thing, the acceleration of gravity, 5088 times greater. Combining the two factors, Mesklin's acceleration of gravity must be

$$\frac{5088}{36}$$

about 141 times greater than on earth, or 141 g. This means that an object would weigh 141 times its earth weight at the equator of Mesklin. Basically, this would make the evolution of life on Mesklin rather unlikely.

But centrifugal force now comes to the author's rescue. Hal Clement gives his planet a rapid rotation. In such a rotating reference frame, as you know, there is always a centrifugal force. From the Rama story, you also can guess that the magnitude of the centrifugal force increases as the speed of rotation increases; more weight was generated as the Raman adventurers went closer and closer to the walls. In a rotating cylinder the walls move the fastest while the speed of rotation at the cylinder axis is zero. Thus, by imagining that Mesklin rotates fast enough, Clement could generate as large a centrifugal force at the equator as he desired, within some limits coming from the requirements of stability of the planet. Now it is the fundamental nature of the centrifugal force that it is directed radially away from the axis of rotation. For the rotating cylinder (Figure 13) this generates an artificial gravity that pins its inner inhabitants to the inner wall of the cylinder, which acts as a floor. On a rotating planet its inhabitants reside on the outside surface, and now the centrifugal force attempts to throw them off the surface radially, in opposition to the planet's gravity which pulls them inward. Thus, the centrifugal force will cancel part of the gravity force of the planet.

Clement assumed in his story that Mesklin rotates just fast enough for the centrifugal force to cancel most of the planet's gravity force on an object. Due to this cancellation, the value of acceleration of gravity at Mesklin's equator was reduced to only 3 times that on earth instead of the 141 times previously calculated.

One more interesting thing. The effect of rotation of a planet is greatest at its equator. Away from the equator and toward the poles, the effect steadily decreases until at the poles there is no effect at all; the poles are on the axis of rotation. So the cancellation of gravity by the centrifugal force is most effective at the equator and becomes less and less effective as one proceeds toward the poles. And to be sure, at the poles there is no centrifugal force at all, and therefore gravity is at its full glory.

This is only part of the intriguing story of gravity on Mesklin. Rotating planets have a characteristic that arises from the action of the centrifugal force over many millions of years. The matter of the spinning planet must redistribute itself to a spheroidal shape, the equatorial radius becoming greater than the polar radius. As you may know, it is also this way for earth; earth is slightly flat at the poles. Of course, Mesklin rotates much faster than the earth, and so the effect is much more pronounced; the equatorial radius of Mesklin is more than twice the polar radius. Since the acceleration of gravity decreases as $1/R^2$, its polar value should be greater on Mesklin than its equatorial value. When Clement combined the two effects—the centrifugal force and the flatness of the poles—he came out with a value of about 700; the value of acceleration of gravity at the poles was almost 700 times the value of earth. Such an enormous rate of fall is quite mind-boggling, and you can guess that living conditions are quite different on Mesklin. The following conversation between a Mesklinite and a human provides a sneak preview to the book. The Mesklinite asks the first question:

"What is throw?". . .

"Well, throw is when you take some other object—pick it up—and push it hard away from you so that it travels some distance before striking the ground!"

"We don't do that up in reasonable countries. There are a lot of things we can do here [at the equator] which are either impossible or very dangerous there. If I were to 'throw' something at home, it might very well land on someone—probably me."

"Come to think of it, that might be bad. Three G's here at the equator is bad enough; you have nearly seven hundred at the poles. Still, if you could find something small enough so that your muscles could throw it, why couldn't you catch it again, or at least resist its impact?"

"I find the situation hard to picture, but I think I know the answer. There isn't time. If something is let go—thrown or not—it hits the ground before anything can be done about it. Picking up and carrying is one thing; crawling is one thing; throwing and—jumping?—are entirely different matters." [p. 8]

ELEVATORS TO THE SKY

Through the hero in his recent Hugo-winning novel, *The Fountains of Paradise,* Arthur Clarke has raised an important issue:

". . . space vehicles are still grossly inefficient. Even worse, their effect on the environment is appalling. Despite all attempts to control approach corridors, the noise of take-off and re-entry disturbs millions of people. Exhaust products dumped in the upper atmosphere have triggered climatic changes, which may have very serious results. . . ." [p. 43]

The situation described here is from the twenty-second century. It may sound ominous to us in the late twentieth century, especially in view of the ozone layer depletion controversy arising from supersonic flights. But is there any alternative to rocket vehicles once the space age is established? Yes, declares Clarke's hero:

If the laws of celestial mechanics make it possible for an object to stay fixed in the sky [by virtue of synchronous orbits], might it not be possible to lower a cable down to the surface, and so to establish an elevator system linking earth to space? [italics in the original, p. 44]

Is this idea total fantasy? Or is there any substance in it? The advantages of such a cable car are obvious. Once we reach the synchronous orbit with its help, the centrifugal force acting outward at the position of this orbit turns out to be exactly equal and opposite to the gravity force of the earth. And objects can achieve orbit with the help of this elevator. This is pollution free, relatively speaking, and also costs less energy than rockets. Even for exploration of outer space, the elevator can take rockets up to a launching platform, where the pollution of the rocket exhaust would present a much less severe problem than on earth.

The only significant problems we find with this functionally marvelous elevator are in the construction phase. As we lower a cable from a satellite in a synchronous orbit, the centrifugal force no longer matches the weight, since centrifugal force is proportional to the distance from the center of the earth. Thus, the cable acquires more and more weight and eventually pulls the satellite down from its orbit. However, a Russian engineer, Y. N. Artsutanov, has solved this particular problem. He suggests that while we extend a cable down toward earth, we must at the same time extend the other end of the cable up from the satellite (that is, away from the earth). The upper cable has greater centrifugal force acting on it than gravity, and thus it pulls the satellite upward, compensating for the downward pull. By careful maneuvering, the net pull can be maintained at zero until the lower end of the cable reaches ground, when of course it can be anchored to the earth. A suitable counterweight placed at the upper end would then balance the system.

The cable, now under full tension, can properly support elevators running up and down its entire length. In fact, this system has an added benefit. As the elevator rises beyond the synchronous orbit, it gains energy, being accelerated by the excess centrifugal force, at the expense of earth's rotational energy. The earth slows down a bit, but no matter, the earth has lots of rotational energy to spare. When the elevator reaches the top, it has achieved escape velocity from the earth, and thus objects can be launched from this elevator into the far reaches of the solar system.

So what's the snag, you may have begun to wonder. The seemingly insurmountable problem is to find a material for the cable that would be strong enough to support the system's weight. Arthur Clarke in his novel suggests a "pseudo–one-dimensional" diamond crystal, but the suggestion itself is pseudo. From the point of view of our present state of technology, it is difficult to see how we can ever manufacture the super-strong material that is needed for this project.

CORIOLIS FORCE

If you were on a spaceship on a long mission, it is likely that you would be provided the comfort of spin to give you some artificial weight. But a spinning ship also has some hazards to which you would have to get accustomed. In fact, on a spinning ship, because of this extra hazard, it is easy to recognize a tenderfoot in space travel. Witness this scene from the novel *The Jupiter Theft* by Donald Moffit:

As Jameson watched, Klein thumbed his mug open and started to pour himself a cup of coffee. Just as Jameson was thinking that it was a little odd for Klein to drink coffee this early in the party, there was a scream and a little flurry of confusion up at the bar. Klein had managed to spill hot coffee over Beth Oliver, and himself, too. The coffee had streamed right past the rim of the mug and splashed them both. Klein hadn't allowed for the sidewise curving effect of the Coriolis force when he poured. It seemed an odd lapse for someone who was supposed to be used to space. [p. 48]

The conclusion from this is that Klein had lied about his space experience. Keep an eye on him, Jameson!

Coriolis force is one other pseudoforce that is encountered in rotating reference frames such as a spinning ship. The explorers of Rama, in *Rendezvous with Rama*, also discovered this:

"Everything OK, Skipper," he [Mercer] reported. "We're just passing the halfway mark. Joe, Will, any problems?"

"I'm fine. What are you stopping for?" [Joe] Calvert answered.

"Same here," added [Will] Myron. "But watch out for the Coriolis force. It's starting to build up."

So Mercer had already noticed. When he let go of the rungs, he had a distinct tendency to drift off to the right. He knew perfectly well that this was merely the effect of Rama's spin, but it seemed as if some mysterious force was gently pushing him away from the ladder. [p. 50]

I hope you noticed in both of these excerpts something peculiar about the action of the Coriolis force. It acts only on moving objects, and its effect is to sway a moving object off its course. On earth you may observe the Coriolis force if you take time to watch how accumulated water in a wash basin or a bathtub swirls as you drain the water. In the northern hemisphere of earth, the effect of the Coriolis force on moving objects is to sway it to the right, which gives a counterclockwise tendency to bathtub water. In the southern hemisphere, bathtub vortices are clockwise.

Imagine that somebody grew up on a world with a lot of Coriolis force—for example, a fast-rotating planet like Mesklin. Any time she tries to move, the Coriolis force will try to push her to her right (assuming she lives in the northern hemisphere of the planet *and* that the rotation of the planet is counterclockwise as seen from the north pole of the planet). In order to travel straight she must learn to balance the Coriolis force by means of sideways friction force from the road. To generate a sideways road friction force she must walk crooked, twisting her ankles sideways as she walks. Indeed, experiments done on laboratory animals, born and reared on a rotating turntable, have confirmed this. Thus, the creatures of a planet like Mesklin, among other peculiarities, should have this additional eccentricity. They walk kind of funny, at least from our perspective.

MASS, WEIGHT, AND WEIGHTLESSNESS

The mass and weight of an object are not the same thing. Weight is a force. Mass is determined by the amount of matter contained in a body. Yet since the weight of an object on earth is m times g—or mg—where m is the mass and g the acceleration of earth's gravity, we tend to think that weight and mass are proportional to each other and therefore can be spoken about interchangeably. If you went to the moon, one of the first things you would have to learn is to get used to the difference between mass and weight. Arthur C. Clarke put it well in *2001: A Space Odyssey:*

A man who weighed one hundred and eighty pounds on Earth might be delighted to discover that he weighed only thirty pounds on the moon. As long as he moved in a straight line at a uniform speed, he felt a wonderful sense of buoyancy. But as soon as he attempted to change course, to turn corners, or to stop suddenly—*then* he would find that his full one hundred eighty pounds of mass, or inertia, was still there. . . . Before one could be properly adapted to lunar living, therefore, it was essential to learn that all objects were now six times as sluggish as their mere weight would suggest. [italics in the original, p. 63]

The setting in *Mission of Gravity* also demonstrates the danger of thinking about mass and weight interchangeably. On Mesklin, the acceleration of gravity varies so much from one place to another that the proportionality of mass and weight is of no use unless you stay at the same place. The weight of an object varies from place to place, but of course mass remains the same. The same effect also occurs on earth and for identical reasons, but the equatorial weight of an object on earth is smaller than the polar weight by only about five parts in a thousand, so we hardly notice it.

The episode quoted previously from *Rendezvous with Rama,* if read carefully, will tell you something else about weight: our feeling of weight has something to do with the support we stand on. If there is no support, we feel weightless. Thus, in free fall under gravity—for example, if you were in an elevator whose cable snapped—you would feel weightless (if other considerations didn't claim all your attention). The elevator floor falls at the same rate as you fall, providing no support and giving rise to that squishy feeling in the stomach that you associate with weightlessness.

So it seems there are two ways to be weightless. The first is if there is no gravity at all, as in outer space far away from any gravitating object. This is true weightlessness. But weightlessness also occurs in free fall, as when an astronaut is in orbit. This is apparent weightlessness.

As we venture into space—to build our first space colonies, for example—getting used to the free-fall condition will be an important challenge. Even more challenging may be the need for a radical change in our thinking. One of the best books I have read on this subject is *Stardance* by Spider and Jeanne Robinson, about a troupe of dancers in free fall. This is how they put it:

"Charlie, I . . . don't even know if I can *imagine* free fall dance. I mean . . . I can't picture it."

"Of course not! You are still hobbled with 'up' and 'down', warped by a lifetime in a gravity well. But you will catch on as soon as you get up there, believe me. . . . You can learn to think spherically, I know you can, and the rest is just recoordination, like getting sea legs." [italics in the original, p. 4]

Spherical thinking! Are you ready for it?

IS GRAVITY A PSEUDOFORCE?

Once we know that gravity can be simulated by means of pseudoforces, it is natural to ask if gravity itself is a pseudoforce. You now know that a person in a free-falling elevator feels weightless. In terms of pseudoforces, we can explain this as follows. The freely falling elevator is an accelerating reference frame, and in accelerating reference frames there is always a pseudoforce. In this case, the direction of the pseudoforce is opposite to the direction of the acceleration of fall, that is, the direction of earth's gravity. Its magnitude is the same as earth's gravity force. Thus, the pseudoforce completely nullifies the effect of earth's gravity on all objects in the elevator.

Suppose a person in a free-falling elevator drops a watch. How does the motion of the watch look to an outside observer, perhaps looking through a window of the elevator? To him the elevator and watch both fall toward earth with acceleration g, according to Galileo's law. But to the inside observer something quite different takes place. In her perception the watch does not fall. So from her "falling body" experiment she concludes that there is no force of gravity on the watch; it is obeying the first law of motion, the law of inertia. To her, the free-falling elevator seems like an inertial reference frame. Of course, due to her prior knowledge about the earth and its force of gravity, she may explain her observation by saying that a pseudoforce on the watch cancels the downward gravity force on it.

Now consider the following intriguing situation. Suppose there is no earth and all of us are in an elevator accelerating "upward" in space with acceleration g. There is now a pseudoforce acting downward on each of us with a magnitude exactly equal to that of the usual earth gravity on us. Thus, for each of us, earth's gravity is exactly simulated; gravity is not needed if we can have an equivalent pseudoforce.

Scientific discoveries are often made by people who have the ability to see things differently. Albert Einstein possessed a greater capacity for this "seeing" than anybody else in this century. Einstein was once invited to dinner by the King of Belgium. (This was around 1911, I think; Einstein had already discovered relativity.) At the dinner table he was seated next to the great physicist and chemist, Marie Curie. Mme. Curie was a kind person who took an instant liking to this young man and asked him what he was researching these days. To this Einstein replied that he was thinking about a person in a free-falling elevator performing experiments. Mme. Curie, unimpressed, probably thought the young man was wasting his time.

But it was out of such thinking that Einstein discovered his famous equivalence principle: gravity cannot be distinguished from pseudoforces. Gravity is equivalent to a pseudoforce.

So are we on an accelerating elevator surging upward in space but held down to earth by a pseudoforce? One problem remains. The earth is round. How about people on the other side? They would be accelerating downward (to them) and therefore the pseudoforce would act on them in the upward direction, forcing them to fall off the earth. So the equivalence of gravity and pseudoforce cannot be correct globally, but only at one place at a time. The equivalence principle is a strictly local principle; trying to apply it to something as big as the earth leads to paradoxes.

Another way to see that gravity over a large region of space cannot be merely a pseudoforce is by considering tidal effects. Tides arise from local differences in gravity's magnitude from one place to another on an extended body. The average gravity force can be regarded as a pseudoforce; but the tidal effects represent a true force—they cannot be simulated or eliminated.

If you are in free fall near a neutron star or a massive black hole, will you simply feel weightless and squishy in the stomach, and nothing else? Unfortunately, no! As previously mentioned, near such massive gravitating objects the tidal force is enormous, and it will rip you apart.

Because of this local validity of the equivalence principle, it is not easy to develop a complete theory of gravitation based on this principle. It took Einstein several years finally to arrive at such a theory based on the idea of curved space. This is his theory of general relativity, to be discussed later.

chapter six

Wave Fantasies

Many people fantasize about waves, at least when they are little children with a lot of time to spend wave-watching. I myself spent hours in my childhood throwing pebbles in a pond and watching the spreading rings of crests and troughs of water waves. My younger brother, however, was more practical and scorned wave-watching. "What are waves good for?" he used to tease me. And I didn't know how to answer him, not then.

But when I got into physics, to my pleasant surprise, I learned that waves are a fundamental and novel aspect of reality. A material body transfers energy from one place to another, but it always remains localized; a wave, on the other hand, spreads out and conveys energy to a large volume of space at the same time. Waves are more global in character. The contrast, local versus global, made a deep impression on me.

What are waves good for? I learned that sound and light, which carry most of our communication, are wave phenomena. So waves are good for something, after all. And when I learned in an introductory course on quantum mechanics that even submicroscopic objects such as electrons, although traditionally looked upon as particles, have a wave character, it just blew me away.

Somebody once asked SF writer Damon Knight, "How do electrons behave like waves?" To which Knight replied, "Electrons are very friendly, they wave at you." To me, this is a perfect description of wave-ness. What are waves good for? If someone asked me that question now, I would say:

> The waves can teach us
> How to listen
> And how to watch.
> Waves can teach us
> Love.

"SILENCE, PLEASE"

Science fiction writers like to fantasize about waves. However, most SF wave fantasies involve light and its sister waves, the electromagnetic waves. The waveness of light is a subtle affair, and before we get into it I want to give an example observable in ordinary experience; a story about sound waves by Arthur C. Clarke is just the thing.

Clarke is a serious writer most of the time, but he also has a light side. He once commented on the prolific writing habit of Isaac Asimov: "Isaac is the only man who can type separate books simultaneously with his two feet as well as two hands." Everybody (except perhaps Asimov) would agree from this one remark that Clarke has a wonderful sense of humor. But SF is a neglected medium for humor, so this sunny side of Clarke has remained relatively obscure to readers—unless, of course, they have read his story about sound waves, "Silence, Please."

But first some preliminaries about waves. If you look closely at water waves, you will see that it is not the water that moves from one place to another, it is the disturbance of the water that moves. The water molecules at any one spot display the disturbance up and down and back and forth, but the molecules don't go anywhere. The wave, on the other hand, moves on, transferring energy from one place to another. Waves are propagating disturbances that transfer energy.

We can display a wave train graphically by plotting a quantity (called the disturbance coordinate of the wave) that specifies the disturbance against distance (Figure 14a). For such a train of waves we can speak of a wavelength, which is the distance between two crests or two troughs. It is the length of a wave cycle. We can also speak about the frequency of the waves, the number of cycles per second. Frequency is measured in the unit of hertz (Hz): 1 hertz is equal to 1 cycle/sec. The frequency and wavelength of waves are connected by a formula that also involves the velocity of the waves:

$$velocity = frequency \times wavelength$$

The maximum height of the wave in Figure 14a is called its amplitude; the square of the amplitude is proportional to the energy (per second per unit area) carried by the wave.

When a sound wave travels through air, it is really the disturbance from a vibrating source that is traveling. If you could look at the air molecules in the path of the sound wave, you would see that the air molecules are condensed in some places (high density and pressure) and rarefied in others (low density

Figure 14(a). The basic features of a wave.

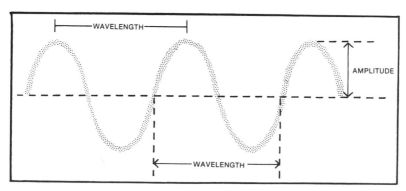

and pressure). Thus, a sound wave is a density or pressure wave; the disturbance coordinate is the air density (or air pressure).

Now to "Silence, Please" (from *Tales from the White Hart*). The narrator of the story, speaking to a group of college classmates, touches the subject of sound waves:

"I do not know," he began, "if you have ever considered the nature of *sound*. Suffice to say that it consists of a series of waves moving through the air. Not, however, waves like those on the surface of the sea—oh dear no! *Those* waves are up and down movements. Sound waves consist of alternate compressions and rarefactions."

"Rare-what?"

"Rarefactions."

"Don't you mean 'rarefications'?"

"I do not. I doubt if such a word exists, and if it does, it shouldn't," retorted Purvis, with the *aplomb* of Sir Alan Herbert dropping a particularly revolting neologism into his killing-bottle. "Where was I? Explaining sound, of course. When we make any sort of noise, from the faintest whisper to that concussion that went past just now, a series of pressure changes moves through the air. Have you ever watched shunting engines at work on a siding? You see a perfect example of the same kind of thing. There's a long line of goods-wagons, all coupled together. One end gets a bang, the first two trucks move together—and then you can see the compression wave moving right along the line. Behind it the reverse thing happens—the rarefaction—I repeat, *rarefaction*—as the trucks separate again." [italics in the original]

One of the most important identifying characteristics of waves is the process of diffraction, the capacity of waves to bend around an obstacle. You can verify that water waves do this by placing a toy boat behind a barrier of sorts in your bathtub and making some waves on the other side of the barrier. The waves will go around the barrier to affect your toy boat. So it is with sound; we all can hear somebody speaking to us from behind an obstacle.

There is another slightly more esoteric phenomenon that is also a characteristic of waves. This is the phenomenon of interference. If two waves meet at one place, the disturbances they produce combine algebraically; if one's crest appears at the other's crest, the two waves are said to be "in phase" and their net effect is a reinforcement, increased disturbance (Figure 14b). On the other hand, if two waves arrive crest to trough at a place (Figure 14c), they are "out of phase," and their effects cancel out. This is something unique with waves; they are able to cancel each other at a place where they meet if the condition is right. The reinforcement and cancellation create a pattern in space wherever two waves meet; the only requirement is that the waves maintain a definite time relationship or phase with each other.

You can demonstrate the interference of sound by playing single-frequency sound on a record-player assembly with two loudspeakers placed about a

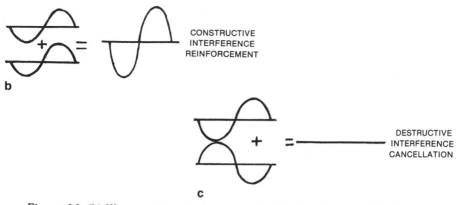

CONSTRUCTIVE
INTERFERENCE
REINFORCEMENT

b

DESTRUCTIVE
INTERFERENCE
CANCELLATION

c

Figure 14. (b) Waves arriving in phase: constructive interference. (c) Waves arriving out of phase: destructive interference.

meter apart. You have two different sound wave-trains from the two loud-speakers, but because they originate from the same source their time relation-ship is guaranteed, they are two "coherent" sources. Thus, they will make an interference pattern in the part of the space where they superpose. You can stand in front of the assembly and move your head. You will find that the sound is reinforced at places, while at other in-between places there is no sound at all, total cancellation.

Now the narrator in "Silence, Please" continues his discourse on sound and explains interference. His explanation is a bit too idealized compared to the true situation, but no matter. After all, he is giving an explanation of a total silencer, even if it doesn't exist. The explanation is cute:

"Doubtless some of you will already see what I am driving at, and will appreciate the basic principle of the Fenton Silencer. Young Fenton, I imagine, argued in this manner. 'This world of ours,' he said to himself, 'is too full of noise. There would be a fortune for anyone who could invent a really perfect silencer. Now, what would that imply . . . ?'

"It didn't take him long to work out the answer: I told you he was a bright lad. There was really very little in his pilot model. It consisted of a microphone, a special amplifier, and a pair of loudspeakers. Any sound that happened to be about was picked up by the mike, amplified and *inverted* so that it was exactly out of phase with the original noise. Then it was pumped out of the speakers, the original wave and the new one cancelled out, and the net result was si-lence.

"Of course, there was rather more to it than that. There had to be an arrangement to make sure that the cancelling wave was just the right intensi-ty—otherwise you might be worse off than when you started. But these are technical details that I won't bore you with. As many of you will recognize, it's a simple application of negative feed-back." [italics in the original]

Why does the machine not work? You figure it out.

STATIONS OF THE (ELECTROMAGNETIC) SPECTRUM

Robert Silverberg's SF novel, *To Open the Sky*, is unique in at least two respects. First, it not only mixes science and religion, but manages to do it without offense to either sector. Second, the leaders of the "scientific religions" depicted in the story are visionary; they are very clear on what mankind's priorities must be, namely, to open the mind (the psychological front) and to open the sky (the exploration of space).

Many of the practices and customs of Silverberg's religious groups may interest you. (Silverberg reveals in the preface that indeed, during magazine serialization, the various sections of his book were being enthusiastically studied by a Buddhist circle.) However, I especially recommend the opening prayer of the book, the Electromagnetic Litany. Repeated once in the morning for a week, this prayer will demystify electromagnetic waves (which are very important for science fiction readers, why else should I be talking about them?). Here it is.

The Electromagnetic Litany
Stations of the Spectrum

And there is light, before and beyond our vision, for which we give thanks.
　And there is heat, for which we are humble.
　And there is power, for which we count ourselves blessed.
　Blessed be Balmer, who gave us our wavelengths. Blessed be Bohr, who brought us understanding. Blessed be Lyman, who saw beyond sight.
　Tell us now the stations of the spectrum.
　Blessed be long radio waves, which oscillate slowly.
　Blessed be broadcast waves, for which we thank Hertz.
　Blessed be short waves, linkers of mankind, and blessed be microwaves.
　Blessed be infrared, bearers of nourishing heat.
　Blessed be visible light, magnificent in angstroms. [1 angstrom = 10^{-10} meter] (*On high holidays only:* Blessed be red, sacred to Doppler. Blessed be orange. Blessed be yellow, hallowed by Fraunhofer's gaze. Blessed be green. Blessed be blue for its hydrogen line. Blessed be indigo. Blessed be violet, flourishing with energy.)
　Blessed be ultraviolet, with the richness of the sun.
　Blessed be X rays, sacred to Roentgen, the prober within.
　Blessed be the gamma, in all its power; blessed be the highest of frequencies.
　We give thanks for Planck. We give thanks for Einstein. We give thanks in the highest for Maxwell.
　In the strength of the spectrum, the quantum, and the holy angstrom, peace! [italics in the original, p. 3]

Before I discuss the various stations of the spectrum of electromagnetic waves, it is necessary to delve into some preliminaries. How do we know that light is an electromagnetic wave? For that matter, how do we know that light consists of waves? And finally, what is an electromagnetic wave? These questions, historically, have baffled many physicists in past centuries. The answers are illuminating.

Because of the small wavelength of the light that we see (approximately 10^{-6} meter), it is a bit hard to perceive that it is a wave phenomenon. Indeed, even the immortal Newton rejected the idea; he went on thinking that light consisted of a beam of particles. Finally, Thomas Young performed his famous double-slit experiment (Figure 15) and demonstrated that two light beams interfere to produce a pattern of dark and light fringes, just as other waves do. Young's experiment finally convinced everybody that light consists of waves.

Actually, plenty of everyday demonstrations of the wave nature of light are possible with very little effort. In particular, diffraction patterns are fairly easy to see with light. Pick up a cloth umbrella and look at a distant street light through the fabric of the open umbrella. If light were a beam of particles, you would see only a continuous blob of light thinning out toward the periphery, not unlike the pattern that appears below a sieve sifting sand. But the light through the umbrella does not make a pattern like the sand from the sieve; because it is a wave, it turns and bends around the small apertures of the umbrella material, and it thus makes a pattern of dark and bright fringes.

One big question about the wave nature of light is the medium. Water waves and sound waves are wave propagation in a medium. Sound waves cannot travel through a vacuum, a fact that pulp science fiction sometimes ignored but modern writers always take into account. Light waves do travel through a medium, but they can also travel through a vacuum empty of matter. Can we have a wave without a medium? This question taunted many physicists for years in the last half of the nineteenth century. Since there was no obvious medium, these physicists hypothesized that there must be a medi-

Figure 15. Young's famous experiment. Light from a monochromatic source splits into two by passing through a double slit. The pattern of bright and dark fringes on the screen shows the interference phenomenon for light. This proves that light is a wave phenomenon.

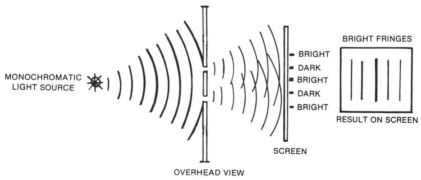

um, which they called ether. But evidence for ether proved elusive. In fact, American physicists Albert Michelson and Joseph Morley looked for many years for this hypothetical ether, or rather the ether wind that earth's motion through such a medium must generate, with a very accurate and ingenious device. They never found any evidence for it beyond the error limits of the measuring apparatus. Today scientists are of the unanimous opinion that there is no ether.

What kind of disturbance, then, does light propagate? It turns out that light is connected with electricity and magnetism; it is really an electromagnetic phenomenon. A light wave is an electromagnetic wave.

The first interpretation of the electrical interaction between two charges is that there is a force between them; for example, for a positive and negative charge the force is one of attraction. But there are some problems with this picture. For one thing, how does the force reach out at a distance? A more adequate picture is this: the existence of the positive charge, say, creates a condition in space, some sort of distortion or tension, such that when we put the negative charge in this space, the latter feels a force. Thus, every charge creates a potentiality of a force, which is realized only when a second charge is put near it. The potential force is called an electric field.

Magnetic phenomena are only slightly more complex in the field description. It takes a moving charge to create a magnetic field. This may be surprising, because we are used to bar magnets, and it is hard to see what they have to do with moving charges. But in the heart of the bar magnet are tiny moving charges, an ample number of electrons. And as far as the interaction between magnets goes, we must again analyze them in terms of fields; each magnet carries its own potential force, the magnetic field.

Now to electromagnetic waves. Physicist Richard Feynman (1964) gives a beautiful analogy to illustrate the principle of generation of electromagnetic waves. Let me quote:

> If we are in a pool of water and there is a floating cork very close by, we can move it "directly" by pushing the water with another cork. If you looked only at the two *corks*, all you would see is that one moved immediately in response to the motion of the other—there is some kind of *"interaction"* between them. Of course, what we really do is to disturb the *water*; the water then disturbs the other cork. We could make up a law that if you pushed the water a little bit, an object close by in the water would move. If it were farther away, of course, the second cork would scarcely move, for we move the water *locally*. On the other hand if we jiggle the cork, a new phenomenon is involved, in which the motion of the water moves the water there, etc., and *waves* travel away, so that by jiggling there is an influence very much further out, an oscillatory influence, that cannot be understood from the direct interaction. Therefore, the idea of direct interaction must be replaced with the existence of the water, or in the electrical case, with what we call the electromagnetic field. [p. 2-5]

Light waves are propagating disturbances of the electromagnetic field.

A look at Figure 16 will tell you that some of the waves very familiar to you in today's technological society—for example, microwaves—are also electromagnetic waves. Microwaves are especially important; the people who plan to send signals out to the stars, in the hope that somewhere some intelligent beings will pick them up, plan to use microwaves. Thus, microwaves are the potential linkers of mankind and extraterrestrial intelligence.

Let's briefly discuss how radio waves bring us the sounds of speech, music, or even an entire entertainment program. In John Cheever's classic story

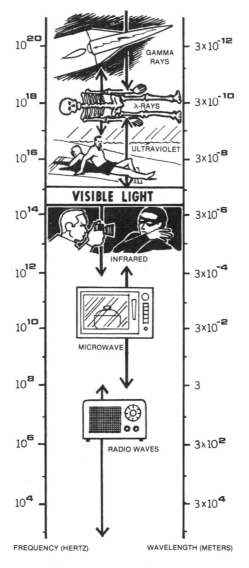

Figure 16. The stations of the electromagnetic spectrum, to use Silverberg's phrase.

"The Enormous Radio," he conjured up a big radio which, through a malfunction, was picking up neighborhood conversations. A gossip would love such a radio, but it would be anathema to all who cherish privacy. Of course, no actual radio could do anything like Cheever's; radios do not receive sound waves, only electromagnetic waves. Sound waves are sent by converting them into electrical waves and then giving these low-frequency waves a piggyback ride on the shoulders of the higher-frequency radio waves. The process is called modulation of the radio wave. At the receiver, the modulated radio wave signal is demodulated by means of elaborate electronic gadgetry, and then the electrical wave is reconverted into sound waves. Only then can you hear the original sounds.

In connection with radio waves, an interesting aspect is that the low-frequency ones used in our AM radio cannot go through the earth's ionosphere, the part of the upper atmosphere that has a large concentration of ions; these signals are reflected back. This fact may have given James Blish the idea for "The Box," a story in which he imagines that the whole city of New York is shielded by an electromagnetic wave screen that creates a total blackout in the city as far as the outside world is concerned.

Very long radio waves are rarely encountered in SF, but in his novel *Imperial Earth*, Arthur Clarke has used them as the mystery element. Could we receive long waves from outer space? Here is a discussion from *Imperial Earth* on the subject:

> But for the *very longest* waves, it's no good merely going up to orbit, or to the other side of the moon. . . . For the sun has an ionosphere, just like the Earth's—except that it's billions of times larger. It absorbs all waves more than ten or twenty kilometers in length. If we want to detect these, we have to go out to Saturn. [italics in the original, p. 250]

The "psychopath" scientist of Clarke's story indeed had set up a project for detecting such long waves in the Saturn system. When the hero of the story discovered this from the notes left by this scientist, who was now dead, the possibilities excited him. Here's an excerpt from a speech he delivered on the independence day of Titan, his home base:

> All our radio telescopes have searched the short waves—centimeters, or at most, meters—in length. But what of the long and ultralong waves—not only kilometers but even *megameters* from crest to crest? Radio waves of frequencies so low that they would sound like musical notes if our ears could detect them.
> . . . We tend to judge the universe by our own physical size and our own time scale; it seems natural for us to work with waves that we could span with our arms. . . . But the cosmos is not built to these dimensions. . . .

These giant radio waves are more commensurate with the scale of the Milky

Way, and their slow vibrations are a better measure of its eon-long Galactic Year. They may have much to tell us when we begin to decipher their messages. [italics in the original, p. 260]

To go back to the electromagnetic spectrum: infrared waves are really the waves involved in the radiative transfer of heat. In science fiction you may have encountered them in two kinds of story lines. Some writers imagine alien beings whose eyes might be sensitive to infrared, and who would therefore see with the help of infrared. Infrared waves also appear in any discussion of the greenhouse effect. You see, heat emission of ordinary hot bodies is in the infrared. Thus, when a planet at night reradiates most of the energy it receives from the sun, the radiation from the planet consists of infrared. However, if the planet's atmosphere contains carbon dioxide, then some of the infrared does not go through this carbon dioxide blanket but is reflected back to the planet, changing the planet's thermal equilibrium. The planet heats up more. The phrase "greenhouse effect" is given to this phenomenon because glass behaves the same way with infrared, and greenhouses with a glass enclosure make excellent hothouses for plants, using the same principle. Thus, the glass or carbon dioxide enclosure lets the incoming high-frequency visible radiation in, but does not let the reradiated infrared out. The presence of too much carbon dioxide in a planet's atmosphere would invariably lead to a hot planet due to the greenhouse effect; Venus is very hot for this same reason. SF writers who involve themselves with "terraforming," making earthlike planets out of uninhabitable ones, have to reckon with the greenhouse effect.

Let's now discuss those electromagnetic waves that have higher frequencies than visible light. The most important characteristic of waves with higher-than-visible-light frequencies is that they are all penetrating; they can penetrate and disrupt matter at its heart by directly interacting with atoms to such an extent as to break the atomic bonds that hold atoms together in molecules. This penetration aspect of radiation is seen spectacularly in the X-ray pictures of human bodies, which reveal the skeletal structure; the X ray goes right through the rest of the body. Superman's X-ray vision is supposed to enable him to see through ordinary buildings; and men other than Superman with X-ray eyes have made several appearances in SF movies. Incidentally, eyes emitting X rays are a very poor idea scientifically. The idea is a remnant of the misunderstanding of the process of seeing that was prevalent in the prescientific age. We see with the light that is reflected from objects, not the other way around. Even if it were possible for humans to emit X rays, ultimately the seeing must be done with the X rays reflected from the bodies. And these X rays would go through the eyes, simply destroying them, certainly not producing a visible image on the retina.

The highest-frequency electromagnetic radiation, gamma rays, is so penetrating that in sufficient dosage it can kill a human being. It is indeed one of the dangerous radiations emitted by radioactive substances. Whereas ordinary light, ultraviolet light, and X rays are emissions from atoms due basically to the jiggle of atomic electrons, the gamma rays result from vibrating charges inside the atomic nuclei.

Pulp science fiction often mentions death rays. Do gamma rays satisfy the description? Not quite. It is practically inconceivable to make a gunlike gadget that would throw a controllable burst of gamma rays selectively on an object. But the SF writer's nightmare has materialized in an unexpected way. The penetrating power of ordinary light can be increased manyfold by laser action. If all the light waves coming from a source dance in unison, in perfect coherence, the togetherness gives the beam the extra power. The laser is precisely such a device; it gives a coherent beam of light (Figure 17). Ordinarily, light waves spread out in all directions; the wave fronts are concentric spheres, and the energy falls off with distance—as $1/(\text{distance})^2$—because of the all-around spreading. What the lasers produce are plane waves; they don't spread out except for diffraction effects in their path. Thus, the laser beam can transfer a lot of power even to a large distance, and can be used to knock down airplanes, for example.

The final topic that I would like to discuss in connection with light waves is

Figure 17. (a) Ordinary incoherent light: dancing out of step. (b) Coherent laser light: a chorus line.

a phenomenon known as the Doppler effect, discovered by Christian Doppler in 1842. Although it sounds technical, this is a very familiar effect, occurring within our everyday experience whenever we hear the sounds of a passing automobile. The pitch of the sound, which is a measure of its frequency, changes from a sharp one corresponding to a higher frequency to a dull lower one corresponding to a lower frequency as the vehicle starts to recede. Thus, the sound from an approaching source is perceived to be of higher frequency and pitch, while the sound from a receding source is perceived to be lower in pitch and frequency. This is the Doppler effect, and it holds true not only for sound waves but also for light and all other cases of wave emission from a moving source. What's more, since motion is relative, even if the observer is moving and not the source, the Doppler effect will show up.

Now for visible light wavelengths, a Doppler shift toward a lower frequency, such as happens for a receding relative motion between a source and observer, will be perceived as a shift toward the red end of the visible spectrum. Such a Doppler shift is called a red shift. Conversely, for approaching relative motion between a light source and an observer, the frequency is increased toward the blue, and such a shift is called a blue shift. This terminology is so popular that it is used not only for visible light but for all electromagnetic waves: in general, a Doppler increase in frequency is referred to as a blue shift and a decrease as a red shift.

LIGHT FANTASIES

Interference and diffraction demonstrate clearly that light is a wave phenomenon, but most often we encounter two other aspects of light, which are directly involved with the way we see things. I am, of course, talking about the phenomena of reflection and refraction that occur every time light encounters a different medium as it travels. Reflection is the turning back of part of the light at the interface with another medium, and refraction is the change in direction that the path of transmitted light takes in the new medium.

In dealing with reflection and refraction, it is convenient to refer to light rays rather than the waves of light. How we pass from the wave description to the ray description is as follows. Light waves are spherical waves propagating in all directions from a source; the wave fronts, the crests and troughs of the propagating light, are spheres concentric with the source. All points on these wave fronts dance in identical steps—in other words, the phase is the same everywhere on a wave front (Figure 18a). Far away from a source, however, a small portion of a large spherical wave front is indistinguishable from a plane. Thus, spherical waves at a distance from a source can be treated as plane waves, waves whose troughs and crests are plane surfaces. If we draw a line perpendicular to the wave fronts of propagating light, we get a light ray.

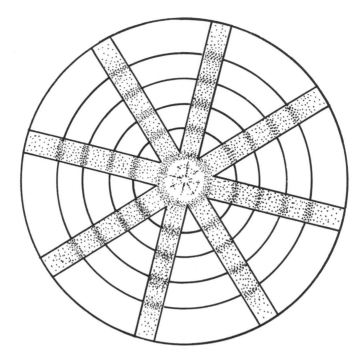

Figure 18(a). Propagation of a spherical wave idealized in two dimensions. The circles represent the spherical surfaces of advancing wavefronts obtained by joining all points of identical phase, in this case the condensation points.

Let's concentrate on refraction, a more curious phenomenon. First of all, why does it occur? Refraction has to do with the change in speed of light in a different medium. Light has different speeds in different media; it slows down considerably in a dense medium like water, even more in denser glass. Even in air the speed of light is a little bit less than it is in a vacuum. Incidentally, this fact that light slows down in glass has been dramatized by British science fiction writer Bob Shaw in his novel *Other Days, Other Eyes*, in which the writer imagines a new technology of slow glass. As the term slow glass implies, this material is capable of slowing down the pace of light so much that light takes days, even years, to get through a slab of slow glass of ordinary thickness. The density of such glass, of course, has to be enormous, a density quite beyond our technology. Furthermore, at such densities glass would cease to be glass. Thus, slow glass is entirely a magic-wand concept. However, once you accept the magic wand, the rest of Shaw's story is quite interesting.

Incidentally, the slowdown in light speed that occurs in a medium is really a slowdown in its average velocity; the instantaneous velocity (the rate of distance traveled as calculated for arbitrarily small time intervals) of light never changes from its vacuum value of 3×10^8 m/sec. In its travel through a medium such as glass, light encounters and spends some time with electrons with which it interacts because of its basic electromagnetic nature. When we compute the average velocity, accounting for the lost time gives us a smaller value.

Now imagine that wave fronts of light (taken to be plane waves for simplicity) are incident on the boundary between two media, say from air to water. If a wave front arrives at the interface slanted at an angle to the boundary, as shown in Figure 18b, part of the wave front encounters the denser medium earlier than the rest of it. This part now is forced to travel at a slower speed; thus, if it continued in the same direction, it would lag behind the rest of the front. To keep pace, the inside part of the front takes on a new direction such that the distance of its travel path is reduced. It makes up in reduced distance what it loses in speed, so that its phase relationship is the same with the rest of the front. Thus, the wave fronts must bend to become more parallel to the interface in a denser medium. In terms of light rays, the rays are refracted toward the normal (perpendicular) line to the interface when light passes from a rarer to a denser medium. The reverse is, of course, true when light passes from a dense to a rarer medium (Figure 18c).

From this reasoning it should be clear that the more light slows down in a medium, the more refractive the medium will be. It is customary to define a quantity known as refractive index when talking about the refractivity of a given medium:

$$\text{refractive index} = \frac{\text{speed of light in vacuum}}{\text{speed of light in medium}}$$

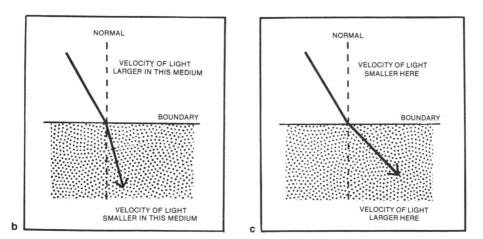

Figure 18. (b) Refraction of a light ray as it travels from a rare medium (where the velocity of light is greater) to a dense medium (where the velocity of light is smaller). The ray bends toward the normal (perpendicular to the interface) in the dense medium. (c) Refraction of a light ray when it propagates from a dense into a rare medium. The light rays refract away from the normal in the new (rare) medium.

With this preamble, we are ready to look at one of the best light fantasies that SF has given us. I am talking about H. G. Wells's *The Invisible Man*. Can a person become invisible? Wells's hero explains the secret to a doctor friend in the following excerpt. In the process he also gives a very clear exposition of how we see things.

". . . visibility depends on the action of the visible bodies of light . . . You know quite well that either a body absorbs light or it reflects or refracts it or does all these things. If it neither reflects or refracts nor absorbs light, it cannot of itself be visible. You see an opaque red box, for instance, because the colour absorbs some of the light and reflects the rest, all the red part of the light to you. If it did not absorb any particular part of the light, but reflected it all, then it would be a shining white box. Silver! A diamond box would neither absorb much of the light nor reflect much from the general surface, but just here and there where the surfaces are favourable the light would be reflected and refracted, so that you would get a brilliant appearance of flashing reflections and translucencies. A sort of skeleton of light. A glass box would not be so brilliant, not so clearly visible as a diamond box, because there would be less refraction and reflection. . . . If you put a sheet of common white glass in water, still more if you put it in some denser liquid than water, it would vanish almost altogether, because light passing from water to glass is only slightly refracted or reflected, or indeed affected in any way. It is almost as invisible as a jet of coal gas or hydrogen is in air. And for precisely the same reason!"

"Yes," said Kemp. "That is plain sailing. Any schoolboy nowadays knows all that."

"And here is another fact any schoolboy will know. If a sheet of glass is smashed, Kemp, and beaten into a powder, it becomes much more visible while it is in the air; it becomes at last an opaque, white powder. This is because the powdering multiplies the surfaces of the glass at which refraction and reflection occur. In the sheet of glass there are only two surfaces, in the powder the light is reflected or refracted by each grain it passes through, and very little gets right through the powder. But if the white, powdered glass is put into water it forthwith vanishes. The powdered glass and water have much the same refractive index, that is, the light undergoes very little refraction or reflection in passing from one to the other.

"You make the glass invisible by putting it into a liquid of nearly the same refractive index; a transparent thing becomes invisible if it is put in any medium of almost the same refractive index. And if you will consider only a second, you will see also that the powder of glass might be made to vanish in air, if its refractive index could be made the same as that of air. For then there would be no refraction or reflection as the light passed from glass to air."

"Yes, yes," said Kemp. "But a man's not powdered glass."

"No," said Griffin. "He's more transparent."

"Nonsense."

"That's from a doctor. How one forgets! Have you already forgotten your physics in ten years? Just think of all the things that are transparent and seem not to be so! Paper, for instance, is made up of transparent fibres, and it is white and opaque only for the same reason that a powder of glass is white and opaque. Oil white paper, fill up the interstices between the particles with oil, so that there is no longer refraction or reflection except at the surfaces, and it becomes transparent as glass. And not only paper, but cotton fibre, linen fibre, woody fibre, and bone, Kemp, flesh, Kemp, hair, Kemp, nails and nerves, Kemp, in fact, the whole fabric of a man, except the red of his blood and the dark pigment of hair, are all made up of transparent, colourless tissue—so little suffices to make us visible one to the other. . . ."

Wells' hero, who is supposed to be the greatest physicist on earth, had figured out how to make all the human body tissues invisible. He was even able to make the pigmented parts of his body transparent; thus, nothing of him—blood and hair included—was visible to another person. And he accomplished all this by treating his body with a transparency liquid such that the body tissues and pigments came to possess the same refractive properties as those of air.

There is a lot of reasonableness in how Wells poses the problem and its solution, and even some truth. There are hairless animals which do have a considerable amount of transparency. For example, in albino frogs you can see the working of the heart muscle or the intestine. But can one treat opaque tissue material to make it transparent? German anatomist W. Spalteholtz first accomplished this about ten years after The Invisible Man was published—but not with live bodies, only with dead specimens. He soaked the specimens in a colorless liquid, methylsalicylate, which has a really high refractive index. When placed in jars filled with the same liquid, the specimens were practically invisible.

Unfortunately, this is as far as one can go. Treating live bodies with a "transparency fluid" very likely would alter the body's organic functions. Moreover, even if the body could be treated like this to become transparent, it still would not be invisible. Invisibility would arrive only if the body were kept immersed in the same treating fluid.

Perhaps Wells should have changed the scenario of his story to imagine a completely different type of intelligent creature who lived in an atmosphere of a refractive index matching that of its body tissue. Would this be a good plot for science fiction? Unfortunately, there is still a problem, because the biggest criticism one finds of Wells's idea also applies here: it is that a completely invisible creature would also be totally blind. Its eye lens, having the same refractive index as its environment, could do no focusing whatsoever of any light reaching it. Thus, the invisible creature would be blind. Indeed, if you look at nearly transparent fish who are close to invisible in their natural environment, water, you will find that their eyes are quite pigmented and are made up of highly refractive material. So nature knows the problem with total invisibility and does not attempt perfection.

Figure 18c does not tell you this, but when light travels from a dense into a rare medium, the situation can be much more intriguing. To see this, consider light propagation from water to air, but this time concentrate on how light is refracted as the angle of incidence (the angle that a light ray makes with the perpendicular to the interface) is increased. Clearly, the refracted ray will fan out more toward the interface as the angle of incidence is increased, and at some "critical angle" the refracted ray will graze the interface (Figure 19a). What happens if the angle of incidence is greater than the critical angle? The refracted ray has nowhere to go but to be reflected back into the original medium. This kind of reflection is called total internal reflection. Total internal reflection is really a refraction phenomenon.

Although none of us has any direct experience of true underwater viewing (our *eye* has a refractive index too close to that of water to see at all well

Figure 19. (a) Rays from a point underwater incident on the water-air interface at an angle greater than the critical angle (in this case 48.5°) do not emerge outside the water at all but are totally reflected. This phenomenon is called total internal reflection. (b) To an underwater creature, the world outside, a 180° arc, is compressed within a much smaller 97° arc (two times 48.5°); the compression becomes increasingly pronounced the farther away the parts of the arc are from 0° (the zenith).

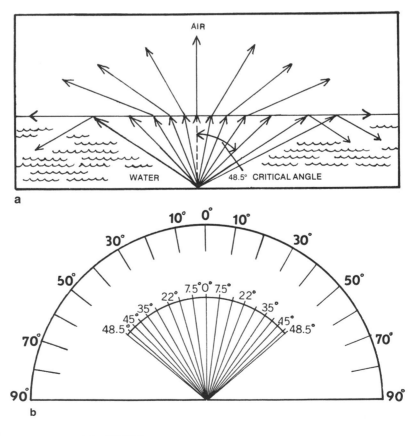

under water), we can reason that the surface of the water looked at from underneath must be like a mirror because of this total internal reflection. From a distance, if one fish looks at another, it must also see an image up above. And it may be confusing that from close, no such image appears.

However, the most confusing thing about being a water creature probably is that the world takes on a very different appearance because of this refraction and total reflection. Look at Figure 19b. Obviously, an aquatic creature sees the outside world to be condensed inside a cone because, although light from everywhere outside can reach inside, it always seems to come from within the cone. Because of this, water inhabitants would think that they live at the bottom of a bowl or crater with slanted walls, the slant depending on the magnitude of the critical angle.

Interestingly, Poul Anderson in *Ensign Flandry* imagined an underwater alien race, but he failed to discuss the variety of optical experiences that such underwater creatures must have, which would have enriched his novel. Fortunately, there is an SF novel, Hal Clement's *Mission of Gravity,* which has a similar scenario. Clement's aliens are not underwater beings, but the atmosphere of their planet simulates the water-air environment. It is very dense down below, but becomes abruptly rarefied at a height. This is not unlike a water-topped-by-air environment close to the ground, and the refraction–total reflection combination thus misleads the inhabitants of Clement's planet into thinking that their world is bowl-shaped.

chapter seven

Time for the Stars

Vincent Van Gogh used to paint trees that reached up to the stars. Once somebody asked him about his strange trees: "Why haven't I ever seen trees like yours?" To this Van Gogh is supposed to have replied, "My trees are dreamers; they want to reach the stars." This is the most important common characteristic of science fiction writers; like Van Gogh's trees, they are dreamers who reach out to the stars.

In an earlier chapter, I presented ideas in connection with the exploration of the solar system. SF writers as a group are supportive of these ideas. But they would ask, Why stop with the solar system? Why not fulfill the star-dream? And most of us SF aficionados would be sympathetic to this star-quest.

But there are problems, one of them being that the stars are very far away. Consider. The highest possible speed that nature seems to allow is the speed of light—a very great speed, but finite: 300,000 kilometers per second. Even traveling at that tremendous speed, it takes light four years to reach us from the nearest star outside the solar system. This is the reason that interstellar distances usually are referred to using the unit of the light year—the distance light travels in one year. Thus, our nearest stellar neighbor, Alpha Centauri, is four light years away.

Can we fathom a light year of distance? As one of the characters in Poul Anderson's novel, *The Avatar,* exasperatedly states, "I've tried and tried to imagine a light year, but of course I can't." If you are trying, perhaps I can help by expressing the distance of a light year in terms of more familiar units of miles and meters. One light year equals roughly the distance of six trillion (6,000,000,000,000) miles; in meters it amounts to about 10,000 trillion. But now your imagination is on its own.

And at the risk of increasing your consternation, let's enlarge our vista. Our galaxy—the huge conglomerate of some one hundred billion stars that we call the Milky Way—is 100,000 light years from one end to the other; we ourselves are situated about 30,000 light years away from the galactic center. Our closest galactic neighbor, the Andromeda galaxy (I am discounting the closer Magellanic Clouds; they are a trifle too small to be called galaxies), is a couple of million light years distant. And there are a hundred billion such galaxies in space as far as we can tell. The entire universe, if it is finite in size at all, has a span of some ten billion light years.

Even traveling at light speed, it would take us four years to reach the nearest star, thirty thousand years to reach the center of our own galaxy, two million years to approach our nearest galaxy, and an incomprehensible ten billion years to traverse the entire span of the vast universe. And at our present speed capability of some twenty kilometers per second, even the nearest star would take a whopping 62,500 years to achieve. These times are so great compared to the human lifetime of a scant 100 years or less, that it seems to make little sense even to talk about star travel.

Fortunately, there are other statistics that give us heart. Speed technology has been growing exponentially in the past century. A mere hundred years ago, the maximum speed attained by humankind anywhere on earth was only a hundred or so miles an hour, and that thanks to the discovery and development of the steam locomotive. The hundred-mile limit extended to four hundred, thanks to airplanes. The four hundred mph speed yielded to new limits established by rocket planes. And today in the eighties, we think nothing of orbital satellites racing at 18,000 miles per hour. This is a very impressive rate of growth.

Many rocket futurists—who, in the absence of proper funding, get to construct their rockets only in their minds—think in tune with SF writers. They admit that today's chemical rockets are woefully inadequate for star travel, but they refuse to confine themselves to chemical fuels. Nuclear fuels, although somewhat scary to use to generate electricity on earth because of their controversial pollution and safety problems, are surely available for use in rocketry. A nuclear-powered rocket would explode hydrogen bombs in the rear of the properly shielded rocket, enabling it to travel at fantastic speeds by today's standards, perhaps as much as one tenth of the speed of light. At such a speed, a round trip to Alpha Centauri, our nearest stellar body, would take eighty years, comparable to the human life span. All of a sudden, the nearby stars at least seem to be within our reach.

And if we can ever learn to build rockets that exceed one tenth the speed of light, the theory of relativity—which gave us nature's speed limit, the speed of light—itself comes to the aid of the space voyager. The voyager's aging processes slow down because of the fundamental nature of time. Even today, more than seventy years after relativity was discovered by Einstein, this idea remains stunning. We'll explore it in some detail in the following pages.

DID EINSTEIN LIKE SCIENCE FICTION?

Did Einstein like science fiction? Who knows? But science fiction writers as a group adore Einstein. No other concept of science has ever turned on the SF world as much as Einstein's relativity. Let's speculate on the reasons for such adulation of a man and his ideas.

One reason is that some of the strange consequences of the theory of relativity seem more like fiction than truth. Relativity proves the old adage,

"Truth is stranger than fiction." It legitimizes not only the adage, but imagination itself. If relativity is possible—inevitable, even, because nature demands it—then we are free to imagine, as the queen did in *Through the Looking-Glass*, six impossible things before breakfast.

Of course, relativity is also very useful to science fiction writers in practical ways; it extends their arena of action-adventure, helping them create new situations that, however strange to our intuition, are perfectly logical. As an example, consider the case of the slowing down of the clocks in a moving spaceship, a very important result derived from relativistic considerations. If clocks slow down for a voyager in a fast spaceship (this includes his biological clocks), the voyager has the chance to complete a long journey to a star while aging little. Thus, space travel, at least to nearby stars, becomes plausible, validated by science. Of course, there still is a catch. Appreciable dilation of time occurs only when spaceships move at near light's velocity, and such speeds could very well be impossible to attain with rockets, even with futuristic designs. But a fiction writer should be allowed at least one touch of a magic wand in a given story.

The phenomenon of time dilation also extends the horizon in another type of imaginative adventure. You know the story of Rip Van Winkle, who slept for twenty years to wake and find his environment aged by twenty years. This "one-way time travel" makes a very interesting setting. Time dilation gives us a means of accomplishing this one-way time travel. Since time becomes slower only in the moving spaceship, people on earth continue at their usual rate; thus, the returning space voyager encounters a situation similar to Mr. Van Winkle's. His story may be even more fascinating because his time travel to the future is achieved so deliberately and "scientifically."

This example makes it amply clear that relativity has changed our view of time in a radical fashion. Before Einstein, the nature of time itself was obscure; only philosophers seemed even to worry about it. I am reminded of a story about the Russian poet Samuel Marshak. While walking the streets of London one day, Marshak wanted to know what the time was. So, in his broken English, he inquired of a passerby, "What's time?" The puzzled man answered, "Why ask me? That's a question for a philosopher." And so it was, but the picture of time that philosophers gave was quite metaphysical. However, since the picture was endorsed by the great Newton, most physicists stayed mum on the issue.

The philosophical picture of time endorsed by Newton was that the universe was ruled by a single absolute time given by an imaginary clock perhaps hidden outside of the cosmos (God's own clock?). Time then would be completely independent of motion, but motion or change, of course, could occur only in time; and all observers could judge these changes using an identical measure of time. This is the absolute view of time. Relativity demolished this picture when it showed that time for a moving observer slows down; moving observers keep time at a different rate than stationary observers. Time depends on motion, on the reference frame of an observer, quite noticeably if the observer happens to have a high speed. This is the idea, that time is relative. The theory that expands this idea and its consequences is called special relativity.

Thus, Einstein had to defy authority of no less stature than Newton in order to develop his new way of looking at time. This nourishes that same blithe spirit found in science fiction, the determined spirit of challenging established dogma. SF enthusiasts, readers and writers alike, love Einstein because he was a rebel at heart.

Did Einstein like science fiction? I don't know if he read even a single work of science fiction. Yet in him I see one of the greatest friends that science fiction ever had. His rebellious spirit, his youth spent as an outcast from the scientific establishment, his power of imagination employed in the pursuit not only of scientific truth but also of social goals to make the earth a better place to live: these are commonalities with science fiction that are impossible to overlook.

THE SLOWING DOWN OF SHIPTIME

In Charles Harness' SF novel *Firebird,* the spaceship courier Dermaq had to face a sad turn of events: on his wedding night he was torn from his beautiful bride and ordered to travel to another planet on assignment:

> Fifteen light-*meda*—fifteen long circuits of Kornaval around the sun—to a backwoods planet to fetch away some village princess (just now an infant in diapers)—another fifteen to return to Kornaval. With the combination of the ship's deepsleep casket and the inherent slowing effect of shiptime, he would age only a few days. But Innae would become an old woman. He ran through the equations mentally and groaned. It had been wrong of him to marry in the first place. Love had unbalanced his reason. [italics in the original, p. 14]

Thanks to relativity and the imagined future technology of cold sleep, Harness creates in the future society in *Firebird* a new class of people who hop from planet to planet with little aging, while years fall like autumn leaves in the lives of those who remain "groundhogs." Relativistic slowdown of clocks on a fast spaceship is a routine affair nowadays in science fiction, used by SF writers fairly often, yet it always makes an impact on me. I felt sad that, when his job was done, Dermaq returned to his wife (on their anniversary) only to find her dead, but especially so because relativity conspired in the tragedy.

Relativity alone allows you to create this kind of drama; you don't need cold sleep if you design your spaceship to travel at speeds 99 percent of the speed of light, and the closer the better. Jan, one of Arthur C. Clarke's main characters in his powerful *Childhood's End,* traveled as a stowaway in an alien spaceship to the alien home planet, some forty light years from earth. But, thanks to the alien technology which could attain incredibly close-to-light speed, he aged only two months during the trip. And when Jan came back, he found the earth fatally changed in the intervening eighty earth years. But that's another story. Jan's speed? 99.999132 percent of the speed of light.

As one of the characters in Joe Haldeman's masterpiece, *The Forever War,* puts it:

". . . you get to nine tenths of the speed of light . . . From then on, you're in the arms of Saint Albert." [p. 176]

Saint Albert Einstein, of course!

In 1973 the relativistic time dilation effect on moving clocks became official. In that year, two physicists, J. C. Hafele and R. E. Keating, arranged an auspicious jet trip around the earth, carrying an atomic clock. At a jet plane's speed, the time dilation effect is minuscule; but an atomic clock, which keeps time in pace with the vibrations of tiny atoms, is so accurate that it measures a slowdown of even 10^{-7} second. Such a slowdown was observed in this experiment, exactly in accordance with Einstein's theory of relativity.

Are you curious yet about what causes moving clocks to run slower? What in the theory of relativity gives us such a mind-boggling phenomenon as time dilation?

Relativity stands on two basic physical postulates, both rooted in experiment. The first is the fact that physical laws remain the same in all inertial reference frames—reference frames such as two spaceships moving at constant velocity with respect to each other. The second is more astonishing: the speed of light remains the same, observed from all inertial reference frames. Let's discuss these postulates in some detail.

The first postulate comes from the relativity of natural motion—the fact that experiments can only tell you about relative motion, relative velocities, never about any absolute motion. When you sit in a moving spaceship and look out at another spaceship, which ship seems to be moving? It's always the other spaceship.

A childhood incident was instrumental in my experiencing relativity of motion. I took my first train ride when I accompanied an elder brother to his wedding. It was a night train. In the morning my brother asked me how the journey was. I said it was fine, but then added bashfully that I was surprised to find out there were really two kinds of trains: one kind that shakes but doesn't go anywhere, like the one I was in the night before, and the usual, moving kind. Everybody within earshot (all adults fortunately) laughed, and eventually someone explained that from inside a moving train one couldn't tell if the train was moving without looking outside.

Perhaps you too can think of a time when, while traveling at constant velocity in a car or a train, you had a momentary feeling that you were not moving at all. It appeared that you were at rest, and that the scenery around you was madly moving away. Very soon, of course, your thinking mind took over. "Trees don't move," you perhaps muttered to yourself, concluding that it was you moving, after all.

But suppose you were in a spaceship moving at constant velocity in deep space. Could you tell if you were moving? Absolutely not, not from the result of any experiment whatsoever that you could conduct inside the spaceship. And even if you looked at the stars through a window, you would not be able to tell which was moving, you or the stars. This is the idea of relativity of motion.

Thus, all inertial reference frames—frames that move at constant velocity relative to each other—are equivalent; there is no preferred frame, and physical laws must be formulated to reflect this relativity. This is the meaning of the first postulate above.

The second postulate is harder to appreciate—that light always moves with the same velocity, irrespective of the frame of origin or observation. Let's face it, it contradicts our everyday experience. When we watch a stone thrown from a moving train, it *does* move with an added velocity—that of the train. And from a moving train, if we were watching a rock moving with a velocity matching the train's, the rock *would* look stationary to us. But in the case of light, Einstein somehow figured out—even as a young boy of fifteen—that things had to be different. He used to imagine that he was running at the speed of light and then attempted to see his face in a mirror held in his hand. Would he see his image? Somehow Einstein felt that he would; he knew intuitively that light is different. Light could not seem stationary even if he were looking at light from a reference frame moving at light speed.

For mere mortals, it is best initially simply to accept the constancy of the speed of light as an experimental fact. The speed of light has been measured from different inertial reference frames with a range of relative motion between them. It always comes out to be the same, 3×10^8 m/sec in vacuum. Let's denote it by c. Thus, we are forced to conclude that the speed of light is independent of the reference frame from which it is measured or from which it originates. So, if you turn on a flashlight while on board a spaceship moving with a velocity v, the light velocity measured from either the spaceship or the ground is always c, not $c + v$ (in the forward direction) or $c - v$ (in the backward direction) as you might have guessed from your experience with ordinary projectiles. Light is very special. It is this special property of light that leads to the slowing down of moving clocks.

To understand this, consider a *gedanken* (thought) experiment—the sort that Einstein specialized in, such as his mirror experiment. Since we are forced to examine time itself in an intimate way, it will help to employ a rather simple clock to measure time, called the light radar clock. In radar, a microwave beam is sent back and forth between an aircraft and the radar station in order to trace the aircraft. The same idea can be used as a clock. If a light beam is kept going back and forth between two mirrors tied to the two ends of a rod (Figure 20a)—with the lower mirror having some sort of ticking mechanism that is activated every time light falls on it (one such device is the photo cell)—then these ticks will measure time.

Suppose we place such a clock in a moving spaceship and watch its performance from an earth-based reference frame. Will its performance, considered from the earth-based frame, be the same as that of an identical clock on earth? To avoid controversy, we synchronize two light clocks; we then put one on the spaceship and keep the other on earth.

One more caution is needed before we unbridle our imagination. The rod that holds the mirrors of the clock in the moving spaceship must be placed at right angles to the direction of motion of the ship. The reason for this has to do with the contraction of the rod's length (another relativistic effect!) if it is placed in any other direction as seen by the earth observer. This could unnecessarily add to the confusion.

The observer on earth, who sees his own light clock as stationary, sees the light rays between the mirrors of his clock traveling in straight up and down paths (Figure 20a). If the length of the rod is L, light according to this observer travels the distance $2L$ between ticks, and thus the time between two ticks of the earth clock is given as

$$t = \frac{\text{distance}}{\text{velocity}} = \frac{2L}{c}$$

according to the earth observer. All observers see their own light clocks ticking at this rate.

However, the earth observer sees the ticking rate of the spaceship clock differently. According to him, the light signals that cause the ticking of the spaceship clock must travel a zigzag path, since the ship is moving (Figure 20b). Suppose the path is AMB, where AB is the distance that the ship travels during the up-down motion of the light ray. Then the time period t' between ticks of the ship clock as measured by the ground observer is given as

$$t' = \frac{\text{distance}}{\text{velocity}} = \frac{AMB}{c}$$

since the speed of light is given by c as always—not faster. Clearly, the distance AMB is greater than the straight up-down distance $2L$. Thus, t' is greater than t; the time period of the moving clock as measured by the ground observer is longer than that of the earth clock, proving that moving clocks run slower compared to stationary clocks.

A little mathematics enables us to derive the following formula for the

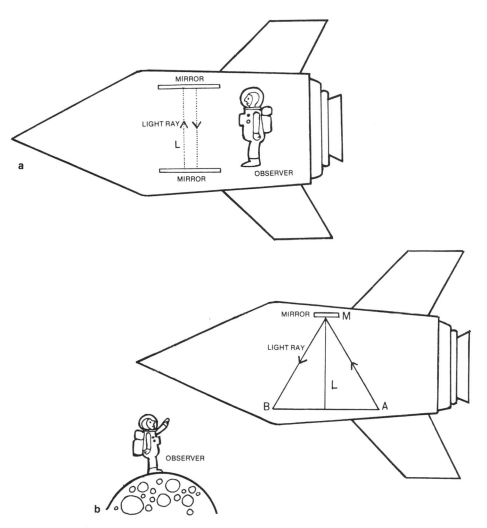

Figure 20. (a) A light clock on a spaceship from the viewpoint of a spaceship observer. A light clock on earth would seem to function the same way to an observer on earth. (b) The path of light of a light clock on a moving spaceship as seen by a stationary earth observer. The path is no longer seen as straight up and down, because of the effect of the ship's motion.

amount of slowing down that moving clocks exhibit. Let v denote the velocity of the spaceship relative to the earth and c denote the speed of light. Then the time between ticks of the moving clock, t', as reckoned by the earth observer, compares thus with the time interval t between ticks of the earth clock, which is stationary:

$$t' = \frac{t}{\sqrt{1 - \dfrac{v^2}{c^2}}}$$

It is customary to denote the relativistic factor

$$\frac{1}{\sqrt{1 - \frac{v^2}{c^2}}}$$

by the Greek letter γ (gamma). Figure 20c shows the variation of gamma with the velocity v of the starship. Notice that gamma is appreciably greater than 1 only when v exceeds 0.1 c—that is, relativistic time dilation is important only when velocities reach to within 10 percent of the speed of light. And notice also how gamma leaps to larger and larger values as v creeps very close to c in numerical value. Thus, the closer the velocity of a spaceship is to the speed of light, the slower runs its clock compared to an earth-based clock.

We can express the time dilation effect in a slightly different manner. Consider the factor

$$\sqrt{1 - \frac{v^2}{c^2}}$$

Figure 20. (c) The relativistic factor γ (gamma) plotted as a function of the ratio of ship's velocity to the speed of light v/c. γ hardly deviates from 1 until v/c is greater than about 0.1. And γ increases rapidly as the speed of the moving object becomes greater than 90 percent of the speed of light.

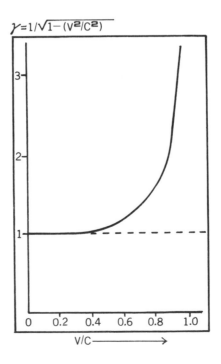

THE COSMIC DANCERS

Call it τ (the Greek letter tau, used by Poul Anderson in *Tau Zero*). Then the interlude between two events (such as the departure from earth and the arrival at a destination star) in shiptime is tau times the interlude between the events in earthtime. To be concrete, if Dermaq's ship in *Firebird* travels at 0.6 *c*, it takes twenty-five years of planet time to reach the destination fifteen light years away, but since tau is 0.8—the square root of one minus $(0.6)^2$, check it out—the elapsed shiptime is only 0.8 × 25, or 20 years. As you see, at this kind of speed it's not too spectacular a gain, so Dermaq has to depend on cold sleep to keep from aging.

I started this section with a sad story, but I'd like to end it on a happy note. Relativity can serve love as well as thwart it, as is clearly revealed in the following letter written by one of the main characters of Joe Haldeman's Hugo-winning novel, *The Forever War*:

11 Oct 2878

William—

All this is in your personnel file. But knowing you, you might just chuck it. So I made sure you'd get this note.

Obviously, I lived. Maybe you will, too. Join me.

I know from the records that you're out at Sade-138 and won't be back for a couple of centuries. No problem.

I'm going to a planet they call Middle Finger, the fifth planet out from Mizar. . . .

It took all of my money, and all the money of five other old-timers, but we bought a cruiser from UNEF. And we're using it as a time machine.

So I'm on a relativistic shuttle, waiting for you. All it does is go out five light years and come back to Middle Finger, very fast. Every ten years I age about a month. So if you're on schedule and still alive, I'll only be twenty-eight when you get here. Hurry!

I never found anybody else and I don't want anybody else. I don't care whether you're ninety years old or thirty. If I can't be your lover, I'll be your nurse.

—Marygay [p. 235]

For Marygay, tau must be

$$\frac{\text{one month}}{\text{ten years}} = \frac{1/12 \text{ year}}{10 \text{ years}} = \frac{1}{120}$$

judging from the results. This value of tau requires a ship velocity of 0.999965 *c*—that close to light speed. This, of course, requires a lot of energy, but no matter, everything is permissible for love! Needless to mention, Marygay did regain William—and as a lover!

TIME DILATION AND RELATIVITY OF REFERENCE FRAMES

Above we proved the slowing down of clocks only for a particular type of clock. How can we be sure that other kinds of clocks slow down also, independent of their specific mechanisms? This is where it is important to recall the principle of relativity of motion between two inertial reference frames. Suppose we have at hand a few other clocks of different mechanisms which we synchronize with the light clock? The spaceship carries along a few of these. Can they keep a different rate, not slowing down like the light clock? No, indeed. This would violate the principle of relativity, because—by noticing the discrepancy of the clocks—an observer *on* the spaceship could tell whether the spaceship was moving. And, according to the relativity of motion, this is impossible. Thus, all clocks must slow down in a moving ship, and this includes all biological clocks: pulse rate, rate of aging, and so forth.

And all this should happen without the passengers of the spaceship having the slightest awareness of any slowing down of their clocks; for them life goes on as before.

Does that mean that psychological time—the time that we *feel*—also keeps shiptime, or does it continue to function as on earth? Most physicists would say that psychological time is not different from biological time, mind is but a function of the brain; yet such assertions are far from established scientifically. Suppose the time we felt *were* different, does that violate the principle of relativity? Not necessarily, because feelings are subjective, and subjective times can vary enormously—even on earth.

You would think that this would stimulate interesting speculations in SF, but you would be disappointed. I have not seen this issue raised in any story. Well, maybe in one, but even then with an escape hatch. In James Blish's story called "Common Time" (included in *The Best of James Blish*), the pilot wakes up on his journey to Alpha Centauri—only to find that his mind perceives all that happens around him in the ship to be extremely slow. Soon he figures out the reason:

> Suppose that this effect of time stretching was only mental? The rest of his bodily processes might still be keeping ship-time. . . . If so, he would be able to move around only in ship-time, too; it would take many apparent months (as judged by his mind) to complete the simplest task.
> But he would live, if that were the case. His mind would arrive at Alpha Centauri . . . years older than his body, but he would live. [p. 182]

Unfortunately, Blish confused the issue (to avoid controversy, I suppose) in his story by claiming that the ship had a superlight drive, which of course is the product of a magic wand; then anything is possible.

CONTRACTION OF DISTANCES OR LORENTZ CONTRACTION

According to relativity, at such speeds that time slows down considerably (shiptime, that is), it should be possible to make voyages to distant stars light years away. Although the ship would take years of earth-time to complete the trip, a much shorter time would have elapsed in shiptime. The traveler would therefore be able to make the trip without sacrificing a significant portion of his life.

But we can ask one important question. How is it that space voyagers are able to travel light years of distance in fewer years of shiptime? Does this mean that in their frame of reference they somehow are able to travel at a speed greater than the speed of light? This would again violate the basic postulates of relativity. The way out of this predicament is to realize that for the spaceship voyagers something strange happens to the distance: the distance in the direction of the ship's voyage shrinks. Since they travel only this shrunken distance, they are able to make good time even with sublight-speed. This contraction of moving lengths or distances is called the Lorentz contraction.

The factor by which the distance contracts from the perspective of a moving ship is again the same relativistic factor, gamma, that appears in time dilation. Thus, if d is the original distance, the contracted distance d' is given as

$$d' = \frac{d}{\gamma} = \sqrt{1 - \frac{v^2}{c^2}}\, d$$

Since all objects are embedded in space, if moving space undergoes contraction, it follows that moving objects contract, too—in the direction of the body's motion, of course. This idea no doubt inspired the following limerick by an anonymous author:

> There was a young fellow named Fisk
> Whose fencing was exceedingly brisk
> So fast was his action
> The Lorentz contraction
> Reduced his rapier to a disk.

WHICH TWIN IS OLDER?

Let's return to the difference between shiptime and earth-time. Time dilation tells us that moving clocks slow down. The basic principle of relativity asserts that motion is relative. When we combine these two ideas, a problem arises: How do we know which clock is moving? Each observer will claim that it is the other observer's clock which is slow.

Going back to the light-radar clocks of a previous section, you may have felt puzzled on one point. Just as the earth observer sees the light of the earth clock go straight up and down, so the ship observer sees the light of the ship clock go straight up and down. Shouldn't the ship observer see the light of the earth clock zigzagging and hence traveling a longer path between ticks? Right. Then in the measurement of the ship observer, it's the earth clock which runs slower.

The problem can be put more dramatically if you imagine the following scenario. Suppose we have twin brothers, one of whom sets forth for the stars in a spaceship, while the other remains on earth. At 80 percent of the speed of light, the space twin can make a round trip to Alpha Centauri, which is four light years away, in ten earth years. When he comes back, his twin brother and everybody else on earth will have aged ten years. How much will he have aged?

According to the earth twin, the space twin will have aged less, only six years, since he has been traveling close to the speed of light and enjoying the time dilation effect. "Not so," says his twin. "In my perception it was you and the earth that were moving away from me. Therefore, you have to be the one to benefit from time dilation and slow clocks, not me." Who is right? When the space twin returns from a space trip at near light speed, will he find himself (a) older than his brother, (b) younger than his brother, or (c) the same age?

This is the twin paradox. Which twin is older? Or maybe time dilation is just an idea, a mirage in actuality, and they both age at the same rate?

Science fiction writer Robert A. Heinlein's beautiful book *Time for the Stars* is about such a twin, except that the author ignores the paradox. When the space twin is moving close to the speed of light but at constant velocity, in between periods of acceleration (presumably, since Heinlein keeps mentioning special relativity, which is about reference frames in natural motion), we read the following description of events (the viewpoint is the space twin's):

Slippage [of time rate] was catching up with us. As anyone can see from the relativistic formulas, the relationship is not a straight line one; it isn't even noticeable at the beginning but it builds up like the dickens at the other end of the scale.

At three quarters the speed of light he [the earth twin] complained that I was drawling, while it seemed to me that he was starting to jabber. [p. 108]

So you see Heinlein's twins don't have a paradoxical situation: one of them, the earth twin, "jabbers"—his clock is fast. And the space twin "drawls" because his moving clock is slowed down. Heinlein chooses to ignore the paradox, perhaps to avoid unnecessarily confusing his readers. Incidentally, if you are wondering how they communicate at all, these twins are telepathic; they can communicate instantaneously over any distance: this is the magic wand of this story.

But for physicists, the paradox is real and severe. If it is not resolved, then the whole of relativity becomes suspect. Einstein, well aware of this, came up with one way to resolve the paradox.

The paradox arises because of the innate symmetry of relative motion. When two objects are in relative motion, the situation has to be entirely symmetrical. But when one of the twins is going away from and returning to the other, is this symmetry preserved all the way? Einstein argued that it was not.

Consider the actual trip as shown in Figure 21. Besides periods of natural motion there must be periods of acceleration in such a trip. And during these acceleration periods, the principle of relativity does not hold. Einstein suggested that during periods of natural motion, each twin observed the other to age at a slower rate than himself. But when the space twin turns around during these acceleration periods, he sees the earth twin's clock speed up enormously as the earth twin ages, becoming older than he. So, Heinlein's description would be more to Einstein's taste during acceleration periods—the earth twin would jabber according to the space twin, and the space twin would drawl according to the earth twin.

Einstein proceeded to develop the theoretical extension of special relativity to a new "general" relativity that includes accelerated reference frames and the resultant effect on time. This new theory—representing a new approach to space, time, and gravitation—will be taken up in a later chapter.

Figure 21. A complete trip to another star system would have to have periods of acceleration (and deceleration, which is negative acceleration).

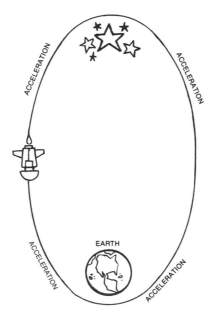

MOVING AT THE SPEED OF LIGHT

One of Einstein's teenage fantasy-inquiries was this: how would time tick for someone rushing through the universe at the incredible speed of light? The mathematical expression for the relativistic factor gamma provides the answer to this question. If we substitute $v = c$ in the equation for gamma, we find

$$\gamma = \frac{1}{\sqrt{1 - \dfrac{v^2}{c^2}}} = \frac{1}{\sqrt{1 - 1}} = \frac{1}{0} \rightarrow \infty$$

(This is the same limit as tau tending to zero, a limit that Poul Anderson alluded to in the title of his novel *Tau Zero*.) As the speed of the traveler tends to c, gamma tends to infinity, and with it the value of t' also becomes infinity. Thus, the time between ticks of a moving clock becomes infinitely long at light speed. This is true time-stop. All physical attributes of such a traveler would cease to change, since change can occur only in time. A trip through galaxies would be instantaneous to the voyager (no matter that such trips would take millions of earth years), for distances would have melted away to naught for such a traveler.

Since motion is relative, to the voyager at the speed of light everything else in the universe would appear to travel at light speed, and thus all their moving clocks would appear to him to be at a standstill. Everything would seem to be part of a universe-wide party in the style of Lewis Carroll's Mad Hatter's tea party, the clock always showing 6. In effect, he would be cut off from the humdrum of the everyday world.

Now, I must disclose the unfortunate (at least to SF writers) but firm conclusion of relativity theory itself: it is impossible for any material object to accelerate to light speed. Matter tends to become infinitely massive when traveling at a speed approaching that of light, and no force is large enough to give the final push to such an object that would be needed to attain light speed.

The relativistic increase of mass of an object when it moves close to light speed is alluded to in many works of science fiction, but seldom as delightfully as in the following excerpt from Donald Moffit's *The Jupiter Theft*, which is about an alien-earthling encounter (the aliens are Cygnans from the Cygnus star system):

"Does Jameson know that as a thing goes faster, it grows heavier?" Tetrachord asked.

By God. The creature was quoting the theory of relativity at him! What Cygnan Einstein, thousands of years in the past, had arrived at the great keystone equation governing the increase of mass with velocity? Jameson dug into his memory for what he had learned in his academy classes long ago.

"Jameson knows that if a thing would go as fast as light is fast, its weight would be . . ."

Damn! What was the Cygnan word for "infinite?" [p. 200]

A little math may be helpful for further understanding: the mass of an object m increases with its velocity v according to the formula

$$m = \frac{m_0}{\sqrt{1 - v^2/c^2}}$$

You will recognize the factor

$$\frac{1}{\sqrt{1 - v^2/c^2}}$$

as our old friend gamma. The mass m_0 is called the rest mass of the object; it is the object's mass measured when it is at rest.

From the above formula we can immediately make a couple of observations. First, gamma is appreciably larger than one only when the velocity v is 10 percent or better of the velocity of light; thus, mass increases are hardly noticeable for objects at ordinary speeds. Second, if we put $v = c$ in the above formula, the denominator vanishes, and the mass becomes infinite. This is what Jameson was trying to express in the Cygnan language in the above quotation.

Now you can understand better why an object can never be accelerated to the speed of light. Because, as the object approaches light speed, the value of the relativistic factor gamma tends to infinity and, accordingly, so does the relativistic mass of the object. Since only an infinite force can accelerate an object of infinite mass—and such a force is not available—we are stuck. We can never push hard enough to enable an object to overcome the light barrier.

But if the mass tends to increase beyond all limits to infinity as the velocity of an object approaches c, the speed of light, you can think of a puzzle for those objects that do travel with the speed of light, such as light itself. You may think that, since light is a wave and waves do not have mass, the problem does not arise. This is not true, because in quantum theory the waveness or particleness of elementary objects becomes hazy; thus, it is perfectly legitimate to talk about light particles, which are called photons. But now that the photons travel at the speed of light, what happens to their mass? The puzzle is solved by assigning a photon a zero rest mass. This is purely formal, of course, since the photon cannot even be slowed down, let alone brought to rest.

Neutrinos, like light, are particles that always move at the speed of light (at least, according to most theories), and are considered to have zero rest mass. (Some recent theories claim that neutrinos may have some rest mass, after all; experiments have not yet ruled out massive neutrinos.) But neutrinos are more exotic than light. We see with light—it interacts with our eyes (and matter, in general) quite strongly via the electromagnetic interaction. In contrast, neutrinos interact with matter very much more weakly; they can pass through an entire star without losing any appreciable amount of energy. They are truly phantom particles.

Detecting and handling neutrinos is very difficult, yet some neutrino technology has been suggested—in science as well as in science fiction. Some scientists have successfully sent neutrino beams through the body of the earth and detected them on the other side. This success has led to the speculation that neutrino beams may be of some future use in communication. The main problem with this idea is that we can't modulate a neutrino beam; thus, the only way to send a neutrino message would be with Morse code or some such combination of long and short signal bursts.

Nevertheless, some SF writers use neutrino communication in their story lines, as in Joe Haldeman's *The Forever War*. The protagonist, Corporal Mandella, is concerned about communication between their spaceship, which is in orbit around a planet they are attacking, and their ground forces on the enemy planet below:

Since the planet rotated rather slowly—once every ten and one-half days—a "stationary" orbit for the ship had to be 150,000 klicks [kilometers] out. This made the people in the ship feel quite secure, with 6,000 miles of rock and 90,000 miles of space between them and the enemy. But it meant a whole second's time lag in communication between us on the ground and the ship's battle computer. A person could get awful dead while that neutrino pulse crawled up and back. [p. 42]

CAN WE BUILD A TIME MACHINE?

Remember the time traveler in H. G. Wells' immortal story, *The Time Machine*? He posed a very important idea to his audience:

"Can an *instantaneous* cube exist?"
"Don't follow you," said Filby.
"Can a cube that does not last for any time at all, have a real existence?" Filby became pensive. "Clearly," the time traveler proceeded, "any real body must have extension in *four* directions: it must have Length, Breadth, Thickness, and—Duration. . . . There are really four dimensions, three of which we call the three planes of Space, and a fourth, Time. [italics in the original, p. 14]

What the time traveler said is quite correct; to specify a body completely, we do need its temporal as well as spatial location. We need to extend our scientific vocabulary, when talking about events, to incorporate the idea that a physical event takes place at a given point in space and a specific moment of time (given by a fourth, time coordinate). Yet, before relativity—when the concept of absolute time dominated our picture of time—such a description of reality in terms of a four-dimensional coordinate system was redundant. This is because the measure of time was thought to be universally the same, independent of spatial location in all situations. Time and space never got mixed up in the old theory; therefore, there was no need to put the time coordinate of an event on the same footing as the space coordinates. However, things are quite different in relativity.

The man who figured this out was Polish mathematician Hermann Minkowski, who also happened to be one of Einstein's math professors. Ironically, when Minkowski was Einstein's teacher, he didn't think much of Einstein; he referred to him as a "lazy dog" who never bothered about mathematics. Yet, when Einstein's relativity theory was published, Minkowski could see that the work should be looked at from a mathematical point of view. You know the proverb about Mohammed and the mountain: if the mountain won't go to Mohammed, then Mohammed will go to the mountain. Perhaps Minkowski felt the same way: if Einstein wouldn't bother with mathematics, then mathematics would bother with Einstein—or at least, with his work. Minkowski spent a couple of years completing his study; then he declared to the physicists of the world (Minkowski et al., 1923):

The ideas on space and time that I wish to develop before you grew from the soil of experimental physics. Therein lies their strength. Their tendency is radical. From now on space by itself, and time by itself must sink into the shadows, while only the union of the two preserves independence. [p. 75]

When you consider that *The Time Machine* was written some twenty years before relativity, it is impressive that H. G. Wells's time traveler talks in a similar vein. The details of the two approaches—Wells' as opposed to Minkowsky's—are, however, very different.

To understand the differences between Wells' view and Minkowsky's, it may serve us well to review the history of a three-dimensional picture of space. Before Newton, space was regarded by many people as merely consisting of two dimensions: the east-west and the north-south acted as the coordinate axes of the two-dimensional system. The up-down direction was looked upon as different—no doubt because of our obvious inability to travel in those directions. The time traveler talks about this:

"Are you so sure we can move freely in Space? Right and left we can go, forward and backward freely enough, and men always have done so. I admit we move freely in two dimensions. But how about up and down? Gravitation limits us there."

"Not exactly," said the medical man, "there are balloons."

"But before the balloons, man had no freedom of vertical movement." [p. 16]

Then along came Newton, and we came to understand the nature of gravity and how it limits our freedom in the up-down direction. Without gravity, we came to realize, space would have a perfect three-dimensional symmetry, with all directions having equal accessibility. Wells' imagination took off from this starting point. His time traveler asked the naturally intriguing question:

"He [civilized man] can go up against gravitation in a balloon, and why should he not hope that ultimately he may be able to stop or accelerate his drift along the Time dimension, or even turn about and travel the other way?" [p. 17]

Just as a balloon can overcome gravity, can a time machine overcome our inability to travel in the time dimension? Wells answered yes to this question and wrote his story.

Einstein and Minkowski proceeded differently. One reason that we need a three-dimensional coordinate system for space is the realization that we can transform one coordinate into another, and sometimes we are forced to do just that. For example, consider a coordinate system (x, y, z) and a rotated one (x', y', z') (Figure 22). As the figure shows, a point whose position could be given just by a y-coordinate in the first system needs x-, y-, and z- coordinates for its specification in the second coordinate system. Thus, the x-coordinate of the first system has changed partly into the other coordinates in the second system. Now Einstein discovered that when you compare the locations of events from two coordinate systems in natural motion with respect to each other, their time and space coordinates get similarly mixed up: time transforms partly into space and vice versa. This is what compelled Minkowski to regard space and time as components of a four-dimensional coordinate system.

Figure 22. The point P can be described by the y coordinate alone in the XYZ coordinate system. But in the X'Y'Z' system, all three coordinates are needed to describe the point; in this system its coordinates are all mixed up.

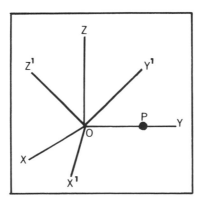

Incidentally, although Wells missed the implication of four-dimensional space-time—namely, the mixing of time and space coordinates of an event (he might have discovered relativity if he had been more alert)—a composer did talk about it, presumably without prior knowledge of relativity. In Richard Wagner's *Parsifal,* the following breathtaking conversation appears:

Parsifal: "I pace hardly at all, nevertheless I feel I have come far already."
Gurnemanz: "You see, my son, that here time transforms into space."

But, if time transforms into space, could the time machine conceivably transform time into space and vice versa, making time travel as versatile as space travel? In short, can Wells' basic idea be right, although his logic is faulty?

Minkowski gave us the answer to this question, and unfortunately, the answer is no. Minkowski's logic is both compelling and instructive. Here are the details.

First, with the help of a *gedanken* experiment, let's consider the idea of the simultaneity of two events as perceived from two different inertial reference frames. The events we choose are simple ones carried out on a spaceship: somebody with a flashlight standing right at the midpoint of the spaceship flashes a signal which is received by two passengers, one at the front of the spaceship and the other at the back. Since the receivers are equidistant from the sender of the light signal, they receive it at the same time. Each reception of the signal constitutes an event, and we can say that the two events are simultaneous as observed from the spaceship reference frame. However, a ground observer will not consider the two events as simultaneous at all. She will see that the signal moving toward the bow observer travels a longer distance than half the length of the spaceship, since the spaceship is moving away from the signal; in contrast, the light beam moving toward the stern travels a lesser distance, because the rear of the ship is moving toward the signal. Since the speed of light doesn't change, remaining the same in both the forward and backward directions, it takes light less time to reach the stern than the bow, according to the ground observer.

Thus, two events which are especially constructed to be simultaneous from one reference frame are seen to take place at different times from another reference frame. In other words, the time interval between two events is not measured to be the same from two different inertial reference frames at relative motion. The same is true for spatial intervals: two events occurring at the same place but at different times in a moving train are perceived from the ground as occurring at different places.

In general, we conclude that observers in relative motion do not agree as to each other's measurement of spatial and temporal intervals between events. In that case, you may ask, how are they going to reach any consensus for the description of events? Minkowski discovered that, although spatial and temporal intervals between events do not possess universality, a certain combination of them remains invariant, the same for all observers. This combination is called the space-time interval between two events. This is a useful mathematical construct from which (with quite sophisticated mathematics) relativistic effects such as time dilation can be derived.

But now a fundamental surprise, the details of which confirm the impossibility of the time machine. Let's consider how we figure out spatial intervals. If there were only one dimension of space, this would be very easy. We take the space coordinates of the two events and the difference gives us the spatial interval—for example, $x_2 - x_1$ where x_2 and x_1 are the two coordinates. For two-dimensional space, things are a little more complex. We have to measure the interval along each axis—for example, $x_2 - x_1$ and $y_2 - y_1$—but how do we combine them? The rule for combination was given by Greek philosopher-mathematician Pythagoras a long time ago: we take squares of each of the intervals, add, and then take the square root of the sum. In mathematical symbols:

$$\text{two-dimensional interval} = \sqrt{(x_2 - x_1)^2 + (y_2 - y_1)^2}$$

Now for three coordinates corresponding to three-dimensional space, we can easily generalize the above expression as follows:

$$\text{three-dimensional interval} = \sqrt{(x_2 - x_1)^2 + (y_2 - y_1)^2 + (z_2 - z_1)^2}$$

where z_2 and z_1 are the z-coordinates of the two events.

Now to the final step: how to generalize this interval further to incorporate four-dimensional space-time. One problem is immediate: time is not measured with the same units as distance. Fortunately, this is easy to solve. If we multiply time by a speed, we get a distance. Thus, (time × speed) has the right unit. So instead of taking time t as our fourth coordinate, we take ct—where c is the fundamental constant of the speed of light. Then, adding a time term, we try to generalize the above expression to something like this:

four-dimensional interval $=$

$$\sqrt{(x_2 - x_1)^2 + (y_2 - y_1)^2 + (z_2 - z_1)^2 + (ct_2 - ct_1)^2}$$

But Minkowski found that this doesn't work, because it is not compatible with the relativity theory. Relativity dictates that the expression of the four-dimensional interval be:

four-dimensional interval $=$

$$\sqrt{(x_2 - x_1)^2 + (y_2 - y_1)^2 + (z_2 - z_1)^2 - (ct_2 - ct_1)^2}$$

Take particular notice of the minus sign of the time term. This introduces a basic asymmetry in the expression. In the formula for the three-dimensional interval, notice how all the coordinates appear symmetrically; this implies that they are interchangeable without reservation. In contrast, we find that the four-dimensional world of relativity that Minkowski mathematically constructed does not possess perfect symmetry: all directions in it are not equivalent. In effect, what this means is that space coordinates and time are not completely interchangeable, a spatial distance cannot be completely converted into a time interval or vice versa.

Thus, even Einstein's magic, the idea that time transforms into space, is not so potent as to make a time machine possible, because the transformation is only partial, with restrictions. Sorry, Wells!

Don't get bogged down in the math, which admittedly retains an amount of obscurity for the nonscientist. What it boils down to is this: space and time, although components of a four-dimensional coordinate system, retain some fundamental differences. They can be transformed into each other to some extent, which is the reason that one-way time travel to the future is allowed as described in previous sections. But the time coordinate cannot be totally transformed into a space coordinate; thus, Wells' time traveler's dream of moving back and forth in the time dimension with advanced technology does not materialize in special relativity.

However, the above arguments rest on the fact that material particles are constrained to move at sublight-speed. Recently, it has been proposed that a different type of matter might exist that *always* travels faster than light. Is it possible to travel backward in time with the help of such matter? We'll discuss this question in the next section.

Finally, there are some commonsense objections to time travel à la H. G. Wells' time machine. One of them is that the earth moves. So somebody leaving in a time machine for another time would have to aim for the earth in another place. The same thing goes for coming back. Even including the effect of inertia, it should be clear that time travel without space travel of quite complicated navigation is out of the question. There is also a second set of objections which is pithily summarized by Larry Niven (1971):

Niven's Law: If the universe of discourse permits the possibility of time travel and of changing the past, then no time machine will be invented in that universe. [p. 121]

Niven's argument is that a time machine in such a universe would create a totally chaotic universe and a total breakdown of causality.

TACHYONS

The relativistic increase of mass makes it clear that it is impossible for ordinary matter to overcome the speed-of-light barrier. From this we may be tempted to conclude, and most scientists did at one point, that there cannot be any faster-than-light particle. This turns out to be a mistaken notion. Conceptually, there is nothing wrong with having particles faster-than-light, provided they *always* travel faster than light. The name tachyon has been given to these hypothetical faster-than-light particles. Ordinary particles of matter are sometimes referred to as tardyons to distinguish them from tachyons.

How is it that the existence of tachyons doesn't violate relativity? Careful examination reveals that none of the *observable* properties (such as the physical mass) of these particles contradicts relativity. For example, consider the expression for relativistic mass,

$$m = \frac{m_0}{\sqrt{1 - v^2/c^2}}$$

For v greater than c—that is, for a particle velocity exceeding the speed of light—the denominator becomes the square root of a negative number: such a number is called an imaginary number. Mathematicians have developed great uses for it, but it cannot describe the value of real physical quantities. It may seem that all is lost, because mass then becomes imaginary for v greater than c, and therefore meaningless as a physical property. Upon introspection, though, the following possibility cannot be ruled out: if m_0 in the numerator of the expression for m is also imaginary, then m —being the ratio of two imaginary numbers—is a real number, strictly kosher according to mathematics. Since the physical mass m is an observable quantity, but m_0 is not (it is impossible to observe a tachyon at rest), it is possible that m_0 is imaginary.

Experimentally, the search for tachyons has been unsuccessful so far. Since we have no idea how tachyons would interact with ordinary matter, it is hard to invent methods for detecting them. We do know that tachyons would have some unusual properties. For example, if we accelerate a tachyon, it loses instead of gaining energy. At infinite velocity, its energy reaches zero! At the other end, if it travels at the speed of light, it ceases to exist; thus, it too can only approach the speed of light, but never be slowed down enough to reach it.

Could tachyons provide us with faster-than-light travel? Suppose we could use tachyons as rocket exhaust. Would such a rocketship travel faster than light? Some SF novels that allude to a "tachyon drive," such as James Blish's *Spock Must Die*, seem to imply so. Unfortunately, since the rest of the ship is made of tardyons, relativity would prevent it from overcoming the light barrier.

The most intriguing aspect of tachyon physics is the possibility of tachyons traveling backward in time. To see how this puzzle comes about, imagine that you are conversing with a friend who is walking toward you at a speed faster than the speed of sound. You will hear her backwards. You see, since she overtakes the sounds which result from her speech, you hear her later sounds before you hear her earlier ones. Now think of your friend coming toward you faster than the speed of light; clearly, you will *see* her actions reversed in time. The following limerick (slightly altered to accommodate the present situation) describes the situation amusingly:

> There was a young woman named Bright
> Who traveled faster than light.
> She started one day
> In the tachyonic way
> And came back yester night.

But beware! This form of time travel has problems with the causality principle, which dictates that cause always precedes effect. For example, if Ms. Bright came back the night before, she would have met herself before she left. This is a contradiction, to say the least, because she started with no such meeting!

Back to tachyons. Tachyons are paradoxical because a moving observer sees tachyons traveling both forward and backward in time. Let's set up a paradox with *Star Treks'* friendly adversaries, Spock and McCoy. McCoy travels away in a rocketship. Unless he hears from McCoy first, Spock is supposed to send him a tachyonic message at a prearranged time. McCoy agrees to send Spock a tachyonic reply as soon as he receives Spock's message. Now suppose Spock sends his message, McCoy receives it and sends his reply as agreed. However, because of their relative motion, Spock may receive McCoy's reply earlier than the prearranged time, in which case he does not send the signal. But then if Spock never sent a signal, how did McCoy happen to send one back? Is this because humans are basically illogical?

Such paradoxes are very difficult to resolve. One way to resolve Ms. Bright's predicament is to say that any attempt she made to see herself is bound to end in failure; this is the escape that SF writers most often choose in dealing with such causality problems in time travel stories (read, for example, Isaac Asimov's *The End of Eternity*). A similar resolution of the tachyonic paradox has been proposed by physicists: In any attempt to see a backward-going tachyon, the detection apparatus creates a forward-going tachyon. Since it is impossible to distinguish between the two tachyons, this means in effect that it is impossible to detect a backward-moving tachyon. This may sound like copping out, but causality is saved! At least, for the moment.

chapter eight

Energize! Energize!

In virtually every episode of the television show *Star Trek,* one or more people stand on a raised platform in a room called the transporter room, and then somebody matter-of-factly says, "Energize." Within moments after a lever is pushed down on a panel, the bodies on the platform dematerialize, usually to rematerialize just as quickly at some predetermined place. How scientific is this process? Can we expect ever to have such a technology?

A physicist of the nineteenth century would be puzzled by such questions. To him matter and energy were concepts as separate as night and day. In contrast, although a physicist of today will be likely to answer no to such questions, he might hesitate a moment before the no, suspecting perhaps that the question may not be nonsense.

Certainly in the view of twentieth-century physics, the concept of matter has become less material. The primary physical idea that contributed to the new view of matter came from Einstein: mass is equivalent to energy. According to Einstein, matter—by virtue of its mass—is equivalent to an amount of energy determined by a rate of exchange inflexibly fixed by nature. And energy, such as a beam of radiation, possesses mass by the same token. Mass and energy are like two different currencies. The rate of exchange between the two currencies is given by the famous law:

$$E = mc^2$$

in which E stands for energy, m for mass, and c for the speed of light, which is 3×10^8 m/sec.

The formula $E = mc^2$ was derived by Einstein as a consequence of his theory of relativity. Every time a radioactive material emits energy in the form of radiation, we are witnessing the conversion of a part of the mass of the radioactive sample into energy. Conversely, in the high-energy physics laboratories of today, when physicists routinely bombard targets with highly energetic particles, a part of the energy becomes manifest as particles of matter. In all these matter-energy exchanges, the exchange rate is always found to be that determined by Einstein's famous formula. Since the speed of light c is a constant of nature whose value never changes, the exchange rate is inflation proof!

Before we proceed further, it is important to grasp the significance of the exchange scale determined by the factor c^2. If we use conventional metric units, the kilogram (mass) and the joule (energy), we notice that c^2 is a very large number, being equal to $(3 \times 10^8)^2$. It becomes clear immediately that a little mass is equivalent to a lot of energy. Conversely, even a lot of energy has a very small mass. Thus, every time we go uphill, gaining potential energy relative to the ground, our mass also increases just a tad; but the increase is so little that we never perceive it.

In earthly processes, change occurs mainly through chemical reactions. But in chemical processes, the energies evolved (change of mass into energy) or materialized (change of energy into mass) are still so small that any change of mass is hardly noticeable. The chemists of old used to think (incorrectly, as Einstein's theory showed) that mass never changes in a chemical reaction. This approximate law of conservation of mass no doubt added to the nineteenth-century belief in the inviolability of matter.

However, mass changes become quite noticeable in nuclear processes, in reactions involving atomic nuclei. In the atomic bomb, as well as in nuclear power reactors, about one part in a thousand of the mass of the fuel, uranium, is converted into energy as each uranium nucleus splits apart into a couple of smaller nuclei. From the mass-energy point of view, nuclear-fission fuels like uranium are about a million times more efficient than their counterparts in chemical fuels, such as coal; that is to say, one kg of uranium fuel can supply us the same amount of energy that we can get from a million kg (1000 tons) of coal.

Uranium is a fission fuel whose active ingredient is uranium-235 (the number 235 stands for the total of neutrons and protons inside the nucleus). Although there is plenty of uranium on earth, this active ingredient, uranium-235, is quite rare; the total amount available might not be enough to last us even fifty years if we were deriving all of our energy from this source. There is, however, another nuclear process, thermonuclear fusion, which also converts about one part in a thousand of mass, but for which the nuclear fuels, deuterium and tritium, are abundant. Thermonuclear fusion is the process that heats the stars; at the high temperature and density present in the stellar core, ordinary hydrogen—which makes up the bulk of a star—undergoes fusion. Incidentally, the hydrogen bomb uses the fusion fuels deuterium and tritium, which are simply "heavier" hydrogen; their chemistry is the same as hydrogen's, but their nuclei are heavier, containing one and two extra neutrons respectively.

Coming back to "energizing" technology, we obviously are already into atomic power, although not yet very deeply (shall we say to the extent of about one part in a thousand?). The basic energizing question is: can we ever find processes that convert all of the mass of a body into energy? It doesn't seem so. Nature has guaranteed the basic stability of matter in the universe by an overriding principle called the conservation of baryon number. Baryons are a family of elementary particles, each made up of three quarks (which are the basic building blocks); the neutron and the proton are the least massive members of this family. Baryon number conservation means that you cannot destroy a baryon without creating another; the total number of baryons always remains the same.* This puts an insurmountable constraint on the convertibility of mass into energy. Conversion is possible only when heavier conglomerations of baryons change into lighter ones without involving a change in the total number of baryons; such changes are hard to bring about, requiring special conditions such as those in the core of a nuclear reactor, and moreover, involve change of only a little mass into energy.

Larry Niven usually keeps his science fairly straight in his fiction. However, every once in a while, his story line demands a magic-wand gadget, as in "The Soft Weapon." In this story the hero discovers an ancient relic from an extinct, highly technologically advanced race. The weapon can assume all kinds of shapes and perform all kinds of functions. In their study of the weapon, the story's characters speculate about the source of its power: "That battery must use total conversion of matter." And indeed, it did. Unfortunately, since such a gadget is incompatible with the baryon conservation law, don't you expect to discover such a weapon.

It is the conservation of baryon number that tells us quite firmly that energizing, *Star Trek* style, is more easily imagined than carried out. Relativity makes it sensible to talk about energizing; after all, if mass and energy are one and the same thing, why shouldn't we be able to energize mass? But baryon number conservation overrules this sensible possibility.

How about antimatter, the fuel that powers the *Star Trek* ship *Enterprise?* Antimatter is the name given to matter made up of antiatoms, which consist of antiparticles of the conventional electrons, protons, and neutrons. Such antiparticles have been observed and produced in our laboratories; they carry electric charges opposite to their conventional counterparts in the case of charged particles, and negative baryon numbers in the case of baryons. Since equal negatives and positives add up to zero, if we start with an equal number of baryons and antibaryons, they can indeed destroy one another to give pure energy, gamma radiation. The conversion of mass into energy is now 100 percent; the matter-antimatter converter of the *Enterprise* is thus about one thousand times more mass-efficient than any nuclear powered engine we can build. Incidentally, the reverse of particle-antiparticle annihilation is the process of pair creation, creation of a particle-antiparticle pair from a gamma ray; it is the materialization of pure energy.

So you can ask if *Star Trek*'s energizing involves, first, this matter-antimatter annihilation process, and then—when the bodies are rematerialized—the process of pair creation. Unfortunately, there are a few snags to energizing this way. First of all, in order to energize Spock, we must find his antiSpock, at least an equal mass of antimatter. You see, although antiparticles have

---

*According to the very recent grand unified theory (GUT), the number of baryons in the universe may decrease ever so slowly over a long time scale, 10^{30} years.

been found, nobody yet has been able to manufacture large quantities of antimatter. Second, matter-antimatter processes are explosive; energizing this way would be a total disaster for the *Enterprise* and its crew. There must be better ways to disembark from a ship!

There are many other problems with energizing technology, even if the principle of baryon number conservation did not exist. For example, it is inconceivable how all the information that makes up a complete human being could be stored in a dematerialized bundle of energy, even assuming that such a bundle could be held together. What is conceivable instead is somehow to decipher all the information incorporated in a particular human, and to transfer that information in the form of modulated electromagnetic waves. Someone receiving these waves could later reconstruct the person. Even if skepticism argues against ever technologically building such a human being (or "carbon unit") of given specifications, there is little doubt that we could build a "silicon unit," or computer, based on such a transmitted blueprint. Fred Hoyle's novel with John Elliot, *A for Andromeda,* is based on such an idea.

THE SCIENCE FICTION STORY OF NUCLEAR ENERGY

The celebrated British physicist Ernest Rutherford once planned an experiment to bombard a certain element with the penetrating radiation known as alpha particles (which are helium nuclei), with the intention of breaking apart the atoms of the bombarded element. His plan prompted a letter requesting that he postpone his experiment until after the letter-writer's birthday. His anxious correspondent was afraid that the energy released from the atom-splitting would destroy the world.

Once Einstein's equation $E = mc^2$ became famous, many science fiction writers saw it as the magic formula that would bring unlimited energy to humankind. Atoms naturally entered the picture after Rutherford's atom-splitting experiments in the nineteen-tens caught the public's eye and imagination. As early as 1909, atomic spaceships were envisioned in G. P. Serviss' SF novel, *A Columbus of Space.* And in 1914 H. G. Wells evidently contemplated the destruction of the world by atomic bombs in *The World Set Free.* But not until the thirties, when John W. Campbell appeared on the science fiction scene, did SF writers become serious about the dream of nuclear power.

Campbell had a keen eye for contemporary physics. Although Rutherford developed the concept of the atomic nucleus in 1911 in order to explain his own alpha-bombardment experiments, the detailed constitution of the atomic nucleus was not known until 1932, when the neutron was discovered. The atomic nucleus then was seen to be composed of charged particles, or protons, and neutral ones, the neutrons. Many physicists immediately started experiments on the bombardment of various elements by neutrons. Eventually, under wartime secrecy in 1942, Enrico Fermi constructed the first nuclear reactor assembly at the University of Chicago. Alone among SF writers, Campbell recognized the importance of neutrons. Under the pen name Don A. Stuart, he wrote a novella, *Who Goes There?*, about an alien invader from space, in which the following scene appears:

Norris grunted. "Leave it for investigation. But I can guess pretty well. That's atomic power. That stuff to the left—that's a neat little thing for doing what men have been trying to do with hundred-ton cyclotrons and so forth. It separates neutrons from heavy water, which he was getting from the surrounding ice [of Antarctica]."

". . . Lord, what minds that race must have. . . ."

"The shimmery sphere . . . I think it's a sphere of pure force. Neutrons can pass through any matter, and he [the alien, who was now dead] wanted a supply reservoir of neutrons. Just project neutrons against silica—calcium—berylium—almost anything, and the atomic energy is released. That thing is the atomic generator." [p. 86]

The physics in this episode, written in 1938, is somewhat premature (we can't use heavy water as a neutron source), but Campbell's vision—that neutrons may be a key element for the future harnessing of nuclear energy—comes loud and clear. And in 1939, German chemist Otto Hahn and his collaborators (among them Lisa Meitner) discovered that when the uranium nucleus (uranium-235) is bombarded by neutrons, it breaks up, releasing a lot of energy in the process. Hahn's discovery led to Fermi's development of the nuclear reactor, and eventually the atomic bomb was developed at Los Alamos.

But, of course, Campbell didn't know what was going on in reactor research, not the details certainly. Yet, under his prodding and guidance, several prophetic stories about nuclear power and atomic warfare were published in the SF magazine that Campbell edited. In Robert A. Heinlein's story, "Solution Unsatisfactory," radioactive dust is used as a war weapon; as you know, radioactive fallout from the atomic bomb is almost as destructive to life as the bomb itself. Then there was "Deadline" by Cleve Cartmill, the publication of which earned Campbell a visit from the FBI; this story contained a not-so-unrealistic description (with which Campbell himself helped the author) of the atomic bomb:

Two cast-iron hemispheres, clamped over the orange segments of cadmium alloy. And the fuse—I see it is in—a tiny can of cadmium alloy containing a speck of radium in a berylium holder and a small explosive powerful enough to shatter the cadmium walls. Then—correct me if I am wrong, will you?—the powered uranium oxide runs together in the central cavity. The radium shoots neutrons into the mass—and the U-235 takes over from there. (*Analog,* 1943)

(Perhaps I should mention that cadmium is a neutron absorber; cadmium or boron, when inserted into fissioning uranium-235, can stop any further fission almost instantly.) Campbell's argument for publishing such details was that they were already available in the literature previous to 1939, which was true. (You may remember the recent furor over the publication of the details of the hydrogen bomb; in this case, the author found all the details in a declassified journal article.)

One of the most famous stories of this era is Lester del Rey's "Nerves." This story depicts an accident in a nuclear power plant; it is especially noteworthy because both the destructive power of the accident and the public's reaction to it are foreseen with remarkable accuracy.

. . . once the blow-up happened, with the resultant damage to an unknown area, the pressure groups in Congress would be in, shouting for the final abolition of all atomic work; now they were reasonably quiet, only waiting an opportunity—or, more probably, at the moment were already seizing on the rumors spreading to turn this into their coup. If, by some streak of luck, Palmer could save the plant with no greater loss of life and property than already existed, their words would soon be forgotten, and the benefits from the products of National [Atomics] would again outweigh all risks.

"Just what will happen if it all goes off?" he asked.

Jenkins shrugged, . . . "Anybody's guess. Suppose three tons of the army's new explosives were to explode in a billionth—or at least, a millionth—of a second? Normally, you know, compared to atomics, that stuff burns like any fire, slowly and quietly, giving its gases plenty of time to get out of the way in an orderly fashion. Figure it one way, with this all going off together, and the stuff could drill a hole that'd split open the whole continent from Hudson Bay to the Gulf of Mexico, and leave a lovely sea where the Middle West is now. Figure it another, and it might only kill off everything within fifty miles of here. Somewhere in between is the chance we count on. . . ." [The Science Fiction Hall of Fame, p. 125]

Campbell wrote in 1946 that science fiction existed in the gap between the laboratory discovery of a scientific fact and its technological application. The stories published in his magazine prove that Campbell practiced what he preached. Science fiction writer Harry Harrison acknowledged the profound influence John W. Campbell exercised on the SF world when he said, "When I was fifteen, I thought John W. Campbell was God."

Of course, things changed in 1945 after nuclear technology became a *fait accompli*. Since then writers have created futurologies of at least three different kinds. The total holocaust was the most popular. But there was still some romance about the possibility of radioactivity-produced mutations leading to a superior race of humans. An outstanding novel of this kind is A. E. van Vogt's *Slan*. And then there was some optimism that nuclear fission, or perhaps controlled fusion, would bring us an energy glut.

This last thesis obviously was inspired by the predictions of scientist-futurologists. Given the trouble we find in today's nuclear energy industry, it may seem irresponsible or simplistic that many SF writers once idolized fission power and many still idolize fusion power. But the success of the atomic bomb project dazzled many people. Thus, when scientists predicted that fission energy would be so cheap that electrical energy would be only a minuscule fraction of people's budgets, the science fiction writer accepted this on faith.

From today's vantage point, it is not difficult to understand where the futurologists went wrong; they underestimated the economics of safety and the problems of environmental pollution with nuclear radiation. These problems have not been overlooked entirely by SF writers.

Optimism about the future must be tempered by the realization that energy gluttony is not viable when we live on a planet with limited energy resources and a finite environment. Energy will never be so cheap that we can afford to waste it, which is no cause for grief since such waste is harmful to the environment anyway. Within the limits of such energy and environmental consciousness, there should nevertheless be some future for nuclear power on earth, especially of the fusion kind.

However, the main thrust of science fiction has always been to get us out into space, out from the finite environment of the earth. And in this area nuclear power undoubtedly will play a major role, thus fulfilling the legacy of John W. Campbell.

In one regard, science fiction's role in the face of the destructive power of nuclear energy has been very satisfying. SF traditionally plays the role of Cassandra, warning us about present and future follies, and it has played this part brilliantly in its nuclear holocaust stories, to which we shall shortly turn our attention.

THE FINAL SOLUTION TO THE NUCLEAR CONTROVERSY (IN THE FORM OF A SATIRICAL ZIGZAG THROUGH THORNY ISSUES)

Much of SF's fiction is based on a fairly optimistic view of the future of nuclear energy. Nevertheless, you can't possibly be unaware of the passion, most of it negatively directed, that flows freely today around nuclear power. I myself keep an open mind on this issue; as a physicist I can see both sides. However, I know some questions here can bother even a science fiction reader, so I decided to visit Dr. Nucleboost, that great futurist and expert on our nuclear future. Planning a tough interview, I fired my first question (why beat around the bush?):

"Do you think nuclear power is too dangerous for the ecosystem?"

"Not really," he said. "Not when you find the right item to compare it with. For example, coal."

"But all that thermal pollution!" I exclaimed. "Do we really need these big plants that put so much heat into our water?"

"Are you thinking about fish?" He was chewing a cigar.

"Among other things."

"The excess heat from large power plants can be used to grow tropical fish, and will be in the future. Power plant employees constantly make new demands for recreation. Getting to watch tropical fish during their lunch break could open a new chapter in employee morale in the U.S."

I could see he had a point. These futurologists do have an oblique way of thinking. But I had to ask all the hard questions that bother my readers. "How about the radioactivity? Isn't that dangerous for the people?" This was a most important question, one that every science fiction reader who plans some day to be on a nuclear-powered rocket has nightmares about.

But Dr. Nucleboost had an answer. "Look, we all get some radiation exposure from natural sources, anyhow—we get used to it. Do you know that you get radiation from sleeping with your wife? Now, how many people prefer to sleep singly just because of a radioactive spouse?"

I was not satisfied. "Isn't the genetic effect of radiation too subtle to trifle with?"

"I'll tell you something. The genetic effects of radiation exposure may turn out to be a blessing in disguise. Do you know an intelligent species like ours can't evolve any further by natural selection? Radioactivity opens a way for the human race to make genetic progress. You read science fiction, you ought to know."

I blushed. He was right, of course, in a science-fictiony sort of way. I remembered Larry Niven arguing in this vein in one of his novels. Also, who could forget the evolved beings of van Vogt's *Slan*? I quickly changed the subject. "New estimates are showing that nuclear power is too costly economically. As our country gets into deeper economic trouble, how can we ever expect to support white elephants such as nuclear power plants, let alone research on nuclear rockets?"

I thought I had him cornered. But this fellow was smooth.

"Baloney!" He sounded almost condescending. "The economic advantages far outweigh the disadvantages. For example, both nuclear power and research on its benefits and perils can keep a lot of people employed: at the power companies, at NASA, at the environmental agencies, even at the colleges where they teach people the art of heckling; nuclear energy keeps a lot of people busy and involved. In a democratic society, we need involvement above all else. You have to learn to do the right kind of cost-benefit analysis."

Trying to penetrate his complacency, I returned to the dangers of radiation. "How about cancer? Science fiction writers don't talk about cancer. Asimov's characters hop around happily wearing radioactive auras, and nothing happens to them! But surely as a scientist you can't minimize the cancerous effects of such radioactive elements as plutonium and tritium involved in the nuclear game?"

"I'll tell you a story. I was sitting at a crowded table in a restaurant when a young woman asked me if she could smoke. I had noticed an antinuclear button on her lapel, so I said, 'Only if you promise to take off your button.' She became angry at first, but when I explained that cigarettes are far more carcinogenic than radioactivity, she shut up. Now why don't you complain instead about science fiction writers continuing to portray cigarette smoking, even in future enlightened societies?"

His counterattack was timed well. I had to change my tack again. "How about people making bombs with plutonium by-products from nuclear power plants? How about nuclear holocaust possibilities?"

He was not bothered at all. "A nuclear holocaust is not necessarily so bad. It will weed out the unfit, if anything. The ones who deserve to survive, will."

He sounded a bit like a Ronald Reagan conservative in that last statement. But I let it pass. I had a key question to ask. "How about the nuclear waste that we keep piling up, the spent fuel from reactors? Those things will stay radioactive for thousands of years. Do you think it's fair to posterity to leave them with such wastes?" I stared at him challengingly.

But he had the answer. "Today's problems are tomorrow's boon. Tomorrow's people have to be better than us in recovering recyclable products from garbage. I'm sure that the people of the twenty-second century will be grateful to us for leaving them so much garbage, especially the radioactive trash. The number of cancer patients is going up exponentially. Our great-great-grandchildren will have good use for nuclear trash in cancer therapy."

(I made a mental note: this may make a good plot for a science fiction story.) This guy sure had all the answers. I couldn't find any more troublesome questions to ask in my role as the opposition's advocate. Then I thought of something. "Look, all you say is irrelevant. Ultimately, it all boils down to psychology. Antinuclear people have an antinuclear bent of mind. And nothing you say can change that."

"Don't be so sure," he responded, lowering his voice conspiratorially. "I haven't told you about our ace in the hole, the McClure idea."

"And what is that?"

"We are working on finding a supply of antiuranium nuclei, the antiparticle of uranium. If you use antiuranium to generate power, the power must be labeled antinuclear power. The people who oppose it will be called anti-anti-nuclear, or pronuclear. And ballots will become so confusing that nuclear power will be voted in in no time."

I was stunned. "Who is this McClure, anyway?" I asked.

"Oh, a physicist friend of mine. No, he doesn't read science fiction."

HOLOCAUST VISIONS

Holocaust stories have always fascinated science fiction writers, but especially so after 1945, the year that saw the first cities devastated by atomic bombs.

The bombs made abundantly clear that natural calamities are no longer needed to ignite a holocaust; humans now can perfectly execute it by themselves. Add to the bomb the threats of various kinds of pollution of our environment by today's technology, biological warfare, and so forth, and you have a rich choice of scenarios for holocaust stories.

Writers seem prompted by a variety of motivations to write holocaust stories. The simplest story lines are found in stories that depict the horror of total destruction in order to arouse our conscience. A good example is Nevil Shute's motion picture, *On the Beach*. In this film, an atomic war causes the first wave of destruction, then the survivors are killed by the lethal radiation left by the bombs. Civilization's impotence against radioactivity is dramatized by the distribution of suicide pills as the survivors begin to succumb to radiation sickness.

In a very different sort of story, the holocaust provides a framework for some other horror. Kate Wilhelm's Hugo-winning novel *Where Late the Sweet Birds Sang* appeared at a time when an alleged case of human cloning was making headlines. In a desperate attempt to guarantee the continuance of humanity, the farsighted survivors of Wilhelm's holocaust—which was brought on by a runaway combination of pollution, pestilential flu and war—create a colony of clones. Ironically, to the horror of its creators, this clone society with its absolute, carbon-copy conformity brings the human race to the brink of extinction.

Since physical survival is one of our basic biological instincts, it is a common theme in holocaust stories. Physical survival is played out in various scenarios. First, there are stories (such as Sterling Lanier's *Hiero's Journey*) in which the survivors form a simpler society in reaction to the "evil" technology that bred destruction. In these stories the holocaust actually rescues humanity from the tyranny of a totally technological society, and returns to individuals some control over their own destinies.

A second group of stories has picked up on a relatively new suggestion. Some politicians today openly express the opinion that survival is not only possible, but inevitable, even if the superpowers engage in nuclear war. The science fiction version of this attitude puts the primitive, postholocaust society under the control of a few technocrats empowered by their secret technology. The revolutionary potential of this situation often produces good action adventure, as in Piers Anthony's novel *Battle Circle*.

The survival theme that is most provocative and compelling to me is this: if survival is a basic biological instinct, then perhaps through further evolution as a species, humans can avoid a holocaust altogether. Perhaps we can evolve a truly peaceful civilization. This does not apply to the postholocaust mutation stories in which a "superior" mutant race emerges as a result of genetic mutation. These stories reflect a gross misunderstanding of the process of mutation, and of the connection between genes and intelligence.

Instead, this theme concerns the evolution of a new awareness that ac-knowledges the relatedness of all peoples who share this finite spaceship, Earth, and recognizes preservation as a common human goal. This extended awareness would erase war from humanity's list of possible behaviors. Theo-dore Sturgeon's beautiful story "Thunder and Roses" (Gunn, 1979) goes at least halfway toward the fulfilling of this theme. In this story, the United States has been virtually destroyed by an atomic attack. A few survivors have the choice of destroying the rest of the world by retaliating with their own atomic weapons. In this desperate climate, a woman singer rises to the occa-sion and argues:

"Let us die with the knowledge that we have done the one noble thing left to us. The spark of humanity can still live and grow on this planet. It will be blown and drenched, shaken and all but extinguished, but it will live if that song is a true one. It will live if we are human enough to discount the fact that the spark is in the custody of our temporary enemy. Some—a few—of his children will live to merge with the new humanity that will gradually emerge from the jun-gles and the wilderness." [*The Road to Science Fiction* #3, pp. 129–130]

In Clifford Simak's Hugo-winning novel *Way Station,* such a transformation toward peace and harmony saves humanity from the holocaust. The Talis-man—a mystical object—and the intervention of the galactic council combine to produce this transformation. In Simak's simple but evocative words,

. . . That was the way with Man; it had always been that way. He had carried terror with him. And the thing he was afraid of had always been himself. [p. 222]

And the Talisman helps cure man of this terror. Perhaps the Talisman is a metaphor and, like the terror, is also within us. But with or without a Talis-man, I believe such an evolution of mankind is inevitable; survival may de-pend on it.

On the other hand, from a mystical point of view, such an evolution is not essential. When I asked Ram Dass (formerly Harvard psychologist Richard Alpert, now a spiritual teacher) his opinion of the possibility of the total destruction of humanity, he responded with equanimity: "Maybe that's what will happen. Either way, it will still be perfect." This mystical view is ex-pressed in one of the most haunting postholocaust stories ever written, Wal-ter Miller's *A Canticle for Liebowitz.* Such a paradoxical title: how can a story about destruction—repeated destruction at that—be a canticle, a song of praise? Actually, Miller's story is about basic human nature in both its strength and its foolish tendency to destroy itself. But he makes the point that there is never total destruction of the human spirit. After the fires of destruc-tion, civilization reemerges with the potential of new wisdom; destruction is part of the human cycle. The canticle is for this cycle. Miller shows that even the holocaust can be transcended; we have only to concentrate, not on the destruction, but on the totality—destruction and re-creation. The book, in some of science fiction's most poetic prose, ends not with death, but with life:

The breakers beat monotonously at the shores, casting up driftwood. An abandoned seaplane floated beyond the breakers. After a while the breakers caught the seaplane and threw it on the shore with the driftwood. It tilted and fractured a wing. There were shrimp carousing in the breakers, and the whiting that fed on the shrimp, and the shark that munched the whiting, and found them admirable, in the sportive brutality of the sea.

A wind came across the ocean, sweeping with it a pall of fine white ash. The ash fell into the sea and into the breakers. The breakers washed dead shrimp ashore with the driftwood. Then they washed up the whiting. The shark swam out to his deepest waters and brooded in the cold clean currents. He was very hungry that season. [p. 278]

But the shark, surviving in the "clean" waters, was hungry for only a season. And a hungry shark is very much alive!

chapter nine

Star Dance

As we look at stars, we feel a sense of wonder; we are swept by a fascination that transcends the mundane, putting us in touch with that communal part of our psyche that thrives on the mysterious and the obscure. Since science fiction attempts to reach that place in us, it is no surprise that so much of SF is devoted to astronomical scenarios. Astronomy comes alive in SF stories. Such astronomical events as the supernovae, superbrilliant explosions of stars, occur in our vicinity only once in a few centuries—few humans can anticipate seeing one. Praise be to science fiction writers, then, who can create this event for their readers in such glorious detail that we can see it at least in our mind's eye. It may not be like the real thing at all, but for a moment science fiction makes us feel a part of the cosmic journey, after all.

Modern astronomy began with Galileo after the discovery of that marvelous instrument, the telescope. The telescope opened up to us such faraway landscapes as the moon and Mars. No doubt inspired by Galileo's discoveries, astronomer Johannes Kepler wrote his "Somnium" (translated "Dream"), which describes his dream exploration of the lunar landscape. And in a series of stories (I don't remember the name of the author) later collected and published as *The Moon Hoax* in 1859, a telescope was envisioned that was powerful enough to reveal even the intimacies of everyday life on the moon; a person with such a telescope could become a Peeping Tom looking at an unsuspecting lunar culture from the faraway earth. And when an astronomer claimed to have observed canals on the Martian landscape, a burst of enthusiastic stories, including the classic *War of the Worlds* by H. G. Wells, began to appear about Mars and Martians.

Recent explorations of the solar system by our space probes have removed some of the mysteries surrounding the solar planets and their satellites; knowledge has its own burden. We have learned that Mars is not a habitable planet; it shows no sign of any form of biological activity. We have been informed that Venus is extremely hot due to the thick carbon dioxide envelope that covers it, like the glass enclosure of a greenhouse. Nowadays, SF scenarios seldom include Mars or Venus unless they have been terraformed, converted into habitability through the marvels of "planetary engineering," a technology yet to be developed. Titan, a satellite of Saturn, has gained popularity, but SF writers are careful to include the adverse elements of the Titan environment in their stories.

Of course, astronomers long ago began to look outside the solar system toward the stars where, in collaboration with astrophysicists, they discovered many new phenomena such as novae, supernovae, and the pulsars. The novae consist of stellar explosions of a minisize, little brothers of the more spectacular supernovae. The pulsars are neutron stars, previously mentioned. And now, due to the brilliant hard work of specialists that we call astrophysicists, we have the basic principles for the understanding of the various stages in the life of a star. As you must know, stars are not forever—although they seem to be so from our human time scale. But expand your imagination to a time scale of millions—nay, billions—of years, and the stars begin to show a pattern of evolution; a violent early childhood consisting of perhaps a few million years; a mature stable adulthood lasting perhaps even ten billion years, and then old age erupting through violent stages leading to eternal quiescence.

Science fiction writers have been interested in the theories of stellar evolution from their very inception. The reason is simple; the writers need extraterrestrial life for their stories. And for life, the supporting star must qualify scientifically; it has to be in a stable and uneventful stage. On the other hand, SF writers also like to write stories about the feelings of the inhabitants of a planet whose star is going nova. Yet another scenario: you have gone off on a space-tour involving many earth years; when you return after a few billion years (how this is possible is another story), our sun has gone nova, becoming much bigger in size—a red giant star. How do you adjust to this new situation? If you read the literature, you will know.

In short, SF writers are right there with the latest astronomers' findings, of which they make good use. Some of their stories even speculate about the origin or nature of astronomical phenomena; right or wrong, they open up our imaginations to new horizons. And most interestingly, they are not unaware of astronomy's pitfall: it is a speculative science in which certain interpretation and reconstruction of the observational data is an essential part; astronomical phenomena are not reproducible at will and certainly are not reproducible under laboratory conditions. As early as 1859, Samuel Butler wrote a story named "The Elephant and the Moon" in which a group of observers interpret their observations as some horrendous events occurring on the moon; only later do they discover that all their observations were produced by the activities of a mouse and a colony of insects inhabiting their telescope. The SF writer, like the astronomer, continually worries about such questions: do the data mean what we assume they do, or is there a mouse in our telescope, a big hole in the theoretical framework we've built to interpret the data?

MOON STORIES

The moon is very close to our hearts. Most of us grow up hearing Grandma's tales about the moon, how it is made of green cheese, or how rabbits are making rice cakes on the moon, and so forth. And then when we grow up, we discover the lifelessness of the rocky moon. The lunar romance tends to be tarnished with this dreary realization.

Science fiction writers of the old genre, such as Jules Verne or H. G. Wells, were not burdened by today's knowledge explosion about the moon. Reading their stories, we regain some of the lost romance. Today's writers have a definite disadvantage; they can talk only about lunar colonies with human inhabitants.

But most of the lunar stories, both old and new, have to be commended for a fair amount of accuracy in the science they portray, although goofs happen occasionally. In one story some people flew a helicopter on the moon, and in another the moon not only had an atmosphere but also possessed air breathable for humans. But these are rarities.

Actually, lunar stories show that the writers are quite tuned in to scientific models about the moon. For example, take the theory of the origin of the moon. The theory that has dominated scientists' thinking on this matter is that the moon and earth were created about the same time—some four billion years ago. The moon of Jules Verne in *Round the Moon* not only was created in this way but followed pretty much the evolutionary history that scientists have traced.

And most impressive are those stories where an innovative but scientifically incorrect model is used with a twist that makes the model plausible. This is the case in the recent novel *Inherit the Stars,* by James Hogan.

British astronomer George Darwin proposed a theory that the earth and the moon originally formed as a single body. They broke up as a result of the incessant action of the tidal force of the sun. Perhaps the Pacific Ocean bears the proof of such a fission—it may represent the hole left over after the vast body of the moon was torn out of the earth's body. If you are wondering how the moon ended up so far from the earth, there is a good answer: angular momentum conservation. The tides caused on earth by the moon also lead to a considerable dissipation of earth's rotational energy due to friction. As a result, the earth slows down ever so little, by about one thousandth of a second per century. But this means a reduction of earth's rotational angular momentum. According to the law of angular momentum conservation, the total angular momentum of the earth-moon system cannot change; thus, whatever the earth loses, the moon must gain. The gain of angular momentum of the moon translates into its moving farther and farther away from the earth, at a rate of about 1 meter per year. Although this sounds like a rather small distance, multiply it by the four billion years that the moon and earth have been around, and you get a distance of four billion meters, or four million kilometers. This is more than ten times larger than the actual distance of the earth from the moon, but the difference between the two figures can be explained away by saying that the rate of loss of angular momentum of the earth has not always been the same, and so forth.

On the whole, a pretty interesting theory! However, few scientists believe it today because more detailed consideration of the sun's tidal force tends to indicate that this could not be a strong enough mechanism to cause the fission. Nevertheless, everyone agrees that originally the moon must have been much closer to the earth than it is today.

Hogan incorporates this theory of lunar origins with an interesting idea of his own. His imagination has it that originally there was a planet named Minerva, whose orbit lay somewhere in between Mars and Jupiter, and that our moon was a satellite of this Minerva. Then one day Minerva broke up (not because of the sun's tidal force but because of nuclear explosions on the planet ignited by the two warring factions of its inhabitants). Somehow, Minerva's moon was blown all the way to earth's vicinity, very close to earth. Since then, of course, it has been retreating as explained above.

The beauty of such expositions in a novel is that the reader not only can be fascinated by them, but also can pick up interesting science material. Add to this the speculation that the asteroid belt between Mars and Jupiter perhaps originated in the blowup of a planet, and you will have your mind going in excited whirls for quite a while before you begin to notice the loose ends that the author leaves in his story.

And another marvel of the moon stories is that you never get bored by having the same scientific theories presented by the writers. Scientists often do not agree on any particular aspect of the moon. The writers are aware of these different theories, and they take advantage of them to present variety for the reader.

For example, take the case of lunar craters. Two mechanisms have been suggested by scientists. One is that the craters are the products of intense volcanic activity, particularly in the moon's early history. The other mechanism is the impact of meteors. Meteoric activities are expected to be more violent on the moon than on earth owing to the absence of an atmosphere.

Jules Verne must have believed in the volcanic theory; in his moon stories, he refers to this theory repeatedly. On the other hand, James Hogan tilts toward the meteor explosion theory; the explosion of his imaginary planet Minerva in *Inherit the Stars* even provides an additional source of the meteors.

Perhaps the most impressive use of legitimate science in moon stories concerns the weakness of lunar gravity compared to earth's. SF writers have created a myriad of adventure stories based on one or another aspect of this weak lunar gravity. In H. G. Wells' *The First Men in the Moon,* this weak gravity of the moon is reflected in the enormous size and structural fragility of the lunar plants and insects, the selenites: each cell of a lunar plant is said to be as big as a human thumb; the selenites are two hundred feet long, yet so fragile that they spin and smash a dozen yards away after one human blow.

Robert A. Heinlein's entire story line in *The Moon Is a Harsh Mistress* is based on the fact that the weakness of lunar gravity makes it technically possible to catapult things from the moon to the earth. Heinlein's catapults are used first for grain shipment, then for the travel of a couple of Lunarians, and finally, for launching warheads at the earth.

THE STARS, MY DESTINATION

Terraformed or not, the solar planets and satellites are not enough to exhaust the creative efforts of such imaginative people as science fiction writers. Sooner or later most SF writers move out into space to invent or to adapt an existing star system as the new hope for their characters. However, any old star will not do. Only certain types of stars can sustain life-bearing planets, the astronomers tell us. So an SF writer has to know something about stellar classification in order to devise an authentic setting for his story.

When you look at the sky with the naked eye, most stars look colorless. But this is due to our faulty vision; stars actually come in brilliant colors. When we see things in dim light, our eyes have difficulty discerning colors. Try it. Photographing the stars with powerful telescopes reveals their colors. The stars also, of course, vary in brightness. Perceived brightness also depends on the distance of the star from us; but if we know its distance, we can figure out its intrinsic brightness, or luminosity—the amount of energy it radiates per second. The color tells us the star's temperature. We organize stars into different spectral classes according to the light they emit.

The blue stars have the highest temperatures; they are classified as O, B, and A, in order of decreasing temperature. Next come the blue-white (F) stars and the yellow-white (G) stars. Still lower in temperature are the orange-red stars (K) and the red stars (M). There are stars with even lower temperatures—designated R, N, and S—but let's not overload our memories. In case remembering is difficult already, the following exercise may help. Get a friend of the appropriate sex and make a request: "Oh, *be a fine girl (guy), kiss me right now—smack!*" Who knows, s/he may—unless s/he catches on to your little play, that you are simply memorizing the spectral classification: O, B, A, F, G, K, M, R, N, S.

Within this broad classification, it is customary to do some fine tuning. Thus, the range between each spectral class and the next is further subdivided into ten regions, and a number is used after the letter to designate the exact temperature region that a star belongs to. For example, F5 would mean halfway between F0 and G0; our sun is designated as a G2 star, two tenths of the way from class G0 to K0.

Now you can appreciate the following astronomy lesson from Isaac Asimov's novel of interstellar politics and intrigue, *The Stars, Like Dust*. The scene refers to a band of rebels star-hopping from one world to another in search of a planet whose inhabitants are supposed to be heading a rebellion against a tyrannical empire.

The outlook was different after the next jump. Biron had set the controls in accordance with the instructions from the Autarch's pilot, and left the manuals to Gillbret. He was going to sleep through this one. And then Gillbret was shaking his shoulder.

"Biron! Biron!"

Biron rolled over in his bunk and out, landing in a crouch, fists balled. "What is it?"

Gillbret stepped back hastily. "Now, take it easy. We've got an F-2 this time."

It sank in. Gillbret drew a deep breath and relaxed. "Don't ever wake me that way, Gillbret. An F-2, you say? I suppose you're referring to the new star."

"I surely am. It looks most amusing, I think."

In a way, it did. Approximately ninety five per cent of habitable planets in the Galaxy circled stars of spectral types F or G; diameter from seven hundred fifty to fifteen hundred thousand miles, surface temperature from five to ten thousand centigrade. Earth's sun was G-0 [now designated G-2], Rhodia's F-8, Lingane's G-2, as was that of Nephelos. F-2 was a little warm, but not too warm.

The first three stars they had stopped at were of spectral type K, rather small and ruddy. Planets would probably not have been decent even if they had had any. [pp. 473–474]

Although the spectral classification of the parent star is the first consideration in terms of its being life-supporting, it is not the only criterion. It is essential that the star be in a stable phase of its evolutionary life. Such stable stars are called main-sequence stars. If you plot the luminosity of stars against their spectral classes (Figure 23), the resulting graph shows that the majority of stars lie on a slightly curved line running diagonally across the diagram. These are the main-sequence stars. The diagram is called the Hertzsprung-Russell diagram (abbreviated H-R diagram). Notice that not all stars are main-sequence; there are other groups. Two other large groups are the red giants in the upper right-hand corner above the line of main-sequence stars, and the white dwarfs in the lower left-hand corner below the main-sequence line. The red giants get their name because they are huge stars, much greater in size than our sun, for example, and because their relatively cool surfaces are red. The white dwarfs, on the other hand, are of smaller size (planet size), high density, and intense temperature (notice that in the H-R diagram the temperature on the abscissa decreases from the left to the right).

The following excerpt from Frederik Pohl's Hugo-winning novel *Gateway* is

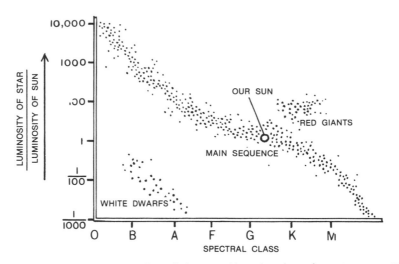

Figure 23. The Hertzsprung-Russell diagram. Note that the ordinate is on a multiplicative scale. The temperature indicated by the spectral class increases from right to left.

part of an ongoing lecture series that Professor Asmenion delivers to the inhabitants of the Gateway. Gateway is an abandoned, alien-built structure which the aliens had used as a base for star expeditions. The alien starships, whose mechanisms are unknown to humans, are nevertheless currently in use by them.

Dr. Asmenion. You all ought to know what a Hertzsprung-Russell diagram looks like. If you find yourself in a globular cluster, or anywhere where there's a compact mass of stars, it's worth plotting an H-R for that group. Also keep your eye out for unusual spectral classes. You won't get a nickel for F's, G's or K's; we've got all the readings on them you could want. But if you happen to find yourself orbiting a white dwarf or a very late red giant, make all the tape you've got. Also O's and B's are worth investigating. Even if they're not your primary. But if you happen to be in close orbit in an armored Five around a good bright O, that ought to be worth a couple hundred thousand at least, if you bring back the data. . . .

Question. Why do we only get the bonus if we're in an armored Five?

Dr. Asmenion. Oh. Because if you aren't, you won't come back. [p. 168]

Now it's my turn to answer some questions. Why are the main-sequence stars so stable? Why are the red giants and white dwarfs relatively rarer, so that their investigation is more worthwhile for the inhabitants of Gateway? And what makes the O stars worth the effort?

A star is born when interstellar matter condenses under the influence of the mutual gravity of the dust and debris that constitute such matter. As the matter falls together toward the common center, its potential energy is converted into kinetic energy; the matter becomes hot as a result. Part of the heat must be radiated away, but never mind. The contraction continues, providing even more heat, especially at the core. At some stage the matter becomes so hot that the atoms dissociate into individual nuclei and electrons. Finally, the matter at the core of a star is a gas of charged particles, usually called a plasma. When the temperature of the plasma is high enough, the individual nuclei (of hydrogen) come together—overcoming their mutual electrical repulsion—and fuse. This "thermonuclear" fusion of hydrogen nuclei in the heart of the collapsing matter now releases a very large amount of heat energy, enough to compensate for the radiation loss and still maintain a constant temperature. The constant temperature maintains a constant outward thermal pressure that now balances the inward pressure due to gravity. The star is now stable at a constant size without any further contraction. Until the hydrogen burns up, that is.

All stars go through such a violent early life before they settle down on the main-sequence curve. Where the star will be on the sequence depends on its mass; if the mass is huge, the star will lie high on the curve toward the upper left-hand corner. Thus, an O star on the main-sequence is also one of huge mass, and must burn its hydrogen nuclear fuel at a very rapid rate to generate enough thermal pressure to keep the enormous gravity of the large mass from crushing into itself. In short, O stars don't stay long on the main-sequence; and as they go off it, they must change. Thus, O stars are relatively short-lived, having a lifetime of maybe a few hundreds of millions of years instead of about 10 billion years for a star like our sun. Short lifetime translates into relative rarity, making them worth more for investigation.

After the hydrogen is exhausted, the star's equilibrium is destroyed and it must start contracting again. The energy released by the contracting core heats up the outer envelope of the star, which must now expand as a result. The star becomes a giant in size and volume. For example, calculations show that when our own sun becomes a red giant, it surely will engulf the earth within its enlarged body.

The red giant phase of a star can stay in equilibrium for a while because the core can become hot enough to burn heavier helium nuclei, fusing to make carbon nuclei. But the helium-burning phase has a relatively short life compared to the hydrogen-burning phase, which makes red giants, too, a rarity.

What happens after the helium-burning phase? More than one scenario is possible, depending on the mass of the star. Let's first consider a star of one solar mass or so. After the helium burns, such a star contracts until its matter becomes "degenerate," a state in which the electrons exist as a plasma, repelling each other with a pressure known as Fermi pressure (named after American physicist Enrico Fermi). This Fermi pressure arises from an innate quantum mechanical principle that the electrons obey against occupying the same space. The Fermi pressure now resists the inward gravity force and holds the star together. This is the white dwarf stage. The white dwarf stage is not permanent, either, but rather short-lived, lasting only until all the energy of the hot star is radiated away. When that happens, the star is called a black dwarf, and is dead to the outside world.

On the path to becoming a white dwarf, a star of a few solar masses will have to sputter away part of its mass. This sputtering often involves explosions, called novae. The spitting off of mass is necessary, since white dwarfs have a maximum mass of about 1.4 solar mass, according to theory. Otherwise, the star can end up as an alternative form of degenerate matter, the neutron star, for which a maximum mass of about 3 solar masses seems to be allowed.

If the star is very massive, say 25 solar masses, the scenario after the helium-burning stage is considerably more involved. Such a star can go through several stages of alternate gravitational contraction and nuclear burning, the nuclear fuel that is burned being heavier and heavier at the core, the temperature being correspondingly higher and higher. For example, after the helium-burning, the next stage may consist of carbon nuclei (generated in the previous stage of helium burning) burning at the core and helium and hydrogen burning at shells outside the core.

Eventually, though, the temperature of the core becomes very high, so high that the star starts cooling by neutrino emission in addition to the usual emission of electromagnetic radiation. Cooling by emission of electromagnetic radiation is rather slow, because the electromagnetic waves take a long time to get through the outer envelope. In contrast, neutrino cooling is very rapid, because neutrinos—being highly noninteractive—can cut through the body of the star to space in a hurry. This rapid cooling causes the core to implode, and as the core collapses, a shock wave proceeds outward and causes the outer envelope to explode. This spectacular explosion, called a supernova, has been known to us since the year 1057, when Chinese astronomers spotted one in the sky. The supernova sheds enough matter so that the massive star finds a new equilibrium state, becoming a neutron star embedded in a nebula (the spent gas residue of the explosion). Such has been the case with the star that went supernova in 1057. It became the Crab pulsar lying in the body of gases that we call the Crab nebula.

The supernovae provide the final important classification that we must bear in mind in the consideration of life-supporting stars. Astronomers have known for a long time that stars in a galaxy can be classified in two major groups; population I, distributed along the disc in the central plane of the galaxy or in the galaxy's spiral arms, and population II, consisting of a bunch of older stars concentrated in the spherical halo about the galactic center. The globular clusters of our own galaxy belong to population II (Figure 24); they are stars of the same age and are useful for making theoretical models

Figure 24. The distribution of globular clusters in our own galaxy (shown schematically). They belong to an older (population II) class of stars.

that study the variations of stellar evolution with mass. Population I stars, on the other hand, are comprised of stars of all ages. Some of them are old; but others are second generation stars formed from the debris left over from the supernova breakup of stars of a previous generation.

Why is this classification important? You see, life depends on certain crucial heavy elements, such as iron. Such heavy elements are not found in population II stars, which mostly consist of only hydrogen and helium. The supernova explosions can generate a huge supply of these heavy elements by a process known as explosive nucleo-synthesis. As a result, some of the second generation population I stars will be rich in heavy elements and just right for the evolution of life on one or more of their planets.

One final note before we end this section. If a heavy star is unable to shed enough mass—even after a supernova—to end up as a neutron star, its collapse must continue until it becomes a black hole, the ultimate stage of stellar collapse.

SOME SCENARIOS FROM *THE AVATAR*

One of Poul Anderson's best novels, *The Avatar,* is about a voyage through space-time that takes its voyagers through our galaxy and beyond. The voyagers use what Anderson calls a T-machine—*T* for American physicist F. J. Tipler, whose ideas Anderson employs in the design of the machine. (The *T* might as well indicate time, since this machine is able to travel not only through space, but also across time.) The first excerpt in the following series of astronomical scenarios from *The Avatar* describes a star being born:

Joelle spoke: "This is a new system coalescing. The sun's energy is from contraction; it isn't yet compressed enough at the core to start thermonuclear reactions. Space remains dusty, rocks of every size plentiful. Falling in on nascent planets, they heat these to incandescence while adding to their mass. . . ." [p. 333]

As you can easily guess, Joelle is the resident physicist. Here is an encounter with another star, quite different from that above:

Jump.
Again heaven was full of stars. . . .
A sun disc hung out there. About the same size as that which Earth saw, it was distinctly greenish—an oath of amazement exploded from him [the captain of the exploring spaceship]—and heavily spotted. According to a meter, the luminosity per unit area exceeded Sol's by some thirty percent. The corona was immense around it, and ruddy; without magnification, he saw flares and prominences like fire geysers; . . .
. . . he scratched his head and plaintively addressed the intercom: "Hey, what's going on? I didn't know the main sequence included green stars."
. . . After a minute, Su Granville's diffident tones reached him: "I t'ink I can guess. Green is not an impossible color, but the range of surface temperature for it is so narrow that we seldom 'ave observed it. . . . I suspect it is simply leaving the main sequence and 'appens to be going t'rough a brief green phase."
. . . "Wait. Doesn't it become a red giant?"
"Yes, in due course. But at first it shrinks and grows very much 'otter. That shortens the peak wavelength. . . ." [p. 282]

The comment on peak wavelength may need elaboration. As you know, light consists of waves, propagating electromagnetic disturbances. Light waves of each color have a characteristic wavelength, the distance between crests. Red has the longest wavelength, and wavelength decreases to violet in the following order: red, orange, yellow, green, blue, indigo, violet. The peak wavelength refers to the light for which the energy emitted is maximum. Let's pass on to a final excerpt:

Jump.
The stellar host was less myriad and brilliant than before, though more than around Sol or Phoebus—save that in one direction towered vast thunderheads of night, relieved only by a few gleams in their foreground. No sun was in view. . . . It [the T-machine] orbited something which the eye perceived as a quivering blue-white spark, Joelle and the instruments as a hellish fountainhead of hard radiation.
Her judgement came to them like God's: "We've approached the core of the galaxy. Those are the dust clouds that have always hidden it from us. Here is a black hole." [p. 345]

As you might guess, I heartily recommend the book, not only for its astronomy, but also for its very engaging story line. Although mushy in places and a bit like soap opera, the human interest comes through. By the time I finished the book, I had learned something about myself, and about humankind. That's a lot to say about a novel.

A GUIDE TO BUILDING YOUR FANTASY PLANET

English writer Oscar Wilde wrote: "We are all in the gutter, but some of us are looking at the stars." And today some of us are even dreaming about getting out of this "gutter"—this earth—beautiful and habit-forming as it is. If, as either an SF writer or dreamer, you are with me in this dream, you will want to construct your very own dream planet to inhabit after you leave the star system and become a child of the universe. Here are some ideas to help you with your dream.

Okay, from the theory of stellar evolution, you learn that the star of your planetary system must be an F, G, or K star—the closer to the middle, the better; it must be a main-sequence star; and finally, it must be at least second generation. If it's hotter than F, its radiation is rich in ultraviolet and X rays and, therefore, too dangerous; if it's colder than K, it will have too little heat to support the required temperate zone. It must be on the main sequence, because the evolution of life may take a billion or more years, judging from our very scant experience. And it has to be second generation in order for it and its planets to be made of the heavy-element-rich stardust that only a supernova can guarantee.

One additional note about choosing the star. Many stars are binary, and in general binary stars do not make a good system for the evolution of life on a planet. Although some science fiction stories have used a binary star system (for example, Clement's *Mission of Gravity*) and even a stellar system consisting of six suns (Asimov's "Nightfall"), your story has to be quite spectacular for the reader to overcome the initial credibility problem of such a case.

Given a proper sun, what makes a good planet that can support life? How many such planets can we expect in our galaxy? Isaac Asimov writes about this in his novel *The Stars, Like Dust*:

There are between one and two hundred billion radiant stars in the Galaxy. Among them are some five hundred billion planets. Of these, some have gravities more than 120 per cent that of Earth, or less than 60 per cent, and are therefore unbearable in the long run. Some are too hot, some too cold. Some have poisonous atmospheres. Planetary atmospheres consisting largely or entirely of neon, methane, ammonia, chlorine—even silicon tetrafluoride—have been recorded. Some planets lack water, one with oceans of almost pure sulphur dioxide having been described. Others lack carbon.

Any one of these failings is sufficient, so that not one world in a hundred thousand can be lived on. Yet this still leaves an estimated four million habitable worlds. [pp. 39–40]

The above quotation gives you some idea of what requirements the planet of your story should satisfy. Although we can easily imagine life forms that inhale ammonia, let's say, instead of oxygen, or that are made up of silicon-based chemistry (there was a *Star Trek* episode based on silicon creatures) rather than carbon, ordinarily such planets would have such a difficult environment for human or humanlike visitors from other worlds that it would be extremely difficult to develop any kind of story without making a gross mistake. In short, just as the sun of your choice should be as sunlike as possible, the planet should also be as earthlike as practical. Of course, you cannot make it too much like earth; that's no fun. So the purpose of this section is to review what factors you need in order to make small changes compared to earth.

One of the parameters at your disposal is the distance of your planet from its sun. There are several factors to consider. How much power the planet receives from its sun depends on the planet's distance and also on the luminosity L of the sun. If you choose greater luminosity for the sun, you can have your planet at a greater distance and still get more or less the same power as we receive from our sun. Remember that the power we receive is inversely proportional to the square of the distance R; this power is called the solar constant S:

$$S = \frac{L}{R^2}$$

There is an advantage in choosing a different luminosity. (Safe choices are a factor of ten on either side of our sun.) If the luminosity is greater, it should be clear from the H-R diagram that the temperature of the star is going to be higher and the color more toward the blue, meaning that the light is going to be richer in shorter wavelengths and poorer in the longer wavelengths. As you must know, the color of our sunset is red because, as the sunlight travels through a greater length of the atmosphere at sunset time, the shorter wavelengths in it get scattered away by the air molecules and suspended dust particles, leaving the red. During the daytime, because we are looking away from the sun, only scattered light reaches us and we see the sky as blue, since the scattered light is predominantly of the shorter wavelengths. Thus, if your starlight contains less red, then the sunset may be more toward the yellow. The color of the sky, however, will not change much; since our eyes are more sensitive to the blue than the purple, we won't see the sky as purple even though there would be more purple in the scattered light. One other thing. If the luminosity is greater, there is also more ultraviolet in the sunlight. This will cause the inhabitants more sunburns; perhaps the skin of most of the people will be deeply pigmented. Also, more cancers will be likely, and so forth.

On the other hand, if you decide to choose a smaller luminosity for the sun, meaning that the color of the star will be more toward the red, you can expect some equally spectacular changes in the opposite direction. The color of the sky will be toward the green; and if we look at the sun directly, even when it is overhead, the light from it will probably not look white, but yellowish.

After you choose your star's luminosity, next make a choice of the solar constant S. If you want your planet to be colder on the average, choose a smaller S; the ice caps of your planet will be more spectacular and the snow line lower compared to earth's. A higher value of S will produce the opposite effect. Incidentally, even if S is smaller, your sun should not look any dimmer to the naked eyes of the inhabitants, because human eyes adjust beautifully to dim light. (But then there will be no intense color on your planet.)

Once your choices of L and S are definite, the average distance of your planet from its sun is fixed. If you want to be quantitative, the formula is:

$$\left(\frac{R}{R_\odot}\right)^2 = \left(\frac{L}{L_\odot}\right) / \left(\frac{S}{S_\odot}\right)$$

Here $R_\odot$, $L_\odot$, $S_\odot$ are the corresponding quantities for our sun.

Incidentally, the above is based on a circular orbit for your planet. If you want to make the orbit very elliptical, the situation will change as the distance varies. It may be advisable to use near-circular orbits to keep things simple.

Some more cautions. If the luminosity of the star is different from that of our sun, so must its mass be, and since stellar densities are similar, you can expect a larger size for the star. Of course, how large the disc of the star looks from the planet also depends on the distance. So if you make statements about such things, be a little careful and check things out.

And once the distance of the planet from the sun is determined, the period of revolution of the planet about its sun (the planet's year) is given from Newton's gravity law. Assuming a circular orbit, the formula for the planet's orbital period T is:

$$\left(\frac{T}{T_\odot}\right)^2 = \left(\frac{R}{R_\odot}\right)^3 / \left(\frac{M}{M_\odot}\right)$$

Let's now talk about the planet's mass. If the mass is too much greater than the earth's, the atmosphere will be thicker because of the increased gravity. You can't afford too massive a planet anyway, since then the atmosphere retains even the lightest of gases, hydrogen, which is inflammable. On the other hand, the planet must be massive enough to retain a reasonably thick atmosphere. Safe choices vary from a factor of half to a factor of two compared to earth's.

Once you choose the mass, this will become a constraint on the size of your planet. However, there is also another factor, the average density. The formula is (the symbol $\propto$ denotes "is proportional to"):

$$\text{size} \propto \sqrt[3]{\frac{\text{mass}}{\text{density}}}$$

So there is some leeway. If you choose the mass to be greater or less (than the earth's), then you must make the density correspondingly greater or less to keep the size the same. There is advantage in contemplating a different density. For example, if the average density is greater, it is inevitable that there will be a preponderance of the heavier elements on such a planet.

However, perhaps you would prefer to keep the same density as earth, but vary the size; this is easier to handle. For one thing, the acceleration of gravity on the planet then varies in exact proportion to the planet's size compared to earth's; that is, if the size is 1.25 times that of earth, so is the planet's g—and so is the weight of a person. This is, of course, assuming that the planet is spherical; it doesn't have to be exactly so—in fact, a rotating planet won't be spherical. But if the rotation is not too rapid, approximate sphericity is a good working assumption.

Now that you have built your planet, close your eyes and set out on a journey in your imagination. You are in a spaceship in orbit around a planet that resembles rather closely the one that you have built. It may be a little hard to find at first; you have to understand that the galaxy is very big.

chapter ten

Entropy and Life in the Universe

Entropy is one of the most popular notions that physics has contributed to science fiction, so let's discuss the idea in some detail. In general, entropy represents the amount of disorder or randomness present in a system. As before, the word *system* takes on a rather precise meaning: it pertains to a body or group of bodies upon which we focus our attention. The rest of the universe is then regarded as this system's environment. The next question is this: how do we figure out the amount of disorder in a system? Sometimes this is quite easy. For example, if you were to compare a clean desk with a cluttered one, it would not take you long to decide that the cluttered desk is marked by entropy. But suppose you have two 8-oz glasses of water, one of cool tap water, the other of hot water; then you mix them together. Now it's not so obvious which has more disorder, and therefore more entropy—the water when it is in separate glasses, or when it is mixed together.

When determining entropy or disorder, we must ask ourselves what kind of order or lack thereof we are concerned with. Order with respect to what? In the case of the desks, it was order with respect to the placement of the paper, books, and other items on the desk. On the disordered desk, all the stuff got mixed up. In the case of the hot and cold water, though, the placement of the water molecules is not any different on the average in the two glasses, so the placement won't do. Here the temperature is the clue, and temperature has to do with the average kinetic energy of the water molecules. The hot water on the average contains molecules of high velocity, and the cool water those of lower velocity. Thus, when the water is in separate vessels, there is an order with respect to the average speed of the water molecules. When we mix the water together, this order gets obliterated, since the result of mixing is a sharing of heat via thermal collisions that leads to a uniform temperature of the mixture. A system of uniform temperature is said to be in thermal equilibrium. The process of thermal collision among molecules that leads to thermal equilibrium also brings about an increase in entropy. Moreover, it is our experience that the state of equilibrium is the most probable; it is extremely unlikely that if we mix hot and cold water we can get anything but water at some uniform intermediate temperature. Thus, the path to equilibrium or increasing entropy is the most probable path of a system.

It is a law of nature that entropy always increases for natural processes. This entropy law is also known as the second law of thermodynamics. And as a result, natural systems—if they are isolated from the environment (that is, closed systems)—show a tendency to run down.

So far we have been talking about local pockets of equilibrium and local maximization of entropy. Can these concepts be generalized globally? That is, suppose we apply the entropy law to the entire universe, taking the universe as our closed system. Although there is some doubt among physicists about whether the concept of global entropy is viable, there is no question that if it is, the entire universe will take the most probable path and attain a state of maximum entropy, the ultimate maximum value that entropy can ever attain. Such a fate for the universe is often called a heat death, for good reason. It is a death because everything in the universe will then be in thermal equilibrium; all its energy will be in the form of a cosmic heat background. No work can ever be accomplished in such a universe, because to get work done you need some onewayness (when you are wet, you cannot dry yourself with a wet towel!). Fortunately, it takes a long, long time for the universe to attain heat death. Physicist Freeman Dyson (1979) recently established this time to be 10^{14} years, assuming an infinite, forever-expanding universe.

In the realm of science fiction, author Philip Dick is quite impressed with the idea of entropy and increasing disorder, and he uses it often. In his book *Do Androids Dream of Electric Sheep?* he coins the word *kipple* to describe entropy; the analogy is quite clear:

Kipple is useless objects, like junk mail and match folders after you use the last match or gumwrappers or yesterday's homeopape. When nobody's around, kipple reproduces itself . . . the entire universe is moving towards a final state of total, absolute kippleization.

In social systems, it is basically the concept of entropy that has given us Parkinson's Law—work increases to keep up with the increase of bureaucracy—and Murphy's Law—anything that can go wrong, will go wrong. George Alec Effinger's novel, *What Entropy Means to Me,* satirizes these popular clichés.

In connection with societies, the notion of entropy—in a somewhat perverse form—has initiated a whole new line of speculation in science fiction. In order to understand this approach, let's ask a question: if there is such an irresistible tendency toward the increase of entropy or disorder, why do we find so much order in nature? For example, among the forms of bulk matter that exist on earth, obviously gaseous matter is the most disorderly; yet we find plenty of earthly matter in more orderly solid or liquid form. What's the mystery behind this? The answer is that so far we have considered only the agency of entropy increase—thermal collisions—but there also are agents in nature that produce order. These agents of order are forces of various kinds. For example, in the case of solid matter, it is the forces between the molecules of the solid that lead to the maintenance of a more orderly state of the molecules. And we can look at the sky for another glorious example. The matter of the sky is not uniformly distributed, but is lumpy in the form of stars and galaxies. The order here is brought about by the force of gravity. Thus, there is a struggle between the agents of order (forces) and the agent of entropy (thermal collisions) that shapes the fate of natural systems. Many SF writers have invoked this struggle as a way to break up a tyrannical social order. Witness the following quotation from *Agents of Chaos* by Norman Spinrad:

Every Social Conflict is the arena for three mutually antagonistic forces: the Establishment, the opposition which seeks to overthrow the existing Order and replace it with one of its own, and the tendency towards increased Social Entropy which all Social Conflict engenders, and which, in this context, may be thought of as the force of Chaos. [p. 11]

The language is slightly different from that about natural systems; for example, the tendency toward increasing entropy is seen as a force. But the idea of the struggle between agents of order (the establishment and its opposition both) and agents of chaos shaping the reality of society is clearly formulated in analogy to physical systems. Here the agents of disorder or chaos, who introduce randomness (like thermal collisions), are human beings who have "the entire chaotic force of the universe" behind them. If you like this idea, you will enjoy the works of Norman Spinrad, Barry Malzberg, Colin Kapp, and James Tiptree, among others.

NEGENTROPY

So far we have confined our discussion to closed systems, systems that have little or no interaction with their environment. Let's now talk about open systems, those that have quite strong interaction with their environment and therefore a large exchange of energy with it. Our own earth comprises such an open system, as it receives a very large amount of energy from the sun during the day and returns most of this energy to its environment at night.

In open systems, because of the availability of external energy, going uphill against entropy becomes possible. Notice that the entropy law is not being violated: the decrease of entropy is at the cost of a greater increase in the entropy of the environment. Life is one of the examples of increased order that becomes possible on earth as a result of this energy flow.

Since in an open system entropy can decrease locally, it is fashionable to talk about an inflow of negative entropy or negentropy to the system. Thus, the sun provides us with negentropy which trees employ through the process of photosynthesis to make more ordered carbohydrate molecules from carbon dioxide and water.

British writer Michael Moorcock, in his books involving the antihero Jerry Cornelius (a collection is available called *The Cornelius Chronicles*), depicts this struggle between negentropy and entropy that shapes the reality of open systems. Jerry and his associates, from episode to episode, jump from one reality to another in a multireal London where they interact with the complex urban society in their search for one place where negentropy wins over entropy, life over death, order over chaos. Unfortunately, Jerry never finds this reality, because he himself carries the seed of entropy. The various structures of order that he dreams up eventually all end in destruction.

Moorcock and other SF writers view the struggle of entropy and negentropy as one between unequal antagonists, David against Goliath. David wins occasionally, but eventually succumbs to the power of Goliath. This is an analogy of how life exists in nature as a temporary and local oasis in the vast desert of entropy. But life ends in death—David loses to Goliath—in the final reckoning.

ENTROPY AND LIFE

The entropy law—that entropy, or disorder, always increases—is a law of evolution; it speaks about the evolution of a natural system. Unfortunately, the final result of evolution under the entropy law is always the same, irrespective of the initial system: a state of no distinction that we call thermal equilibrium. This contrasts sharply with biological evolution in which the evolution leads to nontrivial patterns of structure. How does biological evolution, the creation and development of life, come about in the face of the entropy law?

One answer to this is Maxwell's demon. Nineteenth-century English physicist J. Clerk Maxwell jestingly invented the demon as a way to violate the entropy law. Imagine a container of gas molecules in equilibrium. Suppose we introduce a partition with a trapdoor into the container. Now there are two compartments (Figure 25a), but the compartments are at the same temperature. In terms of molecular velocities, that means that the average velocity of the molecules in each compartment is the same. Of course, the molecules do not all travel with the same velocity, but examine the distribution of velocities of the molecules in the two compartments (the length of the arrows denotes the magnitude of the velocity and the arrowhead the direction of motion). Figure 25a gives an accurate description of the situation: the distribution of large and small arrows is the same in the two compartments.

Now imagine that a demon starts manipulating the system by opening and closing the trapdoor according to a definite plan. Whenever he sees a fast molecule approach the right compartment from the left, he quickly opens the trapdoor to let it pass through; he does the same thing when he sees a slow molecule approach the left from the right. But at other times the door re-

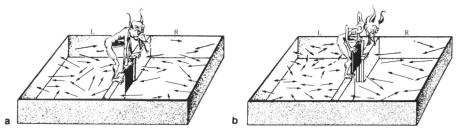

Figure 25. (a) Random assembly of slow (small arrows) and fast (large arrows) molecules in both compartments *L* and *R*. The arrows denote the velocity of the molecules. (b) The slow molecules now have been separated from the fast ones by Maxwell's demon and his trap door trick. Leon Brillouin showed that this feat is impossible to accomplish without expending energy and increasing the entropy of the environment. Thus, information as to which molecules are slow and which are fast costs energy as well as entropy. (From Goswami, *The Concepts of Physics*, D. C. Heath)

mains shut. After the demon plays his trick for a while, the distribution of the molecules in the two compartments is as shown in Figure 25b. There is now a preponderance of fast molecules on the right and slow ones on the left. The system is no longer in thermal equilibrium; we have established some amount of order starting from total disorder. Seemingly, the entropy law has been violated. Many SF writers see life as an act of thousands of Maxwell's demons acting in unison to create order out of the drearyland of entropy.

But Maxwell's demon does not violate the entropy law! French physicist Leon Brillouin pointed out that in order to see which molecule is fast and which slow, the demon must use a flashlight of some sort, a device for gathering information. And information isn't cheap, you can't get it for nothing. Getting the information creates more entropy than the negentropy generated in the container of molecules.

With the exorcism of Maxwell's demon, it becomes unlikely that life is created as a violation of the entropy law. Of course, we can always try chance and say that the large molecules of life were created spontaneously from a random assembly by local chance fluctuations of entropy. Unfortunately, the probability of life coming about in this way, particularly in the complex forms that we see today, becomes minuscule.

Given this situation, some scientists—among them Nobel-winning chemist Svante Arrhenius—have proposed the notion of panspermia: spores of life existing eternally just as matter does. According to this theory, these spores of life are blown from planet to planet and develop into full-grown complex biological forms whenever the conditions are right. An expanded form of this idea has been used in science fiction by Spider and Jeanne Robinson in *Stardance* to explain how humanity is propagated throughout the universe:

"Earth is their spawning ground," I said. "So is Titan. So are a lot of places, outside this system."

"What do you mean?" Silverman barked.

"The alien's last sending was what kicked us over the deep end. It was stunningly simple, really, considering how much it explained. You could render it as a single word. All they really did was tell us their collective name."

Dmirov scowled, "And that is?"

"Starseeders," . . . I went on, "their occupation, the thing they do to be fulfilled. They farm stars. Their lifetime spans billions of years, and they spend them much as we do, trying to reproduce a good part of that time. They seed stars with organic life. They seeded *this* solar system a long time ago. [p. 247]

Physicist–SF writer Fred Hoyle and his collaborator Chandra Wickram-singhe have injected some new excitement (and controversy) into this idea of starseeding. According to them, prestellar gases in nebulae, where there is plenty of negentropy, are the womb of the starseed, small organic molecules that evolve—via processes of competition and survival not dissimilar to the processes of Darwinian evolution—into larger macromolecules and eventually into self-replicating systems of molecules. Borne on comets or even meteorites, they then travel to planetary systems. Indeed, Hoyle suggests (1979) that life on earth "could well have originated about four billion years ago by the soft landing of an icy comet already containing primitive organisms."

Recently, another mechanism for the evolution of life has been suggested by Belgian physical chemist, Nobel Laureate Ilya Prigogine. Prigogine points out that, for open systems which operate far from equilibrium, not all the energy is always "wasted" (toward increasing entropy). Instead, there exists a threshold of complexity; beyond this threshold the system is able to channel a significant portion of its incoming energy to create and maintain new order. The structures that result are called "dissipative structures" by Prigogine. He gives as an example of this the appearance of convection currents in a fluid heated from the bottom. This is obviously a case where there is a sudden onset of order brought about by (1) external energy input to the system and (2) the system's readiness for evolution of new structure once the threshold is reached.

If Prigogine turns out to be right, biological evolution proceeds quite differently than does physical evolution of a system. Physical evolution is dominated by entropy considerations, and order exists only as temporary and chance fluctuation. In contrast, biological evolution occurs through cooperation between the external and internal: the flow of negentropy into the open system *and* the system's ability to evolve in a path of order and structure. It is as if Teilhard is right: there is a certain element of consciousness in a complex system as reflected by the existence of a threshold of complexity beyond which it can organize itself. Could it be that the universe itself is self-organizing, evolving in a pattern following this biological design? And if this were so, might not the universe be an open system, after all—however hard this may be to assimilate in a physical theory? Prigogine's theory opens our minds to such questions. These kinds of questions may have a certain ring of familiarity, no doubt garnered from your reading of science fiction.

EXTRATERRESTRIAL LIFE AND COMMUNICATION

Science fiction treats the question of extraterrestrial life in a variety of ways. In some story lines, notably Asimov's *Foundation Trilogy*, intelligent life in our galaxy started with humanity on earth and then spread elsewhere. Still other story lines invent aliens, which for the most part are monsters; the genre movies especially are full of these. (The recent hit movie *E.T.* may indicate a delightful new trend.) Fortunately, there also are quite a few intelligent explorations of the alien approach. Fictional aliens have been created who not only look different from us, but also communicate and think differently. Stories such as the Robinson couple's *Stardance,* in which the aliens communicate through dance forms, have brought a new kind of excitement to alien stories.

Is there any scientific basis for expecting extraterrestrial life, particularly intelligent life? This question and its possible answers have been popularized by American astrophysicist Carl Sagan in several books. A summary of the extensive work done by scientists all over earth, particularly in America and the USSR, can be expressed through this famous formula, known as the Drake equation (Sagan, 1973):

$$N = R_* f_p n_e f_l f_i f_c L$$

where

N = number of intelligent civilizations in our galaxy
R_* = average rate of formation of stars in the galaxy
f_p = fraction of stars with planetary systems
n_e = average number of planets with life-supporting ecology within such planetary systems
f_l = fraction of planets where life has evolved
f_i = fraction of planets where life has evolved to the emergence of intelligence
f_c = fraction of intelligent life-supporting planets that have attained the technological capacity to communicate with intelligent life outside their star system
L = mean lifetime of such intelligent communicative civilizations

It is relatively easy to write down such a formula. But how do we determine the various components of the formula?

Of all the quantities in this formula for N, only one, R_*—the number of stars per year created in the galaxy—is known with any degree of quantitative assurance. And its value is about ten per year. As for the rest, we can only make educated guesses. Some guesses, based on limited observational data, are quite reasonable. This is the case with f_p, the fraction of stars with planets. (Giordano Bruno, an Italian philosopher at the time of the Renaissance, was burnt at the stake for proclaiming that there are as many worlds as there are stars, because every star is like a sun and carries its own planets.) If we plot a characteristic of stellar rotation, such as angular momentum, against its mass (Figure 26), we find a distinct break in the resultant graph. This can be interpreted as evidence that stars in the lower line in the figure have planets that are taking up the missing angular momentum. Indeed, if we add the angular momentum of its planets to that of our sun, the point for our solar system falls very nearly on the top line of the graph. Most interestingly, those stars which we previously indicated to be most suited for life—namely, those with spectral classes of F, G and K—seem to have planets, according to this interpretation. Finally, it is clear that we can guess f_p fairly well from such data, in spite of the fact that it is impossible to see planets of other stars except in a few isolated cases.

Unfortunately, things get much worse with the rest of the quantities in the formula for N. We have to depend heavily on theory, computer simulation models at best, to come up with even an order-of-magnitude estimate of the quantities n_e, f_l, f_i, f_c. And for a quantity like L, we don't have even a theoretical model from which to make predictions.

So what it boils down to is guesswork. An enthusiast might call this the

Figure 26. The break in the line signifies that F and G stars have planets bearing angular momentum.

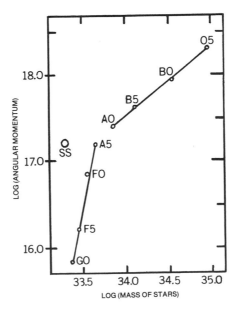

game of "subjective probability estimates." But by whatever name you call it, nobody has any reason to call the estimates in any sense scientific. At best, they are indicative; you must remember that this is a very new field of study.

Nevertheless, let's look at the kind of estimates that are tossed around by Sagan and others, based on the proceedings of an international conference in 1973 (Sagan, 1973). R_* is 10/year, as already stated. The fraction f_p is estimated to be of the order of 1. The number for n_e is also believed to be close to 1. The combined product of the three fractions f_l, f_i, f_c, according to the consensus of the conference, is of the order of 1/100, or 10^{-2}. If L, the lifetime of a technological civilization, is taken to be ten million (10^7) years, we get for N:

$$N = 10 \times 1 \times 1 \times 10^{-2} \times 10^7 = 10^6$$

A million technological civilizations within our galaxy! If they are assumed to be dispersed uniformly, then there should be one within a few hundred light years of us.

Having assured ourselves that we are not alone in the galaxy, next comes the question of communication. Obviously, physical communication would be the best, although that may frighten some people. Such communication obviously has to involve rockets, which will be discussed in the next chapter. A plaque proclaiming our existence and technological coming-of-age has already been sent out from earth on board a space probe to outer space.

Many scientists feel that we should not wait for suitable rockets to venture out of the solar system, but start right now with radio communication. Radio transmissions considerably increase our chance for successful communication. Perhaps within a few hundred years one of our neighbors will receive these signals and answer them! Who knows? However, author James Gunn has written an SF novel, *The Listeners,* reminding us of how boring such eavesdropping for extraterrestrial messages can be. (Gunn also does his readers a great service in presenting a whole chapter full of quotations from various scientists on the pros and cons of the proposed eavesdropping programs.)

One other kind of speculation should be mentioned here. This is the idea that aliens may already have been here, perhaps a few thousand years in the past. The authors of this idea look for the evidence of alien footprints in ancient myths and artifacts. A prominent articulator of the idea, Eric Von Däniken, has written a couple of best-sellers on the subject; he calls these aliens Gods, implying that the god archetype that we humans seem to share may have its origin in this alien invasion of the past. The evidence, not all that impressive, is in some sense degrading to our very talented ancestors. My personal belief is that it is unlikely that we have been visited in the past. Still we must recognize that such a visit in the past by an extraterrestrial civilization is no less probable than the likelihood of a visit in the future. Thus, the concept behind Von Däniken's work is certainly valid.

The theme that Von Däniken has popularized so well has been explored beautifully in science fiction in Roger Zelazny's novel, *Lord of Light*. If you like ancient mythology, you will enjoy this book which recreates stories of Hindu mythology. Hindu gods on a mythical planet are really colonizers from a faraway earth. The technology of these "gods" is so superior that many ideas from Hindu philosophy, such as reincarnation, are depicted as simply technological trickery. Yet the book somehow manages to convey a sense of mysticism, and at the end you wonder. Could it be?

EXTRATERRESTRIAL LIFE IN SCIENCE FICTION

Enough of scientific speculations about extraterrestrial life! There are already quite a few books on the subject. You can find in them a lot more information about many speculative theories than is possible to discuss here. Now let's indulge in a couple of examples of extraterrestrial alien life created by SF writers. Exobiologists admonish that we should never assume that the only possible life forms are those found on earth. This wisdom is cherished in the following examples of alien life. Hope you enjoy these encounters.

A. A Live Black Cloud

Most of the matter in the universe, for some reason, exists in the plasma state, as a gas of charged particles. For example, much of the matter inside our sun consists of plasma—perhaps not surprisingly because of the high temperature within its body. What's more surprising is that even interstellar matter exists mostly as plasma. Even close to earth, in the upper atmosphere, layers of plasma form because of the action of solar radiation on the air molecules; these layers collectively are called the ionosphere. Before the advent of communication satellites, long-distance radio communication was achieved chiefly by bouncing radio waves off the ionospheric layers.

Thus, matter in the form that exists on earth and possibly on other planets is a relative rarity; plasma is the going thing, the common state of matter in the universe. We often assume that life can develop only on a planet and that there is a need for certain chemicals in solid and liquid forms to construct and maintain life. Physicist–SF writer Fred Hoyle speculates otherwise. In his novel *The Black Cloud,* the black cloud—itself a living creature—explains:

". . . Living on the surface of a solid body you are exposed to a strong gravitational force. This greatly limits the size to which your animals can grow and hence limits the scope of your neurological activity. It forces you to possess muscular structures to promote movement, and it also forces you to carry protective armour against sharp blows—as for instance your skulls are necessary protection for your brains. The extra weight of muscle and armour still further reduces the scope of your neurological activities. . . ." [p. 149]

The black cloud, on the other hand, is mostly made up of plasma, although Hoyle never uses the word. The advantages of a life form made up of plasma are emphasized by Hoyle. The electrical processing, communicating, and storing of information is much quicker and more efficient in the neurological system of the black cloud than in ours. Furthermore, the black cloud can absorb solar energy directly at a much greater rate than we can, since we must depend on already inefficient plants. There are, of course, disadvantages. Passage of radio waves or radiation from radioactive substances will affect the state of ionization of the plasma, subjecting the black cloud to headaches or even fatal injuries.

Of course, the neurological systems of the black cloud do need, according to Hoyle, a supply of complex chemical molecules (presumably for storage of information), but again it is the plasma which helps maintain the supply. The black cloud explains this as follows:

"Yes, I do have an equivalent to a blood supply. A supply of appropriate substances is maintained by a flow of gas [plasma] that streams constantly past the units [of the brain] of which I am composed. The flow is maintained by an electromagnetic pump instead of by a 'heart', however. That is to say, the pump is of an inorganic nature. . . . The gas flows from the pump to a supply of chemical foods, then past my neurological structure, which absorbs the sundry materials that are required by my brain operation. These materials also deposit their waste products in the gas [plasma]. The gas then makes its way back to the pump, but before it does so it passes through a filter that removes the waste products—a filter that is rather akin to your kidneys." [p. 157]

If you question that a space creature made up of electrically charged gases should function with such similarity to humans in its basic life processes, Hoyle—through one of the scientists in the novel—gives an interesting philosophical reason:

"It's a little difficult for me to explain, because this is as near as I go to the expression of religious sentiment. We know that the Universe possesses some inner basic structure, this is what we are finding out in our science or trying to find out. We tend to give ourselves a sort of moral pat on the back when we contemplate our successes in this respect, as if to say that the Universe is following *our* logic. But this is surely to put the cart before the horse. It isn't the Universe that's following our logic, it's *we* that are constructed in accordance with the logic of the Universe. And that gives what I might call a definition of intelligent life: something that reflects the basic structure of the Universe. . . ." [italics in the original, p. 158]

B. The Gods Themselves: What Are They Made of?

The Gods Themselves is Isaac Asimov's masterpiece. Asimov's "gods" are the inhabitants of a parallel universe who share with our earth a "positron pump"—a device through which they and we earthlings can tap unlimited energy, or so it seems. In order for the positron pump to work, the parallel universe has to be very different from ours. One of the most spectacular differences is the way the inhabitants of the parallel universe are built. Science fiction has given us many alien creatures, but none so unique (or, incidentally, so charming!).

These gods are a two-phase life-form. In the first phase, they form groups of three separate but complementary individuals, each with a definite function. The individuals are classed as the parental, the emotional, and the rational. The emotional is the "female" of the three, the parental "male" takes care of the offspring, and the rational is the logical "male" of the three. What is the archetype of Asimov's imagination? Some humanistic psychologies recognize three centers (at the psychological level) of our human bodies: the genitals, the heart, and the head or the brain. Thus, we can say that Asimov's triad consists of these three centers. The parental is the sex center, the emotional represents the heart, and the rational the head. Separately each is incomplete, but when they "meld," or join together, they become complete. And when the meld becomes permanent, they become "the hard ones"—their second phase—very much like a human being.

This is one way of interpreting this delightful life-form. However, who knows what was in Asimov's mind when he created these transitory triads? One can ask: what is the nature of the matter that composes the nonsolid individuals of the triad? Is there any three-valuedness in physical matter from which Asimov's archetype might have come?

I am tempted to answer yes. A few years before *The Gods Themselves* was written, American physicists Murray Gell-Mann and George Zweig suggested that protons and neutrons, the particles of which atomic nuclei are composed, are each made of three quarks. According to their theory, quarks are the fundamental building blocks of all matter. I am tempted to think that Asimov's triad is analagous to the quark triad that is thought to make up matter at the fundamental level.

Although most physicists now believe that quarks do exist, being held together inside the core of the protons and neutrons by another class of elementary particles called gluons, there is one snag. No quark (or gluon) has *ever* been found. When we break up protons and neutrons by hitting them hard with other high-energy protons, the result always is other particles of the same type as the protons and neutrons, but never quarks. On the other hand, in experiments where we scatter high-energy electrons from protons without breaking up the protons, the indication is clear: the proton contains other particles within it.

If you like novelist Richard Matheson's character, the shrinking man, it is like this: If the incredible shrinking man shrinks to subatomic size and shakes these candy boxes (protons) of the microworld to which he now belongs, he hears something rattling inside. But if he breaks open the box, to his surprise all he finds is other candy boxes—no candy!

From this strange situation, many physicists have concluded that quarks are perhaps destined to be forever contained inside their proton or neutron boxes. They never see the daylight. Philosophically, this is very nice. Because if we can never isolate a quark, if quarks really are confined objects, they are properly the ultimate elementary particles of nature.

chapter eleven

Interstellar Travel

The bottom line in space travel is adequate rocket technology. How close are we to constructing rockets that can take us to the stars? What are the problems and limitations that we face? Even if *we* cannot solve some of these problems today, is it at least conceivable that rockets capable of travel at relativistic speeds can be constructed? The last question's importance relates to the possibility of a close encounter of the third kind: if other intelligent civilizations from outside the solar system already have acquired such technology, they might pay us a visit.

The rockets we currently use are primitive compared to those we can imagine. Present rocket technology is based on the use of chemical fuels with severely limited mass-energy convertibility, as we have discussed before. Additional limitations arise from our having to make combustion chambers and nozzles for rocket exhaust from materials with very limited heat resistance.

Assuming optimum conditions (which means we shall not worry about such matters as nozzles), let's look at the performance of a chemical rocket.* Ultimately, the rocket lifts a payload to a certain maximum velocity; the acceleration of the payload is accomplished by throwing out the burnt propellant with as high an exhaust velocity as possible. When the fuel is finished, leaving only the payload, the job is done, the maximum velocity has been reached. This, conceptually, is the ideal; the staging of rockets, lifting the payload in five or more successive steps, is simply the implementation we employ to approach this ideal. The important quantity in this ideal performance is the exhaust velocity of the propellant; let's call this v_{ex}, and let's call the maximum (or final) velocity attained by the payload v_{max}. The other important quantity for a rocket is the mass ratio of the rocket's initial mass M_i (which includes the propellant) and the final mass M_p (of the payload); call this ratio M_i/M_p. Then there is an all-important relationship between these three quantities:

$$\frac{M_i}{M_p} = 10^{(0.434\, v_{max}/v_{ex})}$$

This relationship may look very complex and mysterious; for example, you may wonder how one can evaluate 10 raised to a noninteger power. Relax. Leave such computations to pocket calculators. Our interest here is simply to

---

*The introduction to this chapter will be fun for those who enjoy math. For others, feel free to skim, skipping the math; you will get what you need as you read on.

154   THE COSMIC DANCERS

get an idea of what the problems are; for this the details of the calculation are not all that necessary.

Let's consider one concrete example, however. Suppose we design a rocket with $M_i/M_p = 10$, or in other words the fuel is 90 percent of the rocket, the payload only 10 percent. Then from the above relation

$$10^{(0.434\, v_{max}/v_{ex})} = 10 = 10^1$$

If we equate the exponent of 10 on both sides, we get

$$0.434\, v_{max}/v_{ex} = 1$$

dividing both sides by 0.434, we obtain a value for the ratio v_{max}/v_{ex}:

$$\frac{v_{max}}{v_{ex}} = \frac{1}{0.434} = 2.3$$

In other words, even for a mass ratio of 10, we get a maximum velocity of only 2.3 times the exhaust velocity, no more. The best chemical fuels give us an exhaust velocity of about 4 km/sec. For a mass ratio of 10, the maximum velocity attainable by a chemical fuel rocket is thus 2.3 times 4 km/sec or 9.2 km/sec; that is enough velocity to reach orbit around the earth, but a minuscule velocity when pondering travel to the stars.

The picture is clear. The exhaust velocity that we can achieve for the fuel propellant is the really important quantity. Only if we can attain high exhaust velocities can we hope to achieve rockets with a reasonable mass ratio. And clearly chemical rockets are not going to lead us very far.

Futurologists expect the next step of rocketry to consist of ion rockets, which are much used in science fiction literature. Here the low mass-energy conversion efficiency of chemical fuels is overcome by using nuclear-fission fuel. Furthermore, nozzles and high temperature material problems can be avoided by using electrically charged particles or ions as the exhaust, using electric fields to accelerate the ions. One estimates typical exhaust velocities of 100 km/sec with ion drives. However, now there is the added payload due to nuclear reactors and the heavy equipment for accelerating ions. Thus, even with the ion drive, we really do not expect to venture outside the solar system.

It is fairly obvious, all things considered, that to reach the stars we must have rockets that are a couple of orders of magnitude better than the ion drive. With the ion drive, efficiency is reduced by the extra addition to the payload. We can follow physicist Freeman Dyson to think of the next step: use hydrogen fusion bombs (yes, literally) to accelerate the propellant. There are many problems with this idea—absorbing the shock of the explosions, the gamma radiation and so forth—but let's assume that all these problems can be solved. What kind of exhaust speed can we get? Estimates show that the maximum exhaust speed attainable in such fusion rockets, assuming maximum theoretical mass-energy conversion possible in nuclear reactions, is about 1/10 of the speed of light. Since this is finally in the relativistic range, we need to take account of the relativistic mass increase with speed in the rocket mass ratio calculation. The new formula is:

$$\frac{\text{initial mass}}{\text{mass of payload}} = \frac{M_i}{M_p} = \left(\frac{1 + v_{max}/c}{1 - v_{max}/c}\right)^{\frac{c}{2\,v_{ex}}}$$

Suppose we settle for a moderate v_{max} of 0.99 c, 99 percent of the speed of light. This gives a value of the relativistic factor gamma ($\frac{1}{\sqrt{1 - v^2/c^2}}$) of about 7 (which means that clocks aboard a spaceship will be seven times slower than earth clocks), quite reasonable for travel to medium-range interstellar distances. Thus, in the above formula we now have $v_{ex} = 0.1\ c$, so $\frac{c}{2\,v_{ex}} = \frac{c}{0.2\ c} = \frac{1}{0.2} = 5$; and $v_{max}/c = 0.99$. Substituting these values in the formula we get

$$\frac{M_i}{M_p} = \left(\frac{1 + 0.99}{1 - 0.99}\right)^5 = \left(\frac{1.99}{0.01}\right)^5 \simeq 200^5 = 2^5 \times 100^5 = 32 \times 10^{10}$$

In other words, to lift a small one-ton payload, we must start with an initial fuel mass of 320 billion tons. Thus, the fusion bomb drive is quite inadequate for medium-range interstellar travel. However, it can take us to nearby stars, although not in a manner which would permit the crew to take advantage of the relativistic time dilation effect. Notice that if we moderate our demands, let's say to a v_{max} of 0.2 c, then the formula above gives

$$\frac{M_i}{M_p} = \left(\frac{1 + 0.2}{1 - 0.2}\right)^5 = \left(\frac{1.2}{0.8}\right)^5 = (1.5)^5 = 7$$

The above calculation is for a one-time acceleration. For a round trip, the mass ratio would be $7 \times 7 \times 7 \times 7$, since we have to accelerate to the maximum velocity, decelerate, accelerate again, and decelerate again; this comes out to be a mass ratio of 5401. Thus for a 1000-ton payload, we have to arrange for a total initial mass of 5,401,000 tons; staggering but not unthinkable. At $v_{max} = 0.2\ c$ a round trip to Alpha Centauri would take about 40 years, shiptime: not bad at all.

With the fusion drive you can plan generation starship stories easily, stories in which an entire society is spaceborne forever, stopping at different planetary systems only for refueling. But for the true-blue relativistic drive that benefits from time dilation, we must insist that v_{max} be 0.99 or better; in order to achieve this we must consider the best energizing reaction that we can find—the matter-antimatter conversion, for which the efficiency of conversion of mass into energy is 100 percent. There is also a big improvement in the rocket exhaust velocity, since the product of matter-antimatter annihilation is gamma rays, which travel with the speed of light. Let's plug $v_{ex} = c$ into the formula for the mass ratio

$$\frac{M_i}{M_p} = \left(\frac{1 + v_{max}/c}{1 - v_{max}/c}\right)^{\frac{c}{2}\frac{c}{c}} = \sqrt{\frac{1 + v_{max}/c}{1 - v_{max}/c}}$$

since an exponent of ½ is the same as taking the square root. For v_{max} = 0.99 c, we now get

$$\frac{m_i}{M_p} = \sqrt{\frac{1.99}{0.01}} = \sqrt{199} \approx 14$$

Even for a round trip, the requirement now for travel at 99 percent of the speed of light is of a mass ratio of 14 × 14 × 14 × 14 or about 40,000—not bad at all, considering. The only difficult part of this is that half the reaction mass has to be antimatter. Since antimatter is not freely available on earth, we have to manufacture it and store it without allowing it to touch the matter of the spaceship. The technology for storing antimatter is already at hand, although on a rather small scale. For example, antiprotons, which are the negatively charged antiparticles of protons, can be confined by means of magnetic fields to so-called storage rings. But manufacturing antimatter on earth on a large scale, and especially storing it on a spaceship in the huge quantities needed, seems difficult, if not impossible, from our twentieth-century perspective.

If you are a *Star Trek* fan, you are familiar with its matter-antimatter drive. One episode of the show gave us a look at the inside of a matter-antimatter converter. Alas, the imagination of the film makers was many orders of magnitude paler than what the actual situation would demand!

It should be clear from our above estimate that matter-antimatter drives, even assuming less than 100 percent efficiency, are quite adequate for a voyage to nearby stars. In fact, some studies have been made with such a purpose in mind, and the prognosis is good in the sense that getting 100 percent efficiency or close to it may be feasible in the future. Antiprotons annihilate regular protons, giving gamma rays. If these gamma rays can themselves be used as the exhaust (as assumed in the estimate above), employing some sort of laser action, we will have it made. So perhaps our descendants in a few centuries will have such a drive and will operate a regular passenger line to Alpha Centauri. Perhaps the *Star Trek* matter-antimatter converter will look no more ludicrous to them than Daedalus' wings look to us today.

Coming back to ambitious drives, American physicist Robert Bussard has a promising suggestion. Perhaps you are familiar with the drive of today's jet aircraft; they take in air at the front end, accelerate it (spending fuel energy), and then use the air as the exhaust. Bussard has conceived of an interstellar ramjet which is one step better. It will scoop in interstellar matter that will be fed into a thermonuclear fusion engine, where part of it will provide the energy required to generate the high-speed exhaust that consists of the remaining part. Thus, interstellar hydrogen gas will act both as the rocket reaction mass (the exhaust) and as the energy source. In this case there is no limit on v_{max} except for that imposed by relativity, the speed of light. Question: is this feasible?

One of the main problems with this brilliant idea is that the density of hydrogen in interstellar space is really thin, about one hydrogen atom per cubic centimeter. Thus the collecting area of the ship has to be very, very large. For a 100-ton spaceship, Bussard has estimated that the surface area of the ramjet intake has to be a trillion square meters. This corresponds to a radius of 700 kilometers.

Such a collecting area may seem enormously large, but fortunately, the ramjet technologist can count on a big break. Much of the interstellar matter is ionized plasma consisting of charged particles. Charged particles can be collected by a magnetic field. Although the large magnetic fields that will be needed are beyond today's technology, progress in superconducting magnetic field generators is very encouraging to the futurologist.

There is still another problem with relativistically moving spaceships. Since motion is relative, the Bussard ramjet—as it moves through space just short of the speed of light—is sitting still to its crew; but all the matter of the interstellar medium is moving at close to the speed of light, thus carrying a huge penetrating momentum relative to the ship. Such penetrating particles will kill the crew in no time unless some sort of shields are designed to keep these particles out. Fortunately, since most of the particles are charged, they can be handled with a shield consisting of a magnetic field. However, there also has to be some shielding material to dispose of lethal gamma rays, which will be present.

Let's take a break at this point to discuss science fiction. You can easily imagine that Bussard ramjets would be quite popular with science fiction writers, and they are. A story that uses a ramjet for one of the most ambitious journeys through the universe ever conceived in fiction has been written by Poul Anderson in *Tau Zero*. The Greek letter tau, introduced earlier, indicates the reciprocal of the relativistic factor gamma. Tau tending to zero is the same limit as gamma approaching infinity, which is what happens as *Tau Zero*'s spaceship *Leonora Christine* continually accelerates at one g with the help of its Bussard drive:

Consider: a single light-year is an inconceivable abyss. Denumerable but inconceivable. . . .

Nevertheless, such spaces could be conquered. A ship accelerating continuously at one gravity would have traveled half a light-year in slightly less than one year of time. And she would be moving very near the ultimate velocity, three hundred thousand kilometers per second.

Practical problems arose. Where was the mass-energy to do this coming from? Even in a Newtonian universe, the thought of a rocket, carrying that much fuel along from the start, would be ludicrous. Still more so was it in the true, Einsteinian cosmos, where the mass of ship and payload increased with speed, climbing toward infinity as that speed approached light's.

. . . The energies were appalling. Megaroentgens of hard radiation would be released by impact; and less than a thousand r [roentgen] within an hour are fatal. No material shielding would help. Even supposing it impossibly thick to start with, it would soon be eroded away.

However, in the days of *Leonora Christine* nonmaterial means were available: magnetohydrodynamic fields, whose pulses reached forth across millions of kilometers to seize atoms by their dipoles—no need for ionization—and control their streaming. These fields did not serve passively, as mere armor. They deflected dust, yes, and all gases except the dominant hydrogen. But this latter was forced aft—in long curves that avoided the hull by a safe margin—until it entered a vortex of compressing, kindling electromagnetism centered on the Bussard engine. . . .

Starlike burned the hydrogen fusion, aft of the Bussard module that focused the electromagnetism which contained it. A titanic gas-laser effect aimed photons themselves in a beam whose reaction pushed the ship forward—and which would have vaporized any solid body it struck. The process was not 100 per cent efficient. But most of the stray energy went to ionize the hydrogen which escaped nuclear combustion. These protons and electrons, together with the fusion products, were also hurled backward by the force fields, a gale of plasma adding its own increment of momentum. [pp. 32–34]

This is an outstanding combination of present-day physics and fertile imagination. An expert could undoubtedly debate some aspects of this magnificent space drive, but its credibility to the reader is unquestionable. Well done!

INTERSTELLAR NAVIGATION

For nonrelativistic rockets, navigation is not a concern in interstellar space. The reason is that space navigation for journeys at nonrelativistic speed is in some sense even simpler than ordinary two-dimensional navigation on our oceans. In the latter case, we use star charts to guide us. In the former case, even a star chart hardly seems necessary (actually, it is!), for we can see our destination star.

Unfortunately, at relativistic speeds things are not so simple. Two effects enter to complicate matters. One of these is the familiar Doppler effect. As a starship accelerates to within a few tenths of a percent of the speed of light, the light from the stars in front of it is blueshifted beyond the optical range. At the same time, the stars at the aft are redshifted, again beyond visibility.

The second effect, aberration, arises from the directional nature of velocities.

To understand aberration, imagine yourself standing in the rain on a windless day. The rain is falling vertically, so you can ward it off with an umbrella to protect yourself. However, if you start to run, the rain suddenly slants at you and wets you. The reason is that the motion of the rain relative to you is a composite of two motions: the motion of the rain relative to earth and the motion of the earth relative to you. The slant of the rain's direction is the result of this addition of two motions. See Figure 27 for details of how the composition is carried out.

Now forget the rain and imagine starlight coming at you from the side as you move forward in a starship. The light will come at you slanted, from a direction intermediate between yours and the true direction of the star; this is called aberration. It turns out that when your velocity is small compared to light's, aberration is hardly noticeable. But as the spaceship's velocity exceeds 35 percent of light speed, aberration becomes dominant, and the stars in the forward direction begin to huddle as a result. The effect in the rear is just the opposite. There the stars will seem to thin out because of aberration.

Thus, when aberration and Doppler effect both are taken into account, as they must be, the optical monitors of a relativistic spaceship will notice a cone of darkness ahead and an even bigger one behind. To the eye, the only stars that will be visible from such a spaceship will lie in a barrel, the section between the two cones (Figure 28). Interestingly, Doppler shift, although at a minimum when the light comes from a right angle to the direction of motion

Figure 27. When the alien woman runs, the velocity of the rain relative to her consists of the sum of two velocity vectors: (1) the vertical velocity of the rain V_r and (2) $-V_w$, a vector equal and opposite to the woman's velocity V_w. The sum of the two velocities, determined according to the parallelogram rule, has a slanted direction as shown. This is why rain falls slanted toward her. (Notice that she's keeping her tail dry.)

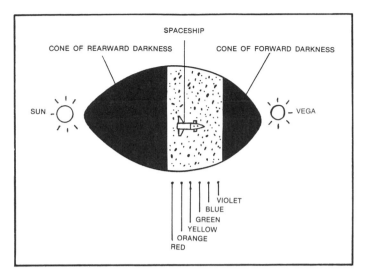

Figure 28. The rainbow effect.

of the spaceship, still shifts the light toward the blue for the forward stars in the visible barrel and toward the red for the stars at the rear. Thus, the spectrum of stars in the barrel forms the sequence of colors of the rainbow, as shown in Figure 28. And indeed, when the spaceship attains a speed within one percent of the speed of light, the barrel thins to a mere ring which would look like a rainbow, if you were there to see it.

In Larry Niven's SF novel *A World out of Time,* there is a reference to this rainbow effect. The hero of the novel is kept in cold sleep during long periods of the voyage, which is relativistic—just right for the rainbow effect. In this scene, he takes a full view of the outside after waking up from one of his long sleeps:

> The stellar rainbow had hardened and sharpened over seven decades. It had lost symmetry, too. To one side, the stars were thickly clustered; the arc of blue-whites blazed like diamonds in an empress's necklace. To the other, the side that faced intergalactic space, the rainbow was almost dark. Each star was sharply defined within its band of color. But within the central disk of violet stars (dimmer than the blue, but of a color that made one squint) was a soft white glow: the microwave background of the universe, at 3° absolute, boosted to visible light by Don Juan's terrible speed. [p. 46]

I shall have more to say about the 3° radiation later, but now the more pertinent question is: how does one navigate in such circumstances? You may think that at least in the forward direction, the Doppler shift should not cause much problem with detection of the stars, since ultraviolet and X rays, although invisible to the naked eye, can easily be detected by instruments with a fair amount of resolution. True enough. But how about aberration, which will make all star maps and charts useless? But if you are worried that there is no solution to this problem, don't be. For a civilization so advanced that it can handle Bussard drive, the navigation problem is relatively simple to solve by computer. Here is an appropriate excerpt from Poul Anderson's *Tau Zero,* showing how to navigate at relativistic speeds:

When *Leonora Christine* attained a substantial fraction of light speed, its optical effects became clear to the unaided sight. Her velocity and that of the rays from a star added vectorially; the result was aberration. Except for whatever lay dead aft or ahead, the apparent position changed. Constellations grew lopsided, grew grotesque, and melted, as their members crawled across the dark. More and more, the stars thinned out behind the ship and crowded before her.

Doppler effect operated simultaneously. Because she was fleeing the light waves that overtook her from astern, to her their length was increased and their frequency lowered. In like manner, the waves into which her bow plunged were shortened and quickened. Thus, the suns aft looked ever redder, those forward bluer.

On the bridge stood a compensating viewscope: the single one aboard, elaborate as it was. A computer figured out continuously how the sky would appear if you were motionless at this point of space, and projected a simulacrum of it. The device was not for amusement or comfort; it was a valuable navigational aid. [p. 40]

PRELUDE TO HYPERSPACE

The technology described in this chapter is some of the most ambitious that humans have ever conceived. The one disconcerting problem for the reader is that it is extremely unlikely that any of it will be forthcoming. In Chapter 4, we spoke of the futility of making ten-thousand-year plans for exploring the solar system, and here we may be speaking of million-year plans. Thus, practical scientists have concluded that it is better not to plan for physical contact with alien civilizations just yet. Instead, we may wait to hear from them, setting up radio communication apparatus for receiving as well as for sending.

Some SF writers and futurologists have their minds set on a different approach. They think they have evidence that we have been contacted already. I mentioned the work of Von Däniken before. You may also have read Anton Wilson and Robert Shea's *Illuminatus* trilogy, in which they imagine that we are being looked after by a civilization based in the Sirius star system. Wilson is quite serious about the relevance of the "Sirius mystery," the claim that some primitive tribes knew about the faint partner of the Sirius double-star system before it was located by astronomers.

If other intelligent alien civilizations are contacting us, how are they doing it? Spaceships with Bussard drive? Possible but unlikely, because their size would have made them very conspicuous. SF writers for some time have used the concept of hyperspace, a dimension outside of ordinary space, to handle extraterrestrial travel. (This concept facilitates considerably story lines involving galactic empires.) Could it be that the purported visitors to earth from outer space have learned the secret of hyperspace? But if so, then why can't we?

In any case, aliens or no aliens, we can appreciate one motivation for hyperspace from the following quotation from Gordon Dickson's SF novel, *Mission to Universe:*

It had always puzzled Ben that people believed that the great creative minds that moved the race forward went *through* the technical barriers in the road of human progress. The fact was just the contrary. They went *around* them. They looked away from the impassable barrier before them to find an alternate solution elsewhere. Men had not solved the problem of ocean crossings by learning to walk upon water, but by building ships. . . . it should have seemed the most obvious consequence in the world that, faced with the limiting speed of light at a hundred and eight-six thousand miles per second, far too slow to permit reasonable exploration of even the nearer stars, men should look out-side the problem for an alternate solution to crossing the vast galactic distances in practical periods of time. [italics in the original, p. 39]

For science fiction writers, this alternative way to get around the light barrier has been the concept of hyperspace. In subsequent chapters of this book, hyperspace naturally will constitute a recurrent theme.

chapter twelve

Curvaceous Space-Time

Suppose you are a traveler in the olden days and in the course of your journey you encounter a huge mountain. One choice you have is to brave the mighty mountain and climb over it. However, besides endangering your life, this choice would involve a big chunk of your time. A second alternative is to look for a mountain pass. If you don't find a pass, you might wish there were a tunnel through the mountain; such a tunnel could be a lifesaver in more than one way.

Of course, in our experience with the curved terrain of our familiar planet, such tunnels are commonplace today and are being used increasingly. Even in ancient times, people knew there was nothing theoretically impossible about digging such a tunnel. Earth was known to be three-dimensional. Although we are more or less confined to its two-dimensional surface, a little deviation from it has always been permitted; large deviations via underground tunnels and airplanes were only a matter of finding the right technology. The ancients were quite clear about this.

When the first science fiction writers began to think of space travel, they were overwhelmed by the vastness of it. Obviously, it was impossible to cover such huge distances within one human lifetime. With Einstein's relativity and time dilation, things were a bit easier; an astronaut now could survive a trip to the stars. Unfortunately, when she returned from her journey, she would find that time on earth had advanced to the extent that she would be a refugee from another time. One could, of course, think of superlight speeds, but such a cop-out in clear contradiction to Einstein's relativity loses too much credibility. And then somebody discovered hyperspace.

Most people, and SF writers are no exception, intuitively think of space as flat, where Euclid's geometry perpetually holds, no matter what distances are traveled. Parallel lines in flat space can be forever extended in either direction without meeting. Although even Euclid was aware that this is not such a self-evident postulate, and many mathematicians over the ages have sought a proof of the parallel postulate, many of us take it for granted for physical space even today.

Unfortunately, this idea of flat space thwarted the writers' imaginations. Then one day, a science fiction writer discovered Einstein's other relativity theory, the one that says space is curved—it is like a mountainous terrain with lots of ups and downs. Now SF writers could take the leap. If there are mountains, why not tunnels through them; if space is curved, why not a short route through its fabric? This short route, this tunnel through space, is one way to think of science fiction's hyperspace.

Perhaps a picture from a novel will help here. The picture in Figure 29 is adapted from one drawn by a scientist in Piers Anthony's masterpiece, *Macroscope*. The scientist is illustrating hyperspace to a befuddled student. Going down the line in the figure means traveling through ordinary space, which is assumed to be one-dimensional for the sake of illustration. "Suppose," the professor says, "it were possible to pass across those connections, instead of traveling down the length of our line in normal fashion?" Passing across would be passing through hyperspace. The student quickly catches on to the idea.

. . . She hesitated, seeing the possibilities. "If Earth and Neptune happened to be in adjacent loops, you might jump from one to the other in—well, virtually, *no* time." . . .

"That depends on its position and the configuration. It might be possible in a single hop, or it might require several months of jumping. By the same token, it might be as easy to traverse the entire galaxy—if this representation of the nature of space is accurate." [p. 241]

And so it goes. In the book the picture is assumed to be accurate, because the macroscope says so. This picture, in one variation or another, has virtually taken over SF, but is it in any sense accurate? We do not know. But this one thing can be said of such a picture: Einstein's idea of curved space gives it respectability.

The theory of curved space that Einstein built does not use the concept of hyperspace. There is no need, Einstein says, to go outside our three-dimensional world to appreciate the curvature of space. We can do it from within, by making careful measurements. Thus, the verification of Einstein's theory, which has been achieved, says nothing about the validity of the concept of hyperspace, or hyperspace travel.

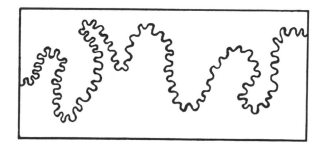

Figure 29. Curved space according to highly schematic representation. (After a similar sketch in Piers Anthony, *Macroscope*)

Besides all the other reasons to be grateful to Einstein, SF writers are generally devoted to him because his theory places hyperspace in the realm of possibility.

WHEN LIGHT RAYS TAKE ON A CURVE

In *Childhood's End* Arthur Clarke has not gone out of his way to stretch his reader's mind with physics. But when he does use physics, he is clearly a master choreographer, as illustrated by the following quotation:

> . . . the immense accelerations of the Stardrive caused a local distortion of space. What Jan was seeing, he knew, was nothing less than the light of distant stars, collected and focused into his eye whenever conditions were favorable along the track of the ship. It was a visible proof of relativity—the bending of light in the presence of a colossal gravitational field. [p. 94]

Jan, one of the book's main characters, was watching the takeoff of an alien ship of the Overlords. The relativity that Clarke refers to in the above lines is general relativity, the relativity theory that includes accelerated reference frames. The physics content of the lines is this: the immense acceleration of the spaceship is equivalent to a colossal gravity field that causes a local distortion or curvature of space; the light from distant stars, following the curvaceous body of the space around the spaceship, bends to produce a huddling or focusing effect.

In a previous chapter, we spoke of gravity in connection with accelerating reference frames; immense accelerations produce physical conditions identical with those of immense gravity fields. Thus, gravity cannot be distinguished from the pseudoforces of acceleration—this is the equivalence principle. What we wish to understand now is how gravity (or acceleration) distorts space.

We can get some idea of this distortion of space in an accelerated reference frame from the following *gedanken* experiment. Suppose we trace the path of a light beam traveling through an elevator which is rapidly accelerating upward in space. To be specific, let's imagine that light enters the elevator from the right where there is a window (Figure 30a); and to mark the path of light we put a few plates of fluorescent glass in its path at regular intervals. If the elevator were stationary, the light path through it would be a straight line—the dotted line in the figure—which intersects the plates at points 1, 2, 3. When the elevator accelerates, light still takes equal time to travel from the window to plate 1, from plate 1 to plate 2, and so forth, but while the light is on its way the plates move. And since the plates undergo accelerated motion, the distance each successive plate moves up is in proportion to the square of the time interval elapsed, in the ratio of 1:4:9. Thus, the spots of fluorescence

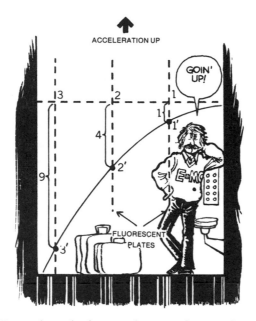

Figure 30(a). Einstein's apple: from inside an accelerating elevator the path of a light beam through it appears to bend like a parabola.

that light makes in an accelerating elevator are 1′, 2′, and 3′; they lie on a parabola and not a straight line. If you are an observer watching this parade of light, in which case you consider yourself to be under gravity (equivalence principle), you must conclude that the path of the light ray is bent by gravity, just as is the path of a projectile such as a baseball.

Now comes the question of interpretation. Since light has mass by virtue of its energy, we quite legitimately can consider the bending of light by either acceleration effect or gravity as nothing but an example of the parabolic fall of a gravitating object in a gravity field. This logic is not faulty, it's quite sophisticated, perhaps too erudite to be true! You remember the story of the high schooler who was experimenting in his biology lab on the effect of cutting off the legs of a frog. Chop, the first leg is gone and the boy says, "Frog, jump." The frog dutifully jumps. Off comes the second leg, followed by the boy's order, "Frog, jump." The frog complies again as the boy notes down his observations. Now the boy cuts off the third of the frog's legs and gives his command, "Frog, jump." Once more the frog does its thing, and the student meticulously writes down the results again in his notebook. Finally, the student dispenses with the fourth leg of the frog. "Frog, jump," he says. But the frog doesn't jump. After a moment's hesitation, the student writes in his notebook: "When you take off all four legs of a frog, the frog loses its hearing."

The student's logic is not inconsistent with his observations, except of course, that there is a simpler answer. The same is true with the bending of light. There is a more elementary way to look at this phenomenon.

One can point out that light rays seek out and follow the shortest paths in space. In flat space, these shortest paths define straight lines. But in curved space, the shortest paths are not the conventional straight lines. If you are not familiar with this idea, consider the two-dimensional curved space of the surface of the earth. Airlines interested in flying the shortest route between any two points always fly the arcs of great circles, circles that are concentric with the globe (Figure 30b). Thus, for the two-dimensional space of the globe, the shortest path is not a straight line, but an arc of a great circle. Now we can understand why the path of light bends in a gravity field in a different way. The light paths indicate the shortest paths, as always, but now the shortest paths (called geodesics) are curved, bent, because the space itself is curved. The gravity field (or equivalently, acceleration) is responsible for the curvature of space.

This provides the starting point of Einstein's general relativity theory, according to which gravity is not like other forces (well, we already know that it is a pseudoforce locally), but exists in the form of the curvature of space near a gravitating object.

Except that a little more work needs to be done. A *gedanken* experiment, however suggestive it is, cannot pass for a fact. You may have heard the story of the three travelers—a philosopher, a theorist, and an experimental physicist—who were looking at a sheep from a distance. "I am taken by surprise," the philosopher said, "I didn't know there are black sheep in this area." The theorist pooh-poohed. "Oh, come, now, don't generalize. All we see is just one black sheep. We can say only that there is *a* black sheep in this area." The experimentalist, not happy with the argument, corrected the theorist irritably. "All we see in front of us is a sheep one side of which is black." Until he saw the other side, he was reluctant to accept that he was seeing a *black* sheep.

So experimental physicists were reluctant to accept Einstein's idea of curved space until they made an actual observation of the bending of light in a gravity field, such as our sun's. Einstein published his theory in 1915; the experimenters had to wait until 1919 to make their observation, because it involved watching the rays of light from a distant star as the light passed very close to the sun's surface, and such observations could be made only during a total solar eclipse.

The observations, needless to say, bore out Einstein's theoretical predictions. In Figure 30c, I have exaggerated the bending of starlight to make the point. The actual bending predicted was only 1.75 seconds of arc. The experimenters observed a value of 1.61 ± 0.40 seconds of arc, verifying the theory within the limits of accuracy of the observations.

Einstein and these experimenters (among them another great physicist, Sir Arthur Eddington) thus paved the way for a general acceptance of the con-

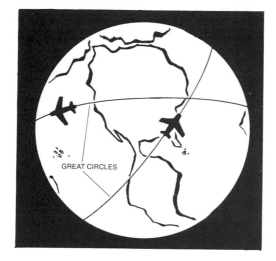

Figure 30(b). The great circles are the shortest paths on a spherical surface.

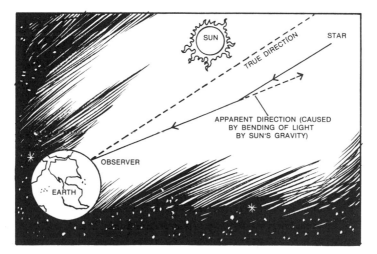

Figure 30(c). The bending of starlight by the sun's gravity field (exaggerated).

cept of curved space. After this, 15 years passed before SF writers used the concept of hyperspace. Perhaps the first such story was written by the great John W. Campbell himself, a story called "The Mightiest Machine." As mentioned before, the idea of hyperspace (looked upon as the fourth dimension of space, from which we can see the three-dimensional space as curved) has not been confirmed by scientists, although theorists have toyed with it to some extent. For all we know, perhaps the idea cannot even *be* verified. But there is nothing inherently wrong with the idea of a space dimension from which ordinary space looks curved, and which is outside ordinary space-time.

THE CURVATURE OF TIME

Special relativity has taught us that space and time are coupled. So if space is curved, what about time? General relativity says it is space-time, or what is called the four-dimensional continuum, that is curved. The geodesics of general relativity are "straight lines" of curved space-time.

However, there are some twists. As you noticed in our discussion of special relativity, space and time have some differences which they retain in their marriage. Although in ordinary space a geodesic defines the shortest possible route, in space-time it is the longest. Yes, longest. This also has to do with the asymmetric sign of the time-term in the expression of the four-dimensional interval in Chapter 7.

Time adds a more spectacular visual element to motion in space-time. This is because, near a gravitating object, curvature in time is more noticeable than the curvature of space. The curvature in time gains by the factor of the speed of light (remember that c times t is the correct fourth-dimensional coordinate) and becomes conspicuous. It's like a small bump in the road, you hardly notice it when you walk on it. But, for the small bump to become truly spectacular, drive over it in a high-speed automobile! The path followed by objects in a gravity field, the parabolic path of a projectile, the curved path of light near the sun—all are examples of geodesics in space-time, but they are curved by different amounts because of this quirk of the curvature of time.

Now we can state the two main ingredients of Einstein's theory of gravitation. The first one, equivalent to the laws of motion in Newton's theory, tells us that objects in a gravitational field follow the geodesics of the curved space-time produced by the field. The second Einsteinian principle is tantamount to a new gravity law that replaces Newton's old one. Roughly speaking, it gives the recipe for determining the curvature of space-time from the matter (or energy) density in the vicinity. (For small curvature, however, Newton's old law remains valid as an approximation.)

Note one more thing. Einstein looks at gravity as a "field" like the electromagnetic field. A massive object produces a curvature of space-time which is the gravitational field. It differs from the electromagnetic field in that the gravity field is not the result of something that happens *to* space, or something *in* space—it *is* what that space becomes. The form of the sculpture cannot be peeled away from the stone: the form *is* the sculpture. So it is with gravity, the gravity field *is* curved space.

Every once in a while you read an SF story which mentions a theory called the unified field theory (for example, in James P. Hogan's *The Genesis Machine*). Einstein worked on this idea of a unified field for the last 30 or so years of his life, trying to unite gravitation and electromagnetism, but to no avail. However, theories of the unification of other fields have panned out quite well; for example, electromagnetism and the nuclear forces are now seen as parts of a grand unified field (the previously footnoted GUT). But nobody yet has succeeded in including gravity in the unification scheme.

GRAVITY AND CLOCKS

A scene from Larry Niven's story "Neutron Star" is of interest here. The hero, if you remember, is off to explore a neutron star. As he approaches his destination, he notices something peculiar about the color of the stars around him.

Were the stars turning blue?
Two hours to go—and I was sure they were turning blue. Was my speed that high? Then the stars behind should be red. . . . And the stars behind were blue, not red. All around me were blue-white stars. [*Neutron Star*, p. 21]

This is not the Doppler effect (the change in observed frequency of light due to the relative motion of source and observer), because then the receding stars would look red. Obviously, this is a different kind of frequency shift— one due to the effect of the strong gravity field of the neutron star, it turns out.

It is easy to understand why gravity should cause a blue shift in all light falling into the field, as in Niven's story. In quantum theory, light consists of elementary particles called photons whose energy is proportional to the frequency of the light. As these photons fall under gravity, their potential energy is converted into kinetic energy of wave motion; greater energy means greater frequency, hence a blue shift. Conversely, if light is trying to come out of a gravity well, it must give up some of the kinetic energy of its wave motion to gain potential energy; such light must suffer a red shift. This is not the most accurate way of describing the situation, but the mathematics works out. Both blue and red shifts of light in relation to gravitational fields have been observed experimentally.

Light, of course, is a form of vibration and thus can be used directly as a timekeeper. Therefore, the slowing down of the rate of vibration of light, its frequency, really means that time itself slows down in the depths of a gravity field; the time clocks of an observer situated in a gravity well appear to be slow to a distant observer sitting at the top of the well. However, the slowing down of clocks in a gravity well is not paradoxical. To the observer at the bottom of the well, the clock of the observer "upstairs" appears fast, since light coming from the top is blueshifted, speeded up in frequency.

Near a source of only moderate gravity, such as a planet or star, the gravitational slowing down of clocks is small; but near a neutron star, especially as we approach the bottom of the well, the effects can be spectacular.

Thus, to the passenger of a starship descending into the gravity well of a neutron star, the stars outside the field all look blueshifted because his clock has slowed down to a crawl.

The most spectacular slowing down of clocks is predicted to occur near collapsed stellar objects called black holes from which even light cannot escape. The light is redshifted by an infinite amount and never makes it up the well. Poul Anderson has used this idea in a brilliant story ("Kyrie") involving a pair of telepaths, people who can communicate mentally across distance without attenuation. One member of the pair goes down a black hole, leaving the other member in an agonizing and incurable predicament:

He made himself pat her hand. ". . . his must have been a merciful death. Quick, clean; I wouldn't mind going out like that."

"For him . . . yes, I suppose so. It has to be. But—" She could not continue. Suddenly she covered her ears. "Stop! Please!"

Szili made soothing noises and left. In the corridor he encountered Mazundar. "How is she?" the physicist asked.

The captain scowled. "Not good. I hope she doesn't crack entirely before we can get her to a psychiatrist."

"Why, what is wrong?"

"She thinks she can hear him."

Mazundar smote fist into palm. "I hoped otherwise," he breathed. . . . "Obviously she does."

"But that's impossible! He's dead!"

"Remember the time dilation," Mazundar replied. "He fell from the sky and perished swiftly, yes. But in supernova time. Not the same as ours. To us, the final stellar collapse takes an infinite number of years. And telepathy has no distance limits." The physicist started walking fast away from that cabin. "He will always be with her." [*The Road to Science Fiction #3*, pp. 486–487]

In the novel *A World out of Time*, Larry Niven describes a near encounter between a spaceship and a rotating black hole of one hundred million solar masses. Fortunately, the spaceship is being navigated by a computer (named Peerssa), which, taking advantage of the immense time dilation near the black hole, guides the ship safely to a universe three million years in the future:

Behind them the Ring of Fire reddened further and was gone. The inner disk grew brighter and bluer and was suddenly past. In the last instant Corbell saw the black hole.

The onboard fusion drive roared beneath him, slammed him down into his chair. Light exploded in his face. It resolved: a blaze of violet light ahead of him, a broad ring of embers around it. Elsewhere, black. . . .

Corbell said, "It's over? We lived through that?"

"Yes." [Peerssa answered] . . .

"What's happening now?"

"Firing a reaction drive within the ergosphere of a black hole has driven us dangerously near lightspeed. I am using the ram fields to ward interstellar matter from us. I won't be able to use them as a drive until we can shed some velocity. We will reach the vicinity of Sol in thirteen point eight years, ship's time, unless we overshoot."

"Did we really lose three million years?"

"Yes, Corbell. . . ." [p. 58]

Before finishing this chapter on general relativity, it is instructive to note that Einstein began his research on the subject with hardly any experimental data as either lure or encouragement. Einstein pushed ahead because he was interested in a complete picture of reality, which his special relativity had rendered very much incomplete. For example, one bothersome question he asked himself was: if time is relational with motion, should space continue to remain absolute in relation to matter? Somehow he didn't think it should, and in general relativity, space does indeed depend on matter in a crucial way. This element of Einstein's quest, the search for a complete picture, is important to remember; the tendency of many physicists and scientists today is to be quite satisfied with compartmentalized successes. They are content to explain experimental data, yet—if there is little or no data—they are very reluctant to examine even large degrees of incompleteness in a theory.

The theory of general relativity remains obscure to most people, partly because it has hardly any consequences in earthly matters. Fortunately, SF writers are not particularly attached to earth; their eyes are on the cosmic dance. The expansion of the universe, one of the cosmic consequences of general relativity, is a wild and fascinating science-fictiony idea. And the black hole, validated as a concept by general relativity, promises the ultimate gift for science fiction, since many people think black holes are doors into hyperspace. These exciting ideas—the expanding universe and black holes—are the subjects of the next two chapters.

chapter thirteen

Black Hole: The Infinity Box

One of the hottest items of interest today, to both physicists and science fiction enthusiasts, is the concept of a black hole. The idea of the black hole, born from the very respectable theory of general relativity, is the most bizarre consequence of that theory. The idea lay dormant for a while in the forties and fifties: most physicists were busy with other things, and science fiction was passing from its golden age into the modern era. Then in the mid-sixties neutron stars were discovered. Previously it was theorized that, depending on its mass, a star could collapse into one of three states: if the star had a mass like our sun's, its likely finale would be the white dwarf; if the star had a mass two or three times that of our sun's, the star should end up as a neutron star; and if the mass of the star exceeded five or so solar masses, nothing would prevent the star from collapsing into a black hole—so says theory, anyway. Now white dwarfs had been known for some time; therefore, with the discovery of neutron stars, two of the three predictions of theory as regards the final states of stars were verified. Can the discovery of the third be far behind? Many physicists think not.

A black hole is collapsed matter, collapsed under its own gravity, producing such an intense curvature in space-time around it that no object—not even light—can escape it. Even light is turned back, can you imagine that? That's why this collapsed matter, this space-time region of intense curvature, appears black to all outside observers. And where goes the matter that collapsed? According to theory, the matter is crushed to a point in space-time, a point that mathematicians call a singularity; at such a point matter density becomes infinite, and physics as we know it perhaps loses its meaning.

How do we ever expect to observe such a black hole without actually going on a voyage and falling into one? But if we fall into a black hole, we can't return. So how can we be sure of the black hole's existence? Fortunately, the black hole, the collapsed matter, does leave a clue behind.

You may remember the Cheshire-Cat in *Alice's Adventures in Wonderland.*

"I wish you wouldn't keep appearing and vanishing so suddenly [replied Alice]: you make one quite giddy."

"All right," said the Cat; and this time it vanished quite slowly, beginning with the end of the tail and ending with the grin, which remained some time after the rest of it had gone.

"Well! I have often seen a cat without a grin," thought Alice, "but a grin without a cat! It's the most curious thing I ever saw in my life."

Like the Cheshire-Cat, the black hole leaves a grin behind, so to say. The black hole's grin is its gravitational force field. The Cheshire-Cat vanished slowly; you could say that as far as external observers are concerned, the black hole takes forever, infinite time, to collapse. And because of the lingering gravitational field left behind, we can continue to "see" a black hole: the black hole will act gravitationally on nearby matter and on any of our probes.

To understand this, recall the slowing down of clocks near a source of intense gravity, which was discussed in the last chapter. Suppose a distant outside observer, by prior arrangement, is looking at the clock of another brave adventurer as he approaches and falls into a black hole. How can one look at the black hole adventurer's clock? It can be done by noting the time that elapses between two consecutive light signals sent to the faraway observer by the black hole explorer. And, of course, as the explorer approaches closer and closer to the black hole, the time between signals as received by the distant observer increases due to the gravitational slowing down of time (Figure 31).

Figure 31. The gravitational slowing down of clocks becomes more and more prominent for a black-hole explorer as he approaches the surface of infinite red shift (denoted here as the Schwarzschild radius).

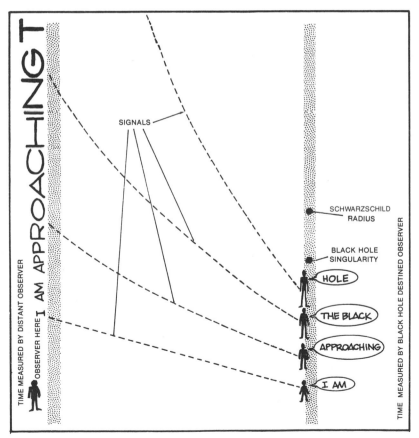

We can imagine from the figure that as the black hole explorer nears the hole, there will be a point at which the time between his signals will approach infinity. He is now at the surface of infinite red shift. After this his signals are curved back, and he is no longer heard from.

Although we cannot have any direct knowledge of the plight of any brave hero who plunges into a black hole, we can make some educated guesses. First of all, he himself is freely falling, which is equivalent to being in an inertial reference frame. Thus, he will not notice any changes in the rate of his time clock. Unfortunately, although he is quite immune to the average gravitational force exerted on him by the black hole, he will be torn apart by the very intense tidal force over the extent of his body.

For a nonrotating black hole, also called a Schwarzschild black hole, the surface of infinite red shift coincides with the "horizon" of the black hole. The horizon defines a region of enclosed space that anything can enter, but nothing can escape. The black hole now can be formally defined as the volume of space enclosed by the horizon (Figure 32). The horizon prevents us from "seeing" the infinity represented by the singularity. Thus, my favorite metaphor for a black hole is an infinity box, a phrase used by Kate Wilhelm as the title of a story.

The likeliest candidate for a black hole is a massive collapsed star, at least four to five times as heavy as our sun (the collapse of lighter stars gives rise to white dwarfs and neutron stars), whose fuel energy has come to naught. So long as the fuel burns inside the core of a star, the pressure of the hot gases balances the inward pressure of gravity, and the star has a stable existence. But with the fuel gone, there is no more heat, the gases cool down, and its outward pressure dwindles. The inward pressure of gravity now takes over, and the star begins a journey of no return toward gravitational collapse, becoming a black hole as its size shrinks below the Schwarzschild radius. Incidentally, inside the horizon the entire structure of space-time changes drastically; space becomes time, and time, space. So the collapse of the

Figure 32. An artist's conception of a black hole. (From Goswami, *The Concepts of Physics*, D. C. Heath)

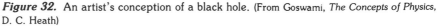
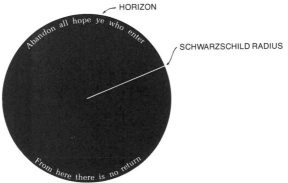

star-matter, once past the horizon, is more to a point in time rather than to a center of space, contrary to what you may feel intuitively. The matter is squished at all points of space inside the horizon as the moment of the singularity approaches. For a collapsing star, from the time the matter passes through the horizon, it's only about 10^{-5} seconds to complete collapse—reckoning, of course, from the point of view of an internal observer, a point of view we can only guess, but never verify.

For a 5-solar-mass black hole, the Schwarzschild radius is about 15 km. Inside the Schwarzschild radius, gravity becomes supreme. The matter that goes in retains no memory other than its total mass, total charge (if any), and total angular momentum (if it began as a rotating star). In any case, these are the only quantities we can measure of a black hole from outside. We cannot distinguish between two black holes with different past histories and initial structures if they have the same mass, charge, and angular momentum. This is the "no hair" theorem: black holes have no distinguishing hair from which to trace their ancestry.

Can a galaxy become a black hole? Galaxies have a hang-up which can prevent the galaxy as a whole from becoming a black hole. Previously, we mentioned angular momentum and how it's conserved. Angular momentum is a vector quantity; when we say it is conserved, we mean that both its magnitude and direction are conserved. Now as far as we know, most galaxies are formed from a sphere of gas. Suppose the sense of rotation is counterclockwise as seen from the top, then the direction of the angular momentum vector for the entire sphere of gas is upward, as shown in Figure 33. It turns out that if the gas collapses in the same direction as the angular momentum vector, the angular momentum is unaffected since the size of the orbit doesn't change—so such a collapse is allowed. On the other hand, collapse in a direction perpendicular to the angular momentum vector is quite impossible, because collapse in this direction would change the angular momentum. Thus, the matter of a galaxy settles down in a saucerlike shape, with the outer parts rotating around the galactic center. Thus, unless we discover a new mechanism which breaks the angular momentum habit of galaxies, it is unlikely that the outer parts of a galaxy will ever collapse inward.

However, the angular momentum hang-up is less inhibiting to the galactic core (because of higher density and smaller orbits), where we can certainly envision some kind of collapse taking place. It is not impossible for a black hole, consisting of the mass of millions of stars, to be at the center of a galaxy, as envisioned in Larry Niven's novel *A World out of Time*.

How about the entire universe? The Schwarzschild radius for a mass of 10^{53} kg (approximately the mass of the universe) can be calculated to be 10^{26} m or 10 billion light years. This is very close to the actual estimate of the size of the universe (assuming that it is finite, of course). Is the universe a black hole? Probably not—at this stage, anyway—as evidence discussed later will

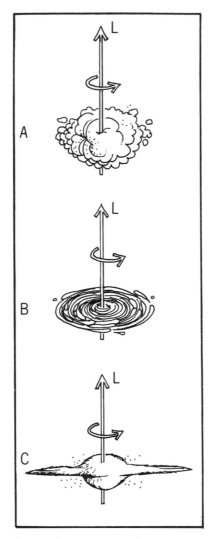

Figure 33. How a galaxy evolves to its typical saucer shape.

indicate. However, it is quite possible that it could become one later, billions of years from today. Also, note that even if the universe does become a black hole someday, its sheer size will keep it collapsing for a long time, for billions of years, before the "singularity" is reached.

HOW TO VISIT AND ESCAPE A BLACK HOLE

Suppose you have got hold of an alien spaceship of unknown mechanism. Somehow the mechanism allows the spaceship to travel through hyperspace to remote parts of normal space. Pretty quickly you learn to program it for destinations on a random basis: the destination depends on the numbers that you punch on a dial. However, you have no idea to what part of the universe a particular set of numbers will take you. Yet you must explore, and in order to explore at all, you must explore blindly.

This is the story line of Frederik Pohl's *Gateway,* which richly details such blind explorations by various crews. In one of these expeditions, the hero and his party have an unprecedented encounter:

Over the static I heard a voice I didn't recognize at first, but it was Danny A.'s. "Do you feel that?" he yelled. "It's gravity waves. We're in trouble. Stop the scan!"

I stopped it reflexively.

But by then the ship's screen had turned and something was in view that was not a star and not a galaxy. It was a dimly glowing mass of pale-blue light, mottled, immense, and terrifying. Even at the first glimpse I knew it was not a sun. No sun can be so blue and so dim. It hurt the eyes to look at it, not because of its brightness. It hurt inside the eyes, up far into the optic track; the pain was in the brain itself.

Metchnikov switched off the radio, and in the silence that followed I heard Danny A. say prayerfully, "Dearest God! We've had it. This thing is a black hole." [p. 292]

By the way, this description of a black hole is quite accurate; from close-up you would expect to see a dim halo of frozen light around the black hole, light emitted from the collapsing surface and also light captured into a standstill by the black hole. There are also X rays emitted in the vicinity of a black hole when matter falls into it, which can hurt the eye as indicated.

So what do you think? Does the story end here? From the discussion so far, it may seem to you that all is hopeless. Nobody can escape the intense gravity of a black hole from that close; the ship and its crew will just spiral toward and go through the horizon, and then into oblivion! However, the hero of the story had the advantage of a lecture by a physics professor. Subject: how to escape from a black hole.

Dr. Asmenion. Now, if you start with a star bigger than three solar masses, and it collapses, it doesn't just turn into a neutron star. It keeps on going. It gets so dense that the escape velocity exceeds thirty billion centimeters a second . . . which is . . . ?

Question. Uh. The speed of light?

Dr. Asmenion. Right on, Gallina. So light can't escape. So it's black. So that's why it's called a black hole—only, if you get close enough, inside what's called the ergosphere, it isn't black. You probably could see something.

Question. What would it look like?

Dr. Asmenion. Beats the ass off me, Jer. If anybody ever goes and sees one, he'll come back and tell us if he can. Only he probably can't. You *could* maybe get that close in, get your readings and come back—and collect, Jesus, I don't know, a million dollars anyway. If you could get into your lander, see, and kick the main mass of the ship away, backward, slowing it down, you might be able to give yourself enough extra velocity to get away. Not easily. But maybe, if things were just right. But then where would you go? You can't get home in a lander. And doing it the other way wouldn't work, there isn't enough mass in a lander to get you free. . . . [italics in the original, p. 262]

Some explanation is in order. For example, what is an ergosphere? We haven't mentioned any ergosphere in the last section. You see, ordinary Schwarzschild black holes don't have an ergosphere, but the professor is talking about a rotating black hole, one with a lot of angular momentum. In such a case, there are several interesting new elements in the structure of a black hole, and one of these is the ergosphere.

For the Schwarzschild black hole, I previously mentioned two concepts: the surface of infinite red shift, where the time clocks practically stop, and the horizon, which defines the surface of a one-way membrane—everything can go in and nothing can emerge. I also mentioned the fact that for a Schwarzschild black hole, the two surfaces coincide. For a rotating black hole, though, they don't. And thus, there is a volume of space bounded by the two surfaces; this volume defines the ergosphere (Figure 34a), so named because it is possible to extract "ergo" or work from this region. Really.

Previously, I also said that inside the black hole horizon, time becomes space, and things evolve toward the singularity. Things cannot stand still when time behaves like space and space behaves like time. In ordinary flat space-time, time always moves on and we have no control over it; inside the horizon, it is space that moves on—it is impossible to stand still in space. Now the most remarkable fact about the ergosphere is that here too time changes into space, and things cannot stand still. Why does this peculiarity happen even though there is no singularity within the ergosphere? The rotating matter that collapsed to form the black hole continues to exert influence on matter in the vicinity; matter that enters the ergosphere is forced by the collapsed matter to rotate in the same direction as the collapsed matter itself. Thus, everything is dynamic inside the ergosphere, and time has become spacelike.

But this fact can enable a spaceship trapped in the ergosphere to return to normal space. In ordinary space-time, the energy of a body is always positive if you count the total energy to include the mass energy. But when time becomes spacelike, this restriction goes away, and the total energy of a body is allowed to be negative or positive or zero. So the trick is to split the ship into two (say, by an explosion) in such a way that one of the fragments falls into the black hole and has negative energy. The other fragment then gets additional positive energy equal to the amount of negative energy of the first

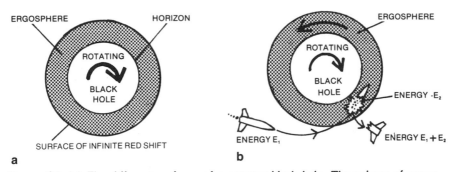

Figure 34. (a) The different surfaces of a rotating black hole. The volume of space bound by the surface of infinite red shift and the horizon is the ergosphere. (b) How a ship can escape a black hole ('s ergosphere). The incoming ship has energy E_1. It explodes in two inside the ergosphere. One fragment goes into the black hole across the horizon with negative total energy $-E_2$; from energy conservation, the other fragment must get an energy boost. Note the sum of the final energies, $E_1 + E_2 + (-E_2) = E_1$, the initial energy.

fragment. This follows from the conservation of energy (Figure 34b). Having gained a boost, the second half of the ship—with some luck—can escape to normal space.

But wait! This still doesn't solve the problem faced by the crew of the *Gateway* ship, because, even if half the ship escapes to normal space, it's still in the middle of nowhere. The crew can never return home in half a ship. But what if they had two ships, one whole ship to spare?

There was no way we could get out considered as a unit. Our ships were caught well inside the point of no return, and there just ain't no way home from there. But old Danny A. . . . knew all about the loopholes in the laws. Considered as a unit we were stuck.

But we weren't a unit! We were two ships! . . . And if we could somehow transfer acceleration from one part of the system to the other—you know, kick part of us deeper into the well and at the same time kick the other part up and out—then part of the unit could go free! [p. 300]

And the method worked, too, and with yet another suspenseful twist! But I don't want to spoil the thrill of that suspense when you read the book.

MINI–BLACK HOLES

Stephen Hawking is one of the most original physicists of today. Restricted to a wheelchair because of a severe, incapacitating illness during his college years, he does most of his mathematical work in his head. In 1973, one of his ideas shook the world of physics. According to the currently popular big bang model of creation, the universe was created in a huge explosion. Hawking suggested that during the first few moments of creation, the density was so great that pockets could have been formed—small regions of space of the same size as elementary particles but containing the mass of a mountain—where the matter would collapse and form a horizon around themselves. These pockets would be similar to the black holes from stellar collapse, they would be mini-black holes. Hawking said many mini-black holes could have been created during the early history of our universe.

Ever since the suggestion was made, mini-black holes have been popular with SF writers. It is quite possible for a mini-black hole to be rotating and therefore to possess an ergosphere. If we inject matter into this ergosphere and make it explode so that one of the pieces is captured by the black hole, the other piece can come out with increased energy, as we have indicated before. Thus, the mini-black hole can be used as a source of energy. Because of its small size, it conceivably is manipulable even by our present technology. For example, we could think of putting some charge on one. Charges can be manipulated with a magnet. Such a mini-black hole put in orbit around earth or other planets could then act as the source of energy for mankind for a long time, as imagined in John Varley's novel *The Ophiuchi Hotline* (Varley calls them "holons").

Arthur C. Clarke gives a vivid description of a mini-black hole in his book *Imperial Earth*. Clarke's black hole is human-made (he calls it a node), although it is extremely unlikely that we could ever carry out the manufacture of a mini-black hole; but perhaps you will like Clarke's style:

"Take a look," he said, when he was finally satisfied.

Duncan floated to the eyepiece and fastened himself rather clumsily in place. He did not know what he had expected to see, and he remembered that the eye had to be educated before it could pass intelligible impressions to the brain. Anything utterly unfamiliar could be, quite literally, invisible, so he was not too disappointed at his first view.

. . . for a few seconds he could still see nothing. Then he realized that a tiny bulge was creeping along the hairline as he tracked the microscope. It was as if he was looking at the reticule through a sheet of glass with one minute bubble or imperfection in it.

"Do you see it?"

"Yes—*just*. Like a pinhead-sized lens. Without the grid, you'd never notice it."

"Pinhead-sized! *That's* an exaggeration, if ever I heard one. The node's smaller than an atomic nucleus. You're not actually seeing it, of course—only the distortion it produces."

"And yet there are thousands of tons of matter in there." [italics in the original, p. 81]

Perhaps you are curious about the gravity force you would feel in the proximity of such a black hole. Since a mini-black hole is about as massive as a mountain, its gravity force at a distance is similar to that of a mountain, not much. Of course, if you get real close, the gravity force on you will increase, but as you know we never have to be worried about the magnitude of the average force on us. It's the tidal force that counts. Arthur C. Clarke talks about this also.

"What would happen," Duncan asked, "if I tried to touch it?"

"You know, absolutely *everyone* asks that question."

"I'm not surprised. What's the answer?"

"Well, you'd have to open the vacuum seal, and then all hell would break loose as the air rushed in."

"Then I don't do it that way. I wear a spacesuit, and I crawl up the drive tunnel and reach out a finger . . ."

"How clever of you to hit exactly the right spot! But if you did, when your finger tip got within—oh—something like a millimeter, I'd guess—the gravitational tidal forces would start to tear away at it. As soon as the first few atoms fell into the field, they'd give up all their mass-energy—and you'd think that a small hydrogen bomb had gone off in your face. The explosion would probably blow you out of the tube at a fair fraction of the speed of light." [italics in the original, p. 82]

A comment on the "node" drive of *Imperial Earth*, which is called the Asymptotic Drive in the book. It is proposed as a kind of reactionless drive. Although the description of the drive is as mysterious as can be to give it credibility, you will have no difficulty in figuring out that the drive can never work; it violates Newton's third law of motion. It's in the same class as the Dean drive.

THE POSSIBILITY OF SPACE AND TIME TRAVEL THROUGH THE BLACK HOLE

The name black hole creates an image in our minds of a hole in space—albeit black, difficult to find, and hazardous to investigate. If you are tuned to hyperspace thinking, you invariably will ask: can we go into hyperspace through the black holes? If we did, could we ever return? How about time travel? Parallel universes? And so forth.

The concept of black holes is the SF writer's supermarket. Physicists are the sellers. The merchandise consists of possible solutions to the SF writer's problems. Here are the specials on space and time travel that have earned the respectability of physics. Or have they?

Item: a method of travel to a parallel universe.

The geometry of the Schwarzschild black hole can be mathematically extended to what is called the maximal geometry. In the extended geometry, the black hole has a counterpart called the white hole. Matter cannot fall into the white hole, but can only go out; white holes are like cosmic geysers. Likewise, there is a counterpart to our universe, a counterpart we can call a parallel universe (Figure 35a). Mathematically, there is nothing to prevent the existence of such a parallel universe. Unfortunately, if you insist on the validity of physical laws as we know them, there is no possibility of any communication with this parallel universe. But if you are willing to inject a science fiction idea, that inside the black hole it is possible to travel with faster-than-light velocity, it may be possible to travel to this parallel universe.

Item: space travel to remote places of our own universe.

This is a variation of the above theme. Actually, there is no compelling reason why a tunnel through the black hole–white hole complex (called officially a "wormhole" or an "Einstein-Rosen bridge") should not lead to some other part of our own universe. Physicist John Wheeler devised a theory called quantum geometrodynamics, according to which—if gravity has a quantum nature—wormholes can exist in the fabric of space-time even without a black hole. Such wormholes (they are alluded to in Pohl's *Gateway*) can take you to other parts of the universe. One minor problem: wormholes are truly minuscule, matter has to be crushed or dematerialized (energized in *Star Trek* jargon?) before it can pass through a wormhole.

Item: time travel.

For time travel, you have to find a charged or rotating black hole. There are not supposed to be charged black holes in significant numbers, but most black holes, since they originate from the collapse of rotating stars, should be rotating. In a rotating black hole, apart from the ergospherical peculiarity, there are two horizons (Figure 35b). In between the two horizons, space becomes time and therefore a voyager loses his usual navigational freedom in traveling through space; there space moves on just as time does in our ordinary experience. But after crossing through the inner horizon, space and time interchange again, and two interchanges bring us back full cycle to ordinary space-time. It is now possible to choose space travel again, and you can choose to travel to the singularity or you can try to avoid it and get out. If you get out, you cannot retrace your path through the horizon, which is a one-way membrane, but will emerge into a future, parallel universe. People from the past can enter our present universe this way.

Item: travel to negative space.

If there are astronauts who really want to dare going where nobody has gone before, the rotating black hole furnishes another exotic idea. The "singularity" of a rotating black hole is not a point, but a ring. So it is perfectly possible to pass through the ring without encountering the singularity: just pass through the hole in the ring as a thread does through the eye of a needle. What is waiting for you on the other side? Mathematics says negative space, whatever that means. Some physicists translate negative space to mean a negative-gravity universe. So mathematically, at least, we can think of

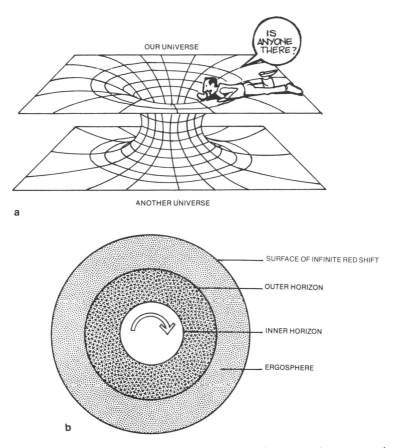

Figure 35. (a) Looking for a parallel universe? Unfortunately, it is much more complex than the figure indicates. (b) The different surfaces of a rotating black hole again, this time showing both the outer and inner horizons.

a negative-gravity universe or negative space and even of taking a trip to such an exotic place.

Actually, one can theorize even further. Once you are inside the negative space, you can rotate in a direction opposite to the direction of rotation of the black hole itself; then you will be going backward in conventional time. After doing this awhile, if you find your way out, you can travel to the past. Thus, theoretically speaking, the rotating black hole is something like a time tunnel. With its help, you can describe what is called a "closed time loop," and catch up with your own past. Note that this does not violate causality in our universe, since you can never return here.

Unfortunately, there are other physicists (the spoilers?) who don't believe in any of this mathematical, highly conjectural stuff. They abhor such things as closed time loops. Every SF reader who has read Heinlein's "All You Zombies" (Gunn, 1979), in which the same person is mother, father, and offspring—due to peculiarities of time travel—knows how exciting closed time loops can be, and how liberating. No longer would we be creatures bound by the rules of causality. Unfortunately, many physicists feel just the opposite. And they work diligently to close such exotic paths with suitable logic. Many claim that the routes to these parallel universes or hyperspace are all closed by today's physics.

Joe Haldeman, who has written a good novel called *The Forever War*, does use a black hole (he calls it a collapsar) for space travel, but with a twist: here's an excerpt (the hero of the book is talking):

Twelve years before, when I was ten years old, they had discovered the collapsar jump. Just fling an object at a collapsar with sufficient speed, and out it pops in some other part of the galaxy. It didn't take long to figure out the formula that predicted where it would come out: it travels along the same "line" (actually an Einsteinian geodesic) it would have followed if the collapsar hadn't been in the way—until it reaches another collapsar field, whereupon it reappears, repelled with the same speed at which it approached the original collapsar. Travel time between the two collapsars—exactly zero.

It made a lot of work for mathematical physicists, who had to redefine simultaneity, then tear down general relativity and build it back up again. [p. 7]

This is perhaps the safest approach an SF writer can take in using black holes in space travel stories. If some day—and it is certainly possible—somebody discovers new methods of space and time travel, an enlargement in the scope of the Einsteinian concepts of space-time spelled out in general relativity will certainly be needed, perhaps even a complete revision.

As it stands right now, at least one futurologist, Adrian Berry, feels that the technology of manufacturing a black hole, and hence traveling to remote corners of the universe, is in our hands already; we have only to get on with it. If you are interested in exploring Berry's idea, read his book, *The Iron Sun*.

WHERE ARE THEY?

How do we "see" a black hole? Since no light can come out of it and its frozen light halo around the horizon is too faint to see from afar, one of the few ways we can hope to see it is as a partner of another star forming a double-star system. If one of the components of a double-star system is invisible and massive, we can suspect that it may be a black hole. However, it could also be a neutron star or just a dead star. Fortunately, the black hole can do something special. It can continuously attract matter from the companion star into itself. Matter, as it falls into a black hole, gets very hot and emits X rays. A neutron star can also emit X rays, but a dead star cannot. However, a neutron star is expected to be only a couple of solar masses; an accurate determination of the mass of the invisible partner can rule out the neutron star option if the mass is found to be greater than, say, five solar masses. In addition, X rays coming from a neutron star are expected to be pulsed, since they are emitted by a different mechanism.

X rays are difficult to observe from the earth's surface. No matter. Astronomers have sent X-ray telescopes to space in a couple of missions. Both missions have discovered that there is an invisible massive star in the double-star system Cygnus X-1 which fits the black hole picture pretty well. X rays coming from it have been traced to a small, compact region. The X rays are not pulsed but instead fluctuate erratically. So this is a likely candidate for a black hole, although many physicists think otherwise. Only time will tell.

There is also some evidence that black holes, perhaps a million or so times heavier than our sun, inhabit the centers of some galaxies. Some physicists have further suggested that the huge energy that comes out from quasars is due to the infall of a star or two a year into the gravitational gullet of a black hole.

As for the mini–black hole, some people have suggested that one caused a catastrophe in Siberia in 1908. There is really no way to confirm this. And to date there is no evidence of any mini–black hole. Further clouding the issue is a recent suggestion by Hawking himself that mini–black holes actually decay away to nothingness, and that most have already done so since their creation. If Hawking is right, then our chance of seeing a mini–black hole from the early history of the universe is infinitesimal.

Most disturbingly, even for stellar-mass black holes, the implication of Hawking's theory may be devastating to the black hole scenario that we have built. Although Hawking originally calculated that a stellar black hole's decay time would involve 10^{66} years or so, physicist F. J. Tipler recently claimed that perhaps the decay time is as short as one second, even for massive black holes. Other physicists promptly refuted Tipler's work. It makes sense to me that, because of the intense time dilation effect near a black hole, faraway observers will "see" a black hole star's decay for a long time. But it might be that a black hole explorer who went to watch the black hole from up-close would not find the black hole; for him Tipler might have called the shot correctly, after all.

But these are all theories; what we need is observation.

A HOLE-Y DREAM

I was astounded. I didn't expect to see him there. Black Hole himself. "Well, Mr. Black Hole," I said, eager to begin a conversation, "you certainly have been in the news lately. What do you think was the turning point for your spiraling popularity?"

"Your society needs something to look forward to, I suppose. The usual escape syndrome," he muttered.

"But look forward to a black hole? One cannot even see you."

If you're wondering how I myself was able to see him, let me tell you. You can see the shadow of a black hole. This black hole was with his girl friend, a companion star. Very pretty. I could see his shadow on her.

"Precisely," Black Hole was answering me. "Your kind is always fascinated by the unseen, the unknown. Your whole culture glorifies the unknowable. Now where can you find anything as unknowable as I am?"

"True," I acknowledged. He had a point. However, I wanted some first-hand information rather than talk about humanity's myriad idiosyncrasies. So I fired another question. "Say, did any of your cousins cause that havoc in Siberia in 1908?"

Many people heard the sound of a big explosion in Siberia around 1908 when trees burned and land was upturned. I was referring to that incident, which has yet to be scientifically explained. The incident made the list of the most outstanding mysteries of this age, although some people have suggested that a minuscule black hole passing through the earth might have caused it.

Black Hole was noncommittal. "Maybe, maybe not." He was going to be difficult.

I changed the subject. "Who should get the real credit for your discovery?" I asked. "Pierre Simon de Laplace, who was the first to speculate on your existence? Or perhaps Einstein. You are really Einstein's protege, aren't you? It is his theory that gave you respectability. Or perhaps John Wheeler should get much of the credit. He acted as your agent for quite a while, didn't he? But maybe you're most partial to your latest agent, Stephen Hawking. After all, he humanized you. Now your kind can be manifest as a speck, a mini–black hole which lets us think even of harnessing your power."

Black Hole stopped me. "Who says I have been discovered? I don't want to be discovered. Once I am discovered, you guys will lose all interest in me."

Unfortunately, that was true. We humans are fickle in our fancies. Remember Neutron Star? His heyday lasted only a couple of years after his discovery. However, Black Hole is different; he is important to us. We may solve our energy crisis with his help. I reassured him, concluding, "In fact, why don't you sign this form so that I can officially declare your discovery?"

"No way! I am not going to sign any paper." Black Hole was adamant; I had to accept his decision. Perhaps the time is not yet ripe, anyhow, for his discovery. One more mystery would be gone. One less topic with which physics professors can create interest in the hardened hearts of their students.

"One last question," I said. "What is your relation to the Black Hole of Calcutta?"

"That does it!" He was visibly angry—I mean his shadow flickered. "Giving my holy name to that concocted incident of your history . . ." Black Hole vanished from my sight, taking his girl friend with him.

"Don't go! Don't go, Your Black Holiness!" I was shouting. Suddenly, I felt myself being shaken.

"What's all the commotion about?" My wife was speaking to me.

"Darling, black holes exist," I babbled excitedly. "I just spoke to one in my dream."

"You have a black hole in your head," she said.

chapter fourteen

Where Are the Universemakers?

Cosmology is the science that concerns itself with no less than the nature, origin, and the structure of the universe itself. Scientists have pondered such matters since the dawn of civilization; however, the observations that mark the beginning of modern cosmology are relatively recent. And also, although today the observational techniques used in cosmology are highly sophisticated, the observational data are of limited availability depending on the kindness of nature. We cannot reproduce at will any cosmological process, and thus cosmology remains a speculative science.

From the speculative nature of cosmology, you may assume that there should be abundant samples of cosmological ideas in science fiction. Unfortunately, this is not the case. Although eminent authors such as Edgar Allan Poe (in the story "Eureka") and Olaf Stapledon (in his novel *Star Maker*) have hypothesized on the nature and origin of the cosmos, their works are the exceptions. By and large, science fiction has been rather quiet about cosmology. We can speculate about why this is. The time scales involved in cosmology are far too great compared with human time scales. Thus it is difficult to blend cosmological ideas with those of human interest.

Although reluctant to propose new theories of the cosmos, science fiction writers should be given ample credit for keeping track of the major observational and theoretical breakthroughs that have occurred in the field. For example, by far the most spectacular observational feature of modern cosmology is the expansion of the universe. The expansion reveals itself in the fact that all other galaxies are found to run away from ours. Most physicists today accept a primordial explosion as the reason for the expansion, but an SF story written in 1935 (Edmond Hamilton's "The Accursed Galaxy"), before the scientific big bang theory took shape, is based on the idea that all other galaxies are fleeing from ours because we are infected with a disease called life. Sound utterly nonscientific? Perhaps it is an indication of how difficult it is to humanize cosmological events such as the expansion of the universe.

In 1948, SF writer Fred Brown wrote the novel *What Mad Universe?* in which he explored this question how does a science fiction fan fantasize the universe? In the novel, an editor was pondering what kind of universe a fan would dream up, when he suddenly was zapped with the explosion of a rocket into the fan's dream universe. It was a world where everybody read science fiction. But that was the good news. The bad news was that nobody called it science fiction any more, because

In a world where interplanetary and interstellar war and purple moon monsters were actual facts, cold reality, then stories about such things would be *adventure* stories, not science fiction at all.

Of course, you have to remember that this was in 1948.

THE EXPANDING UNIVERSE

The cosmological evidence for the expansion and the underlying big bang explosion came in three stages. First, in the last century, a German physician named Heinrich Olbers made a paradox out of a well-known fact: the night sky is dark. Second, in the twenties, American astronomer V. M. Slipher made some observations, and another American astronomer, Edwin Hubble, interpreted his data to indicate that, indeed, distant galaxies do seem to move away from ours. And third, if the expansion were due to a primordial big bang—a cosmical creation event not unlike the Biblical command, "Let there be light"—then we should be able to see that first-born light. And indeed in 1965, two American astrophysicists, Arno Penzias and Robert Wilson of the Bell Laboratory, accidentally discovered the fossil light from the big bang that bathes the universe. Let's now go into some details.

Why is the night sky dark? Olbers added some spice to this question by pointing out that in an infinite universe, the night sky should be very bright. (Actually, Olbers was not the first to suggest this, but the paradox has immortalized his name.) The paradox may defy our reasoning faculty a bit, because we expect the faraway stars to contribute less and less light to the luminosity of the night sky; in fact, the intensity of light does fall off inversely as the square of distance. Thus, the infiniteness of the cosmos seems irrelevant at first look. Olbers pointed out that there is a second factor; the number of faraway stars at a given distance from us increases as the square of the distance. The two factors then compensate for each other, and the light contributed to the total luminosity of the night sky by a spherical shell of stars at any distance is the same, irrespective of the distance (Figure 36a). Since in an infinite universe there are an infinite number of such spherical shells of stars, we must conclude that the night sky should be infinitely bright. Instead, the night sky is dark! This is the paradox.

The expansion of the universe provides us with a way out of this paradox because the frequency of the light from the faraway receding galaxies is lowered toward the red (via the Doppler effect). Light of lowered frequency has less energy, so the energy content of the light does decrease with distance; stars at infinite distance do not contribute the same energy or luminosity to the night sky as nearby stars, after all.

What Slipher discovered was this redshift of light from distant galaxies, except that he erroneously thought the light he examined was from nebulae, conglomerates of gases within our own Milky Way. Hubble interpreted Slipher's data correctly and, adding some new data to it himself, came up with a remarkable conclusion about the expansion: the speed of recession of the galaxies is directly proportional to their distance from us. If a galaxy is

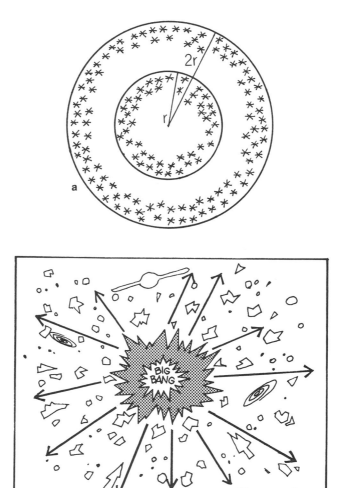

Figure 36. (a) At a distance 2r from us, the intensity of starlight that reaches us is less by a factor of four compared with the starlight from distance r. However, the number of contributing stars is four times greater at distance 2r. As a result of this compensation, we receive the same amount of light from both surfaces. Since for an infinite static universe the number of surfaces as shown is infinite, we should receive an infinite amount of starlight, and the night sky should be very bright. This is Olber's paradox. **(b)** The big bang. The distance traveled by one fragment relative to another should be equal to its velocity with respect to the other times the time of travel since the explosion.

twice as far, it recedes twice as fast. If we denote galactic velocity by v, and distance by R, Hubble's discovery can be summarized as

$$v \propto R$$

or, introducing a proportionality constant H (now called Hubble's constant)

$$v = HR$$

This mathematical relationship is known as Hubble's law.

Hubble's law can easily be understood if we assume that the universe began in an explosion, from a singularity. This assumption is the basis of the big bang model of the universe. In an explosion—of a bomb, for example—the various fragments are given greatly different velocities. If the velocities remain constant during the entire journey, then the distance traveled by one fragment relative to another should be given by the product of the relative velocity of the fragment and the time of travel (Figure 36b). The time of travel is given by the age of the universe, the time elapsed since the creation. Thus, according to the big bang theory, the galactic distance R is given as

distance of galaxy R = age of the universe $\times$ velocity of recession v

Now Hubble's relationship can be written in a similar form:

$$\text{distance of galaxy } R = \frac{1}{H} \times \text{velocity } v$$

The two expressions for R are identical if we identify the reciprocal of Hubble's constant, $\frac{1}{H}$, with the age of the universe.

Thus, the big bang theory not only gives an explanation of Hubble's law, there is even a bonus. We can determine the present age of the universe from the observationally determined value of Hubble's constant H. Unfortunately, H has never been known too well. The determination of H involves accurate estimates of galactic distances, very difficult to obtain in practice. Even the velocities, which are given accurately from the measurement of the Doppler shift, have to be corrected for special motions of the earth that are not part of the universal expansion. Some of these special motions—for example, the motion of our galaxy toward the Virgo cluster—have come to light only recently, and are not all well known.

The lower limit for the value of H is about 1.5×10^{-18} per second. This gives the age of the universe as

$$\frac{1}{H} = \frac{1}{1.5 \times 10^{-18}} \text{sec}^{-1} = \frac{10^{18}}{1.5} \text{ sec}$$

$$= \frac{10^{18}}{1.5 \times 3.2 \times 10^{7}} \text{ years} = 2 \times 10^{10} \text{ years}$$

or twenty billion years. Anyhow, this gives us an order-of-magnitude estimate of how long the universe has been around.

This is all very nice, but some physicists have contemplated alternatives to the big bang hypothesis. Let's face it. The big bang theory has at least one ugly aspect in its philosophy, best expressed through the following story about Saint Augustine. One day, Saint Augustine was giving a discourse on heaven, hell, creation—this kind of thing. A guy from the audience spoke up—in fact, challenged him. "Look, Augustine," he said, "you have told us that in the beginning God created heaven and earth. And then you have told us that God is immortal, with no beginning and no end. Can you tell me what God was doing before He created heaven and earth?"

So this is the problem with any creation model for the universe: what preceded the creation? Incidentally, Saint Augustine gave a rather sardonic but unscientific answer, "God was creating hell for people who ask such questions."

One way to avoid such questions is to make models in which the universe has neither a beginning nor an end. One such model is the once popular steady state model proposed by astrophysicists Fred Hoyle, Hermann Bondi, and Thomas Gold. (The same Fred Hoyle has written *The Black Cloud* and other SF novels.) In the steady state universe, the expansion is offset by the continuous creation of matter, which fills in the space left empty by the expanding matter. As a result, the universe always looks the same; the distribution of matter in any part of the universe is the same today as it has always been, even billions of years ago (Figure 37a). In contrast, according to the big bang theory, the matter of the universe thins out with time (Figure 37b). To be sure, the creation of matter in the steady state universe violates the law of conservation of energy, but the needed violation—the rate of creation of matter—is so small that it could never be detected from earth-based observations.

The steady state theory is philosophically attractive because it supports an age-old belief that the universe does not change with time, that it looks the same at all times. Incidentally, most present cosmologies accept a similar view about the matter distribution of the universe as far as space is concerned—that is, the matter distribution is believed to be the same everywhere in the universe. This is the cosmological principle. The steady state model hypothesizes a little more by demanding that the distribution of matter be the same not only at all places but also at all times. Charles Harness, in his 1968 novel *The Ring of Ritornel,* gives a penetrating exposition of the philosophy behind the steady state and other cosmological theories.

Unfortunately, the final word on theories is spoken not by philosophy, but by observations. And in 1965, a chance observation by Penzias and Wilson ruled out the steady state theory in favor of the big bang.

What Penzias and Wilson found is a microwave background that bathes the

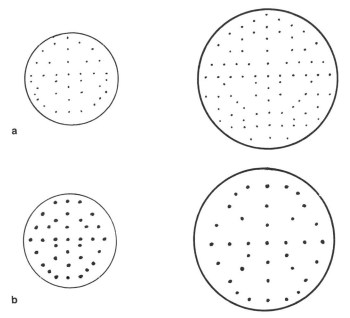

Figure 37. (a) In the steady state model of the universe, new matter is created as the universe expands, keeping the distribution of matter in any segment of the universe always looking the same. (b) The evolution of the universe according to the big bang model. The matter distribution thins out with universal expansion.

earth almost uniformly from all directions. It is then logical to assume that this background prevails throughout the entire universe. The radiation is found to have frequencies in the range 5×10^8 Hz to 5×10^9 Hz, typical of the thermal emission from a black body at a temperature of 3° on the absolute scale, or −270°C. Hence, the name "three degree radiation" is often given to it. The big bang theory predicts such a radiation background left over from the early, violent days of the universe. This radiation decoupled itself from the matter content of the universe when its temperature was about 5000°C, still very hot—as much as the surface of our sun today, but not hot enough to prevent the decoupling. The radiation has cooled since then due to the universal expansion and the resulting Doppler shift.

There are other ways than the steady state postulate to avoid Saint Augustine's consternation. One very interesting way for the universe to be timeless is the following. Suppose that the universe expands to a maximum size, and then contracts back to a collapse only to recreate itself and expand again. This picture is known as the cyclical model (Figure 37c). Here, on the whole, the universe is atemporal because everything repeats cyclically; of course, within each cycle the concept of progression of time exists, but there is no overall direction of time. The Hindus of ancient India proposed such a model. According to them, Brahma, the God of creation, starts the universe. The God Vishnu looks after it during its temporal cycle. The end of each cycle is

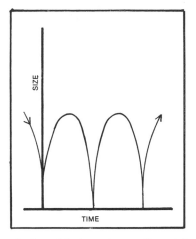

Figure 37(c). In the cyclical model, the universe alternately expands and contracts.

marked by destruction at the hands of Shiva, the king of the dancers. But the destruction is not permanent; Shiva himself declares the message of impending creation. Incidentally, if all these Hindu names are familiar to you, you must have read the novel *Lord of Light* by SF writer Roger Zelazny, who recreates the Hindu mythology in a quasi-scientific framework in this book.

This cyclical model has earned a lot of popularity with science fiction writers, perhaps because it provides an opportunity for humanizing cosmology. In *Tau Zero,* author Poul Anderson has described the plight of near-light-speed travelers in a spaceship who survive the end of the universe to begin life in a new universe. If you are curious about how this incredible feat is accomplished, the following excerpts will give you some idea. The first question is one of time. Here time dilation in the fast-moving reference frame of the ship is invoked to prolong the lives of the inhabitants beyond the end of the universe. Witness the following comment:

". . . we should be able to circle the shrinking universe repeatedly. . . . At a rough estimate, I would say that the time we experience . . . from now to the ultimate collapse, will be three months." [p. 171]

But time is not the only problem of survival. The scientists of the spaceship have further reason to worry:

". . . the universe does indeed oscillate. It will be reborn. But first all matter and energy must be collected in a monobloc of the highest possible density and temperature. . . . We can scarcely pass through the primordial nucleon. My personal suggestion is that we cultivate serenity." [p. 172]

But the hero of the novel maintains hope:

". . . That's the kind of oversimplification which helps our math along but never does tell a whole story. I think the central core of mass is bound to have an enormous hydrogen envelope, even before the explosion. The outer parts of that envelope may not be too hot or radiant or dense for us. Space will be small enough, though, that we can circle around and around the monobloc as a kind of satellite. When it blows up and space starts to expand again, we'll spiral out ourselves. . . ." [p. 172]

And, of course—as in all good stories—the hero was smarter than the doomsayers. The ship survived the creation as depicted in the following words:

They must hold *Leonora Christine* [the spaceship] well away from the growing monobloc, whose radiation would otherwise surely kill them; at the same time, they must stay where the gas was so dense that tau could continue to decrease for them, turning these final phoenix gigayears into hours; and they must keep the ship riding safely through a chaos that, did it ever strike her full on, would rip her into nuclear particles. No computers, no instruments, no precedents might guide them. It must be done on instinct and trained reflex.

Gradually Reymont entered the pattern, until he could steer alone. The rhthms [sic] of rebirth were wild, but they were there. Ease on starboard . . . now *push* that thrust! . . . brake a little here . . . don't let her broach . . . swing wide of that flame cloud if you can. . . . Thunder brawled. The air was sharp with ozone, and cold.

The screen blanked. An instant later, every fluoropanel in the ship turned simultaneously ultraviolet and infrared, and blackness plunged down. Those who lay harnessed alone, throughout the hull, heard invisible lightnings walk the corridors. Those in command bridge, pilot bridge, engine room, who manned the ship, felt a heaviness greater than planets—they could not move, nor stop a movement once begun—and then felt a lightness such that their bodies began to shake asunder—and this was a change in inertia itself, in every constant of nature as space-time-matter-energy underwent its ultimate convulsion—for a moment infinitesimal and infinite, men, women, child, ship, and death were one.

It passed, so swiftly that they could not tell if it had been. Light came back, and outside vision. The storm grew fiercer. But now through it, seen distorted so that they flew, fountaining off in two huge curving sheets, now came the nascent galaxies.

The monobloc had exploded. Creation had begun. . . . *Leonora Christine* . . . flew out into a reborn light. [italics in original, p. 179]

Tau Zero is a really remarkable story in the scope of its science. Yet most physicists will criticize the above scenario. It's impossible to be a spectator at the collapse of the universe, they would argue. Their rationale is based on a very fundamental ground, which I will now elaborate.

You see, many people, science fiction writers and some scientists among them, picture the big bang as the explosion of primordial matter from a center in a preexisting space. Likewise, the final collapse represents to them the implosion of this matter to a point, as if the space remains "out there" from the imploding matter. And when the matter reexplodes, the space outside receives the exploding matter as a mother does a child. And if you happen to stay out there in that space, why can't you survive this chaos?

But most physicists have an entirely different point of view of what actually happens. To them, the explosion—in the big bang or any re-creation of the universe—is one of space itself. And when the universe contracts, it is again the underlying space which contracts. In both expansion and contraction, the matter is simply carried back or forth by the contracting or expanding space, as the case may be. *All* matter is affected; this includes any spaceship. Nothing can escape the contraction and collapse; there is no "out there" where you can wait while space collapses.

If you are having difficulty with this way of looking at things, think of the expansion (or contraction) as that of a balloon on which galaxies are marked by ink dots. As the balloon expands, the ink dots separate because the fabric of the balloon expands between the dots. The same is true for the galaxies. The galaxies recede from each other because new space "grows" between them. It is space that expands. And in the event of collapse, it is space which is collapsed—and everything else with it.

Notice that this model is very clear on one thing: there is no center. From every vantage point of an expanding balloon, every other point appears to be receding. Thus, every point can be considered as a center, which is to say that none is.

This view that space does not preexist as a box in which matter comes and goes, but that space and matter both are created (and/or collapsed) is largely due to Einstein. In general relativity, it is the underlying geometry of space that determines the fate of the universe, its size and evolution. We will see in the next section how this comes about.

It should be noted in passing that the story line in *Tau Zero* is nevertheless not nonsensical. It presupposes that space is absolute, boxlike, and that matter just hangs in there, expanding or contracting or whatever. Matter does its thing, space remains unchanged. This is not the Einsteinian view, but never mind. In this absolute space picture, the collapse of the universe is a gravitational many-body problem, and mathematically you can find examples of solutions in which part of the universe can escape collapse. Freeman Dyson (1979), a physicist highly respected for his fertile imagination, speaks of this in yet another vein:

Suppose that we discover the universe [to be] doomed to collapse, is it conceivable that by intelligent intervention, diverting matter and radiation and causing energy to flow purposefully on a cosmic scale, [we might] change the topology of space time so that only a part of it would collapse and another part of it would expand forever?

Dyson admits, of course, that he doesn't know the answer. Nobody does. But it is important to realize that there may be an answer that goes against the grain of conventional Einsteinian wisdom and agrees more with Poul Anderson and *Tau Zero*.

THE CURVATURE AND FUTURE OF THE UNIVERSE

What does the theory of general relativity have to say about the expanding universe? Plenty, as Einstein himself realized back in 1915, when he was writing down the equations of curved-space geometry and gravity. Unfortunately, Einstein at the time had a pinch of what psychologists call "functional fixedness": the inability to perceive something new if it contradicts your belief system. Einstein had a belief that the universe is static, unchangeable with time. And thus, even if the solution of his general relativity equations—when applied to the entire cosmos—told him otherwise, he refused to see the implication of his result. Instead, he concluded that his equations as they stood did not apply to cosmology; there should be an additional term (now called the cosmological term) in his equations, which he then concocted. The added term made his solution for the universe static, and Einstein was happy.

But only for a short while. In a couple of years, another physicist showed mathematically that Einstein's static universe was not stable. And in a few more years, Hubble discovered the expansion of the universe, which Einstein's original equations had tried to tell him in the first place. When Einstein heard about Hubble's work, he called his own fudging of his equations "the worst blunder of my life."

General relativity, with some help from observational astronomy, can guide us to find answers to some of the most important questions of cosmology. Is the universe finite or infinite? Is the expansion going to stop some day, or will the universe expand forever? These questions can be tackled quite naturally within the context of general relativity. General relativity reframes these questions into one blanket paramount inquiry: what is the nature of the curvature of the entire cosmos—of space itself on a global scale?

Previously, we talked about curved space in connection with the curvature of space near a massive body. In curved space, the shortest distances between points are not "straight" lines, as in Euclidean geometry and flat space, but curved lines called geodesics. Let's now ask: how many kinds of curved space are possible for the universe as a whole?

The surface of a sphere is a two-dimensional example of one type of these curved-space geometries. On a spherical surface, the geodesics are the great circles, as any airline pilot should know. And you can readily verify that all great circles eventually meet each other, so there are no parallel lines on a spherical surface. Thus, this kind of curved-space geometry is characterized by the absence of parallel lines. This is the conceptual basis that led to the discovery of this "spherical" curved-space geometry by German mathematician Bernard Riemann. Spherical space is also called Riemannian space.

In contrast to the surface of a sphere, consider the surface of a saddle. Take a point P on the saddle (Figure 38a), and ponder how many "straight lines" you can draw through P that are parallel to (that is, never meet) a given line L. Of course, since the lines that you draw must be the shortest distances between points on the saddle, they are curved by ordinary standards. You will find that there are an infinite number of such lines. Thus, the saddle surface is a two-dimensional example of still another curved-space geometry.

Geometries of the spherical type define space of positive curvature, and those of the saddle type define space of negative curvature, whereas Euclidean geometry defines flat space—zero curvature. Question: how do we distinguish between these spaces in a more pragmatic, measurement-oriented fashion? The answer is to consider geometrical relationships involving figures in these spaces. For example, construct a triangle made up of "straight lines" in each of these spaces. In Euclidean space, the sum of the angles of a triangle is exactly equal to 180°. But in spherical geometry (Figure 38b), the space is bulged between the vertices of the triangle and this leads to an inflationary value for the sum of the angles; the sum is actually greater than 180°. In contrast, in the space of negative curvature, the angles of a triangle add to a sum of less than 180° (Figure 38a).

Operational ideas like these enable us to comprehend curved space even from within it. Author Dionys Burger has written a delightful story about curved space named *Sphereland,* in which he depicts the lives of imaginary two-dimensional people living on the surface of a sphere (they think they inhabit flat land). Then one day a creature from three-dimensional space comes and tells them that their world is curved. The result about the sum of the angles of a triangle tells us that we can discern between the three geometries even without the help of a creature from hyperspace, the supposed fourth dimension of space from which our "hypersphere" looks curved. We can construct a space triangle using a distant star, and the two positions of the earth in its orbit around the sun six months apart (Figure 38c). True, we cannot measure the apex angle $\angle A$, but we can measure the two base angles, $\angle B$ and $\angle C$. Since for very distant stars $\angle A$ is very small, we can ignore it and concentrate on the sum of $\angle B + \angle C$. If the sum of the base angles exceeds 180°, we must conclude that our space has a positive curvature. A result of the angles adding up to something less than 180° will lead to the conclusion that space has a negative curvature. And if perchance the base angles add up

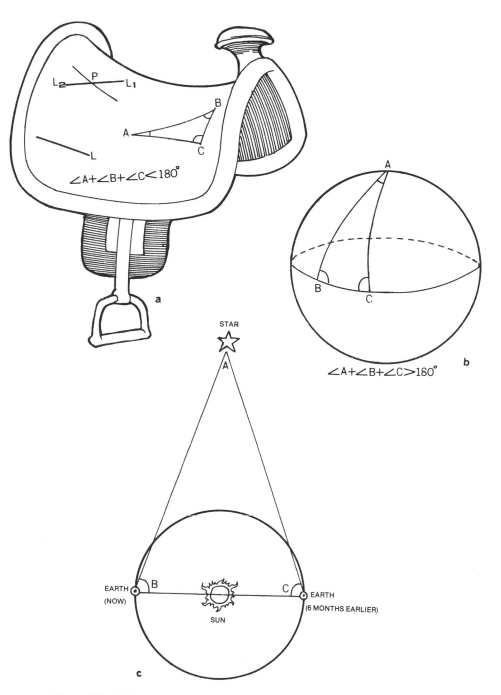

Figure 38. (a) Geometry on a saddle surface; it's different from Euclid's flat geometry. (b) The geometry on the surface of a sphere is also different from Euclid's. (c) If the sum of the base angles, when we look at a distant star in this fashion, is ever found to exceed 180°, it would be direct evidence that our cosmos obeys curved (spherical) geometry of positive curvature.

to 180°, we must accept the fact that Euclid was right, after all—space is flat.

Such measurements are now being carried out, with no definitive result as yet. Up to the explored distance of about 10^{20} m, there doesn't seem to be any deviation from Euclidean geometry. But this may mean that the result of the curvature of space becomes appreciable only at an even larger scale. The curvature of the cosmos is small!

Let's learn to visualize curved space. Thinking in terms of spherical and saddle two-dimensional surfaces may be confusing because we look at these things from outside, perceive them being curved extrinsically, whereas for the three-dimensional space we inhabit we have to perceive the curvedness intrinsically, from within. Something analogous to what mapmakers do can help us here; they know that in order to represent the curved surface of the spherical earth on a flat plane, they have to distort the scale. Thus, in the map, Canada looks bigger than the United States, although it is not. You can directly verify this distortion of scale by taking a portion of a basketball and trying to lay it flat on a table. You won't succeed unless you stretch the ends, just as the mapmaker does. So this is one way we can visualize space of positive curvature: we can think of it as space where the scale distorts, expanding at the edges.

How about negatively curved space? If you want to lay a portion of a saddle on a plane surface, you will discover that now you need to shrink the edges. So in a map of this kind of space in two dimensions, the scale distorts in such a way that it seems to have shrunk as we look farther and farther toward the edges, something like the drawing in Figure 39, which flowed from the genius of M. C. Escher.

Escher's picture makes one thing quite clear, that space of negative curvature is infinite; the scale gets shorter and shorter, but the space never ends. Flat space is also infinite, but here there is no distortion of the scale. In contrast, space of positive curvature is finite; here the geodesics do not extend to infinity but instead turn back on themselves.

Some words of caution here. Finiteness of space does not mean that space is bounded. Space obviously cannot have a boundary like a wall, because then you could always ask, What's on the other side of the wall? You could extend your hand while standing on this wall—and where would your hand be? No, space can be finite only because it has positive curvature. Just as the surface of a sphere (a two-dimensional space of positive curvature) has no boundary, neither does three-dimensional spherical space have any boundary. Think of it as a boundless (hyper-) surface of a four-dimensional sphere.

We now can understand what general relativity predicts about the future of the expansion of the universe. The future depends on the curvature of space. If space has a negative or zero curvature, the universe is infinite, and the expansion will go on forever. If, on the other hand, the curvature is positive,

Figure 39. The map of space of negative curvature, thanks to the genius of M. C. Escher. Called *Circle Limit III*, this drawing properly represents the distortion of scale inherent in drawing a two-dimensional map of a three-dimensional object of negative curvature. *(M. C. Escher, Circle Limit III, © Beeldrecht, Amsterdam/V.A.G.A. and Vorpal Gallery, Haags Gemeentemuseum—The Hague, 1981)*

the universe is finite; it can expand only to a maximum size, then start contracting and eventually collapse (Figure 40). The point of collapse is the SF writer's monobloc, or the mathematician's singularity.

Thus, if we could measure the curvature, we could know the future of the universe. Since the prospect is dim of directly measuring the curvature in the cosmic scale needed, people have tried to figure out things in an indirect fashion. The curvature of space is determined in general relativity by the

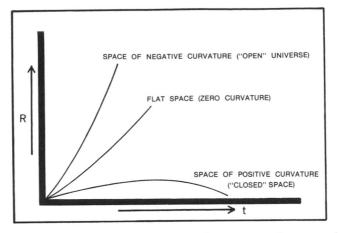

Figure 40. The expansion of the universe can be represented on a graph of the size parameter *R* (the ordinate) against cosmic time *t* (the abscissa). The three curves correspond to the three possible geometries of space.

cosmic energy density itself. If there is sufficient energy density, then space will be finite with positive curvature and the expansion of the universe will be arrested. On the other hand, if the energy density is not large enough, space will be open, with negative or zero curvature, and the expansion will continue forever. Unfortunately, determining the energy density is not easy, either, because it is very hard to account for some of the energy—that which doesn't reside in the matter of the galaxies or in the radiation background.

So here we are, very uncertain about our cosmological future. Although astronomers have not given up on this—far from it—I wish all of us would join in the effort. We could use some entirely new ways of thinking here.

THE CYCLICAL UNIVERSE

It is the astronomers and the physicists who are confused about whether the universe will turn back from its present expansion, and if so, whether it will ever bounce back again. Science fiction writers are more enthusiastic about the idea of the cyclicity of the universe. In his novel *The Final Programme*, the first of the Jerry Cornelius sagas, Michael Moorcock has one of his characters quote ancient Hindu mythology to reinforce the idea of a cyclical universe:

"The *manvantara* is divided into four *yuga*, or ages. The current cycle is nearing its end. The present age is the last of four."

"And what are they?"

"Oh, let me think . . . The *Satya Yuga*, the Golden Age. That accounted for the first four tenths of the cycle. Then we had the *Dwaparu Yuga*, the Second

Age. That took care of another 864,000 years. The Third Age—the *Tretya Yuga*—can you hear the echoes of an ancient common language?—lasted for only two tenths of the whole cycle. The *Kali Yuga,* of course, is the current age. It began, as I recall, on February 18, 3102 B.C." . . .

"Then at the end of the *manvantara* the cycle repeats itself, does it? The whole of history all over again!"

"Some believe so. . . . The strange thing is that modern physics begins to confirm these figures—in terms of the complete revolution of the galaxy and so on. I must admit that the more I read of the papers published these days, the more confused I become between what I was taught as a Hindu and what I have learned as a physicist. It requires increasing self-discipline to separate them in my mind." [italics in the original, p. 11]

There is a symbolic reason for Moorcock to mention this idea at the beginning of his novel, since he creates Jerry Cornelius and company in a sort of cyclical reality: they are destroyed at the end of a story only to be recreated again in the next. Their existential dance is choreographed repeatedly, each time with new steps, but the basic music doesn't change.

Can the universe really be this way? General relativity, even for space of positive curvature, does not predict an oscillating universe, only expansion and subsequent collapse. There exists no mechanism in general relativity itself that leads to a re-creation event, such as is so popular with some science fiction writers.

Physicists have come up with some tentative ideas for a mechanism of bounce from the collapse. One idea is to use the cosmological term (the term that Einstein called his "greatest blunder") in the equations of motion of the universe. In this case there is a solution to the equations where the universe contracts and then expands, but it never contracts all the way to a singularity. But the solution has defects and is suspect.

Another idea is to invoke considerations of quantum mechanics. Unfortunately, physicists so far have not been able to formulate a quantum theory of gravity, although the belief is strong that when such a quantum theory is discovered, it will provide us a bouncing remedy.

Still another idea is to say that continuous creation, à la steady state theory, operates in tandem with the big bang and general relativity. Such continuous creation of matter can be expected from a symmetry principle. Expansion means, in general relativity, creation of new space. If space and matter in a cosmological theory should have the same footing—identical importance (as the philosophy behind general relativity dictates)—then creation of space should be accompanied by the creation of matter as well. Such creation of matter at a varying rate can lead to a bounce.

I want to develop a fourth, and I think compelling, reason at some length. We are all aware that time is a one-way street—going from the past through the present into the future, and not the other way. Surprisingly, the equations of physics do not display this asymmetry of time; usually they are time-symmetric. Thus if a process can be shown to occur one way in time, these equations of physics also permit the process to go the opposite way in time. So if we make a cause-effect description of a future-preserving event, in the time-reversed process, cause and effect also are reversed. This is against the principle of causality—that cause must precede effect—and thus many physicists feel that it is causality which precludes the time-reversed process.

If a light source emits light, we find the light waves emerging outward from the source. But in his fantasy novel, *A Voyage to Arcturus*, author David Lindsay writes about a different kind of light beam:

"What are back rays?"
"Light that goes back to the source," muttered Nightspore.
"And what kind of light would that be?" [p. 32]

Strangely, the mathematics of physics answers this question: advanced light. In physics, regular light waves that diverge from a source are called retarded waves, and light waves that go back to the source are called advanced waves. Mathematically, both kinds of waves are allowed. But since most physicists are partial to the causality principle, which no one yet has proved, they simply disregard the advanced wave. And experimental data on wave propagation seem to bear them out.

However, there are a number of people who believe in a different sort of principle. Novelist T. H. White triggered this train of thought. In his novel *The Once and Future King*, about young King Arthur and his mentor, the magician Merlin, White created a scene in which Arthur (with Merlin's help) has become an ant and is investigating an ant colony. Above each tunnel leading to the ant castle, Arthur sees the following boldly written words: "Everything not forbidden is compulsory."

According to some physicists, if advanced waves are not forbidden by some agency, then they are compulsory. According to them, causality does not forbid advanced waves; it is the other way around. Because advanced waves are cancelled by some other agency, the world appears to us as causal. These physicists believe that there must be a universal conspiracy of sorts that cancels the advanced waves.

Physicists of no less stature than Nobel Laureate Richard Feynman and his doctoral advisor John Wheeler have suggested that the advanced waves in each case of wave emission are cancelled by opposite advanced waves sent forth by the universe itself. But then, responds physicist Jayant Narlikar, there is a problem. Not all models of cosmology allow a universe that is capable of producing just the right cancellation of the advanced waves. For example, the forever-expanding universe model does not. Narlikar votes in favor of the steady state universe, which does have such an allowance. Unfortunately, the steady state theory has been ruled out for all practical purposes by other evidence.

For the oscillating model, Narlikar says the mathematics is ambiguous. That is, in a cyclical universe it is possible, though not inevitable, that advanced waves are cancelled. And this is just fine for those who would like the universe to oscillate between expansion and contraction. Although mostly causal, acausality is not ruled out in a cyclical universe.

One final quotation from the science fiction literature about a re-creation event will end this chapter. It is interesting here that James Blish, in *The Triumph of Time,* talks about continuous creation *and* the big bang from a monobloc, and bounce.

Amalfi lifted his glass reflectively. It was silky in his fingers; the Hevians made fine glass.

"This frame of reference I'll find myself in," Amalfi said. "It will really have no structure at all?"

"Only what you impose on it," Retma said. "It will not be space, and will have no metrical frame. In other words your presence there will be intolerable—"

"Thank you," Amalfi said drily, to Retma's obvious bafflement. After a moment the scientist went on without comment: "What I am trying to say is that your mass will create a space to accommodate it, and it will take on the metrical frame that already exists in you. What happens after that will depend upon in what order you dismantle the suit. I would recommend discharging the oxygen bottles first, since to start a universe like our present one will require a considerable amount of plasma. . . . As the last act, discharge the suit's energy; this will, in effect, touch a match to the explosion."

"How large a universe will be the outcome eventually?" Mark said. "I seem to remember that the original monobloc was large as well as ultra-condensed."

"Yes, it will be a small universe," Retma said, "perhaps fifty light years across at its greatest expansion. But that will be only at first. As continuous creation comes into play, more atoms will be added to the whole, until a mass is reached sufficient to form a monobloc in the next contraction. Or so we see it; you must understand that this is all somewhat conjectural. . . . [*Cities in Flight,* p. 579]

And so it is, quite conjectural. But it makes a fascinating story.

chapter fifteen
Taking the Quantum Jump

Just as the relativity theories taught us new ways to look at space and time, quantum mechanics forces us to take a new look at the nature of reality itself. Quantum mechanics is the domain of nature where uncertainty, probability, and indeterminacy reign; in it we see the beginning of new paradigm. The old order, "yielding place to new," to quote Alfred Lord Tennyson, changed with the discovery of quantum phenomena. The new order is characterized by discontinuity, jumps from one level of energy to another that are called quantum jumps. Has science fiction taken the quantum jump?

SF writers have a problem. The domain of the new quantum physics is the world of submicroscopic particles—electrons, atoms, and such. In the macro world, where most SF stories take place, it is classical Newtonian mechanics that holds true most of the time. Quantum effects in the macro world are infrequent and subtle in character. So what does the SF writer do?

Take a quantum jump, of course. No one says that the reality of the science fiction writer, the reality of his story, must always be in one-to-one correspondence with our familiar reality. The writer can speculate about new worlds where the quantum reality is the going thing not only for microscopic objects but also for macro objects. This is one way of taking a quantum jump.

But there is something about the quantum jump itself that makes us wonder: could we build a machine that would enable us, macro objects, to take such a jump? There are popular SF stories that capitalize on an affirmative answer to this question. What these writers have invented is no less than a new method of space travel. Of course, it's all fictional now, but in the far future who can tell?

One thing I can say for sure: although the concept of the quantum jump has been around for about seventy years now, it remains as exciting and provocative as when new. To see what's exciting about it, let's start with a discussion of the atom; it was the study of the atom that led to the discovery of the quantum jump.

WHAT'S INSIDE THE ATOM?

What is the nature of reality in the microphysical domain? In this are we truly guided by well-known archetypes? Psychologist Carl Jung especially mentions the Tibetan Mandala (Figure 41), which depicts the microcosm and the macrocosm in the same picture. A similar idea is that, by reducing the dimensions of objects in the macroworld, we can get a fairly good idea of how the

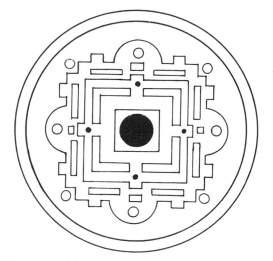

Figure 41. A Tibetan mandala (improvised).

microworld looks. Mathematically, this process is called scaling; changing the geometrical dimensions of an object without changing its shape.

Jonathan Swift, considered by some a true precursor of the science fiction writer, gave us *Gulliver's Travels* based on this scaling idea. His Lilliputians are scaled-down versions of humans. In fact, the adventures of the incredible shrinking man, the famous SF character, are based on the "Gulliver effect," world within world within world. If you want to read other SF stories based on this world-within-world idea, try "He Who Shrank" by Henry Hasse, "Microcosmic God" by Theodore Sturgeon or, one of the best stories of this kind, "The Diamond Lens" by Irish writer Fitz-James O'Brien. This last story is narrated by a young microscope maker who, not surprisingly, wants to build the most powerful microscope ever. Following instructions from a spirit (received through a medium), the narrator steals a 140-carat diamond, passes an electric current through it, and constructs the perfect ("science fictiony") microscope. He then looks through it:

On every side I beheld beautiful inorganic forms, of unknown texture, and colored with the most enchanting hues. These forms presented the appearance of what might be called, for want of a specific definition, foliated clouds of the highest rarity; that is, they undulated and broke into vegetable formations, and were tinged with splendors compared with which the gilding of our autumn woodlands is as dross compared with gold. . . .

While I was speculating on the singular arrangement of the internal economy of Nature, with which she so frequently splinters into atoms our most compact theories, I thought I beheld a form moving slowly through the glades of one of the prismatic forest. . . .

It was a female human shape . . . I cannot, I dare not, attempt to inventory the charms of this divine revelation of perfect beauty. Those eyes of mystic violet, dewy and serene, evade my words. Her long, lustrous hair, following her glorious head in a golden wake, like the track sown in heaven by a falling star, seems to quench my most burning phrases with its splendors.... [Cournos, 1967]

I hope you get the idea. One can see in the inner world of matter what one wants to see. What would a scientist expect to see? To a physicist, the most beautiful symbol of the macro world is the solar system, with the sun as the center around which the planets travel. This picture was one of the starting points of modern science. Thus, when physicists found that the atom resembles a tiny solar system, their ecstasy was as overwhelming as that of the microscopist of "The Diamond Lens." The atom has a central core, the nucleus, which carries almost all its mass, but is about 100,000 times smaller in size than the overall atom. Orbiting this nuclear sun are other tiny pointlike particles called electrons, which are the analogue of planets in the atom. In the macro world the gravity force keeps the planets orbiting instead of flying off on tangents pursuing their natural motion. In the micro world, gravity plays no role. The nucleus holds the electrons in orbit by means of electrical interactions. The nucleus is positively charged, whereas the electrons carry a negative electrical charge; the attraction between the positive and negative charges gives the electrons the force toward the center necessary to keep their orbits.

Thus, the atom is not quite a miniaturized version of the solar system; the force is different. Actually, many other things are different also. Physical attributes do not necessarily scale following the same rules of scaling as size or volume. Let's discuss this point a little further, going back to the Gulliver stories of Swift. Can the giant of Brobdingnag be a scaled-up version of a human? The answer is no, and here's why. Suppose a giant creature of Brobdingnag is a 10 times scaled-up version of a human. How much is his weight compared to a human's? Weight is the product of mass and g, the acceleration of gravity. The value of g is fixed on earth, so weight scales as mass. But mass is the product of volume and density of the body. If you assume the giant is made of human tissue, then the density of the giant's body material is the same as a human's and doesn't change in scaling. Thus, mass (and therefore weight) really scales as the volume. But volume is the quantity of three-dimensional space occupied by the body; it's equal to the cube of the linear dimension. When the linear dimensions are changed by a factor of 10, the volume must change by the factor of 10^3, or a thousand; so the weight of the Brobdingnag giant is a thousand times that of an ordinary human being.

Unfortunately, the giant's bone structure cannot support such an increase in weight. This argument also is based on scaling, this time the scaling law of the strength of the bone structure. When an external force acts on a bone, stresses are set up in it. These internal stresses bring the bone back to its original shape after the deforming external force is removed. It turns out that the relevant quantity is external force per unit area, which is then taken as the measure of stress. Now if the bones of the giant are made up of the same stuff as ours, then the stresses are the same also. The external force that his bones can support is equal to the stress times his area. But the stress doesn't scale (assuming the bone material is the same); thus, the force the bones can support scales as the area. Area is the square of a linear dimension and scales as the square of the same. Thus, when we scale up a human 10 times, the area goes up by a factor of 10^2 or 100. So, whereas the giant's bone structure can support only 100 times greater weight, his actual weight has increased one thousandfold. Such a giant obviously is structurally unstable.

What is the moral of this story? You cannot just scale up or down from one realm of reality to another, because not all physical quantities scale the same way. The Brobdingnag creature must be made of bones structurally much stronger than human bones (or, like the bones of a dinosaur, much thicker than simple scaling would suggest).

So although the microworld of the atom has a superficial similarity to the solar system, we must not expect the physics to be the same. Initially, many physicists had misgivings about this. But after three decades of concentrated research, it became clear that the physical principles that apply to this world within a world are radically different from those that apply to the solar system. This new physics is quantum mechanics.

ATOMS, LIGHT, AND THE QUANTUM JUMP

Danish physicist Niels Bohr had a few personal reasons for unhappiness when he was a postdoctoral research associate under the guidance of the celebrated British physicist Ernest Rutherford. Many people had difficulty with Bohr's accent, which made young Niels self-conscious in communicating with his peers. Moreover, Rutherford wanted Niels to work on an experimental project that his heart wasn't in. He was a theorist in his approach to physics, you see.

But his years in England were well-spent for just one thing. He learned about the solar-system model of the atom, which Rutherford had developed. Bohr felt that Rutherford's thinking about the atom as a tiny solar system could not be literally true. An electron going around the nucleus in an orbit as a planet does around the sun is an accelerated electron. Such an electron must radiate light, according to classical physics. However, if the electron loses energy by radiating light, its orbit must shrink and eventually the electron must fall into the nucleus. Thus, a literal solar-system model of the atom as envisioned by Rutherford is not stable.

In making a picture of the atom that is stable, Niels Bohr was the first to inject the quantum idea into the model of the atom. In a paper published in 1913, he said that an atomic electron can assume only a set of discrete values of energy—its energy is "quantized." If this sounds difficult to comprehend, an everyday example of such quantization is provided by our monetary system; money exchange can take place only in denominations of a cent, which is the quantum of monetary exchange. Adding pennies together, we build the ladder of coins, such as the nickel, dime, and so forth. According to Bohr, the atomic orbits are not continuous, but instead they form a discrete energy ladder for the electrons (Figure 42). Additionally, Bohr postulated that an electron cannot radiate energy when in one of the orbital "energy levels," the state of the electron when in one of these levels is stationary, nonchanging. Only when an electron jumps from a higher level to a lower one, from a faraway orbit to an orbit closer to the nucleus, is energy emitted. (Energy will have to be absorbed by the electron to jump from a lower level to a higher one.) And when the electron is in its lowest orbit, the "ground" energy level, it is stable because there is no lower level to which it can go. This explains the stability that atoms exhibit.

The jump from a higher level of the electron's energy staircase to a lower one is a quantum jump. According to Bohr, light is emitted when an electron makes such a quantum jump, as described in the following poem, "The Tuning Fork," by Louise McNelle:

> Hush—the electrons sing
> Dropping
> Down
> Through their orbits
> From ring
> To glowing ring
> Lower
> And lower
> Hush—

Light is the music the electrons make when they jump, but surprisingly we know nothing else about the electrons while they make their jumps. If you ask a physicist where an electron is during its jump, the physicist will stay mum or murmur something to the effect that it's none of our business, since what the electron does between jumps has no measurable significance; you should be happy that you have some idea where the electron is before and after the jump.

We can wonder if this bizarre phenomenon of the quantum jump gave the idea of "jaunting" to SF writer Alfred Bester. I am, of course, referring to the incredible Gully Foyle in *The Stars My Destination,* who could "jaunt" instantly from one definite station to another, but in between was nowhere to be found. This is very much like the quantum jump of the electron, and the idea has been used with even more sophistication in such novels as Poul Anderson's *Ensign Flandry,* Clifford Simak's *Way Station,* and James Blish's *Star Trek*–based *Spock Must Die.*

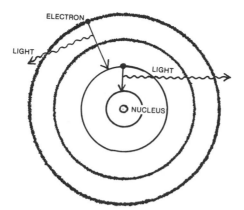

Figure 42. The energy ladder of the Bohr atom, and quantum jumps, each from one of its steps to another.

In Poul Anderson's *Ensign Flandry,* one of the characters explains hyperspace travel as:

". . . A series of quantum jumps which do not cross the small intervening spaces, therefore do not amount to a true velocity and are not bound by the light-speed limitation." [p. 91]

Later in the same novel, we find a little added elaboration:

"We travel faster than light by making a great many quantum jumps per second, which don't cross the intervening space. You might say we're not in the real universe most of the time, though we are so often that we can't notice any difference." [p. 208]

Since the *Star Trek* transporter is the best known of the supposed quantum-jump devices, let's talk about this. If you have watched even a single *Star Trek* episode on TV, you already know that the transporter works by energizing the body of a human or other object. "The transporter turns our bodies into energy and then reconstitutes the matter at the destination," explains Dr. McCoy in *Spock Must Die.* Engineer Scott explains things differently:

"What the transporter does is analyze the energy state of each particle in the body and then produce a *Dirac jump* to an equivalent state somewhere else. No conversion is involved—if it were, we'd blow up the ship." [my italics, p. 3]

McCoy's explanation follows the literal meaning of "energizing," which, of course, as pointed out in an earlier chapter, doesn't work since it would violate the conservation of baryon number—unless, of course, you make an antimatter prototype of the body and annihilate it with the original. This *would* blow up the *Enterprise,* as Scott says. But Scott's explanation is more sophisticated. He sees the function of a transporter as a quantum jump (Dirac is the name of a prominent physicist connected with quantum mechanics). In my judgment this gives the transporter an aura of respectability.

My point is this. We do not, in spite of a fifty-year-old study of the subject, understand the quantum jump to everyone's satisfaction. Since we do not understand its nature, we can speculate. And such speculations do not necessarily exclude machines like the transporter. I have one misgiving, however, which has to do with causality. Quantum jumps of single electrons turn out to be acausal—they cannot be predicted or caused with certainty at a given instant. Quantum mechanics, as I will elaborate below, is a probabilistic theory. Although you could predict the time of transporter jumps of a hundred million Spocks on the average, when a single Spock will make the jump just cannot be known in advance. You can readily see that this could cause an enormous problem to the usual action-adventure format of *Star Trek* story lines.

Coming back to physics, what is responsible for the discreteness of the energy that an atomic electron can have? Why can't the electron assume any old energy value in between two allowed steps? German physicist Max Planck had suggested in 1900 that light has a graininess, a discrete quantum nature. Einstein called the quanta of light "photons." Since light is emitted when an atomic electron makes a quantum jump, then if light energy is quantized, it makes sense that the electron's energy should also be quantized.

French physicist Louis de Broglie made the final connection. Being a lover of symmetry, he surmised that if light can be both wave and particle, then why can the electron not be both particle and wave? Being also a lover of music, he was keenly aware that musical notes have an inherent discreteness. If we strike a note on a piano, what we hear is a combination of several notes—a fundamental note of lowest frequency which determines the pitch of the music heard, and a discrete bunch of harmonics whose frequencies are integral multiples of the fundamental note; the admixture of these harmonics determines the quality, the character that distinguishes a musical note played on one instrument from the same note played on another. People who study music understand these things perfectly. They say that the discrete structure arises because musical instruments have confined waves. Said de Broglie, let's assume that the atomic electrons are confined waves.

De Broglie's idea, refined by several other physicists, developed into quantum mechanics—the rule book in the atomic world. The basis of this new mechanics is a new kind of duality; that light and electrons (and other submicroscopic objects) consist of both waves and particles: they are "wavicles." To an examination of this duality and of the experimental evidence for it, especially, we now turn our attention.

LIGHT QUANTA AND MATTER WAVES

Ordinarily, we perceive light as rays, but when we look deep we discover that light consists of waves; it is traveling disturbances—not localized, but spread out like water waves. For example, recall looking at a distant street light through an umbrella: you see not just a central spot, but a whole pattern of light dots. So light does not always propagate as rays, after all; like waves it bends around obstacles, displaying a phenomenon called diffraction. (The same phenomenon lets us hear sound waves around a corner.) It is light diffraction that causes the pattern you see when looking through an umbrella at a point source of light.

Regarded as a wave phenomenon, light energy is expected to be continuous, capable of subdivision to as small a unit as we desire. Yet, experimentally, there is also a certain graininess about light's energy. A grain of light energy is a particle, a quantum, of light: a photon.

All you need to convince yourself of the graininess of light is an analysis of the process of seeing in dim light. When we see objects in dim light we do not see sharp outlines; the shapes of objects are not distinct but seem to merge into each other. If light were continuous energy, then some light from the objects we view would always illuminate the optical receptors of our eyes. Of course, the contrast between light and dark would not be so good in dim light because of low intensity, but this would have no effect on the sharpness. Yet it is the sharpness that is most affected. If light consisted of photons, then dim light would mean fewer photons falling on the eye. Fewer photons means the stimulation of only a few receptors at any one time, the ones that are hit by a photon. Instead of all the receptors being excited at any one time, as in the wave picture, in the quantum picture only a few receptors—too few to give us a sharp outline—are stimulated simultaneously.

The question may occur to you, why can't the brain put together the fragmented information from the few receptors that fire at one time by waiting until it has all the info? Alas, this doesn't work because the receptors store the information for only a brief moment, not long enough for the brain to compile the information into a sharp outline. So every time you wave good-bye to a friend in twilight, watching his silhouette become more and more obscure as he moves away, you really are witnessing the quantum nature of light.

Thus, it is an experimental fact that light is dual, it has both a wave and a particle nature. Which nature is revealed on a particular occasion depends on the situation. Quantitatively, the wave and particle pictures of light are connected through a mathematical equation (discovered by Max Planck himself), which expresses the energy E of a photon in terms of the frequency ν (the Greek letter nu)—the number of wave cycles per second of the light wave:

$$E = h\nu$$

Here h is a fundamental constant of nature, known as Planck's constant, and has an extremely small numerical value in conventional units. It is this smallness of h that obscures the dual aspects of light and other submicroscopic objects. (If you find it difficult to remember the important quantum relationship $E = h\nu$—which is as important as Newton's $F = ma$ and Einstein's $E = mc^2$—the following true story may be of some comfort. Once a professor was giving a test. Pointing to the formula $E = h\nu$ written on the blackboard, the professor asked a student, "What is ν?" "Planck's constant," came the [wrong] answer. The puzzled professor queried, "Then what is h?" "The length of the plank," replied the unabashed student.)

Let's now discuss matter waves. At the macroscopic scale we experience matter as localized, but how about particles of the submicroscopic world, such as electrons? Is an electron always localized, always behaving as a particle, as it does when it leaves clearly defined tracks in the cloud chamber? The electron has a definite mass and a charge; it is hard to imagine how the mass and charge of the electron could be spread out. Only experiments can tell us for sure. What we seek are suitable umbrellas through which to look at electrons.

Since electrons are constituents of atoms, it is easy to guess that in order to see electron diffraction, the grid of the umbrella must be of atomic dimension, and that means the minuscule size of 10^{-10} m. Fortunately, there are substances known as crystals in which the atoms are arranged in a regular pattern in three dimensions (a three-dimensional umbrella!) separated by distances of about the same order as the atomic sizes. And indeed, it is found that when electrons are allowed to pass through a crystal, they too show a diffraction pattern (Figure 43). Thus, electrons do have a wave nature. Like light, they too are dual. In fact, objects in the submicroscopic domain of nature all possess this duality; they have both wave and particle characteristics: they are all wavicles.

The quantitative relationship between the wave and particle behavior of electrons was discovered by Louis de Broglie. It connects the electron's momentum (the product of mass and velocity) with the wavelength (the crest-to-crest distance) of the electron wave:

$$\text{de Broglie wavelength} = \frac{\text{Planck's constant}}{\text{momentum}}$$

Notice the appearance again of Planck's constant in this relationship.

If matter is waves in the microscopic scale, we can wonder if some of the wave properties persist even in the macro scale. Wouldn't it be nice to be able to drive a car in Eugene, Oregon, while one little part of me is strolling through Central Park in New York City? Unfortunately, this is unlikely. If you use de Broglie's formula for calculating the wavelength of macro matter, you discover that the wavelengths are of the order of 10^{-33} m. This is infinitesi-

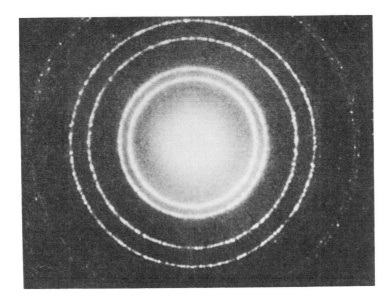

Figure 43. Diffraction pattern of electron waves. *(Courtesy: J. T. Shipman)*

mally small compared to the dimensions of macro matter. The net result is that the wave characteristic gets suppressed.

But, of course, this is true in the real world as we know it. Suppose there were pockets of the world where quantum effects were much larger; for example, suppose Planck's constant h were much greater in value through some kind of quantum inflation. If you have the imagination of Kurt Vonnegut, you would call each of these imaginary pockets a "chrono-synclastic infundibulum." To understand what that means, read his book *The Sirens of Titan*; it's all explained there.

Winston Niles Rumfoord had run his private spaceship right into the heart of an uncharted chrono-synclastic infundibulum two days out of Mars. Only his dog had been along. Now Winston Niles Rumfoord and his dog Kazak existed as wave phenomena—apparently pulsing in a distorted spiral with its origin in the Sun and its terminal in Betelgeuse.

The earth was about to intercept that spiral. [p. 13]

How does a quantum physicist observe an electron that exists as a wave? By intercepting its path with a cloud of dust: for example, in a cloud chamber. The electron will become localized and show us its track. When earth intercepts the wave of Mr. Rumfoord and his dog, they too become localized for others to see them. Vonnegut knows his physics!

You are not satisfied. Trying to think of electrons—objects with definite mass and definite charge—as waves can be hazardous to your mind, but you will not be happy until you understand how this can be.

Try to remember the case of light waves. There too you went through a temporary deadening of your senses when the statement was made that light waves exist without a medium. In trying to understand light we were forced to examine a new nonmaterial concept of field. Perhaps, an examination of the nature of electron waves will lead to something new.

It does. It was Erwin Schrödinger who first studied matter waves mathematically in the mid-twenties; his equation is now called the Schrödinger equation. Like Newton's $F = ma$ in classical physics, the Schrödinger equation enables us to figure out the time development of a quantum system. In Schrödinger's treatment, matter waves appear to be a multitude of simple waves. Call this wave combination a wave packet. Schrödinger was able to show mathematically that these wave packets, although capable of remaining localized for a short time, eventually spread out over a large region of space. This is, of course, what we see on the photographic plate in a diffraction experiment, but there is a problem. How can we associate an individual electron with a multiple of spots on the diffraction photograph? In fact, the electron has a charge, and whenever experimenters try to measure where an electron's charge is located, they always find it highly localized. Doesn't it then make sense to say that one single electron is responsible for just one spot on the photographic plate? But then how do we explain a multitude of spots?

One way to answer all these questions is to borrow a notion from statistics—the notion of probability—as German physicist Max Born did. The electron wave is not like a water wave, physically spreading everywhere; instead, it is a probability wave—it gives us the probability that the measurement of the electron's position (or momentum or other such quantities) would obtain a certain value. The diffraction spots on the photographic plate correspond to those locations where the electron's wave amplitude—called its wave function—is large. These are the places where the electrons are most likely to arrive when we pass a large number of them through a diffractive crystal. The square of the wave function determines the probability of the electron to be found at a given place on the photographic plate.

Let's look at the implication of this probability interpretation by examining the results of a coin flip experiment: let's use runs of 30 flips of a coin. How many heads should show up? The chance of a head at each flip is fifty-fifty; thus, about 15 heads should result in a run. Of course, you would not be surprised if in some runs only 12 heads show up and in others 17. There would be a statistical distribution, you would say.

Let's be more specific. Suppose you ran 2000 such coin-flip experiments,

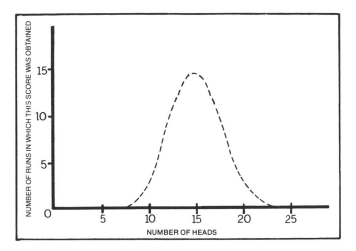

Figure 44. The bell curve of probability for the coin flip experiment.

each run consisting of 30 flips. You determine the number of runs in these experiments that show between 14 and 16 heads, the number of runs that show between 11 and 13 heads, and so forth. When we plot the data (Figure 44), a bell-shaped curve results, centered around 15 and tapering off on both sides.

If we plot an electron's probability distribution—the square of its wave amplitude or wave function—as a function of its possible positions or momenta, we get similar bell curves (Figure 45). Thus, for the position of the electron (Figure 45b), we may find that the probability is maximum for the electron to be at a position x_0, but the probability is nonzero in a region around this point. Similarly, for the momentum (Figure 45a), the probability is maximum for the electron to have a momentum p_0, but there is a distribution of momentum values around this maximum. Clearly, there is an uncertainty in

Figure 45. (a) The momentum probability distribution and uncertainty. (b) The probability curve for position and position uncertainty of a quantum object.

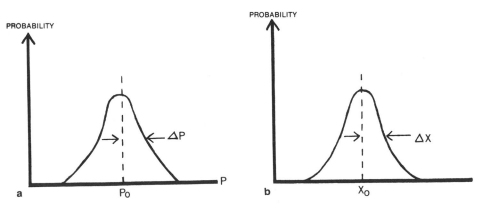

both the electron's position and momentum, given by the widths of the respective bell curves—denote them by Δx (pronounced "delta ex") and Δp (pronounced "delta pee").

Enter Werner Heisenberg, a German physicist of great intuitive capacity. Heisenberg knew that the complete determination of the whereabouts of a particle involves the knowledge of its position and momentum (or velocity) both at the same time. He now asked the crucial question: what is the limit of accuracy, or the uncertainty Δp for determining the momentum (say), when we have ascertained that the position is given within an uncertainty of Δx? The answer he found was a profound surprise. If we try to minimize the position uncertainty in a given situation, the momentum uncertainty becomes greater—it doesn't matter what kind of experiments you perform—and vice versa. The position and momentum uncertainties are related. Thus, in 1927, Heisenberg gave us his famous uncertainty principle, often expressed as the following mathematical relation:

> The product of the position and momentum uncertainties
> is greater than or equal to Planck's constant h.

In symbols,

$$\Delta p \, \Delta x \geqslant h$$

in which the symbol $\geqslant$ denotes greater than or equal to.

Thus was born quantum physics, which is specifically probabilistic; its mathematical equation determines only probabilities, not actualities. When we are predicting the behavior of a large number of submicroscopic objects like electrons, the probabilistic theory is able to predict the result of an experiment with all the accuracy needed. Since in all experimental situations in the micro world we are always dealing with a large number of submicroscopic particles, quantum mechanics is quite satisfactory as a predictive theory for the outcome of any physical process. Yet the determinism implied by this claim is entirely statistical, and it is extremely significant that we cannot predict the behavior of a single electron with much accuracy at all. There seems to be an ultimate indeterminacy in our ability to perceive reality; the uncertainty relation is the reminder of this basic indeterminacy.

If the uncertainty relation between the position and momentum uncertainties has not been mystifying enough already, consider this. Suppose we determine the momentum of a quantum wavicle exactly: now there is no uncertainty in our knowledge of momentum; the momentum uncertainty is zero. What happens to the position uncertainty? From the uncertainty relation:

$$\text{position uncertainty} = \frac{h}{\text{momentum uncertainty}} = \frac{h}{0} \longrightarrow \infty$$

The position uncertainty has become large without bounds, infinity, because a nonzero quantity when divided by zero gives an infinitely large number.

SF writer Gordon R. Dickson, in his novel *Mission to Universe*, toys with an interesting idea for using this aspect of Heisenberg's uncertainty relation—that the position uncertainty becomes infinite if the momentum or velocity is completely known—for hyperspace travel between two points:

> If distance divided by a fixed speed limit gave an impractical answer to star travel and the speed limit could not be changed—then how about changing the distance factor? Specifically, was it not possible to look at the universe in terms that assumed that the distance between points in the universe did not exist?
> Walt's mathematics had found that [to be] the way, using the Heisenberg Uncertainty Principle as a departure point—that declaration by Werner Heisenberg in 1927 that stated it was impossible to specify or determine simultaneously the position and velocity of a particle as accurately as wished. The determiner could be precise about position only at the expense of being uncertain about velocity—and vice versa.
> Assume therefore that velocity could be absolutely determined—this was the proposition that had fascinated Walt, . . . Then, theoretically, the position of the particle would be ubiquitous—it would have all points in the physical universe as its position. Starting with this desired end, . . . came the mathematics of his phase physics [from which] had come first the theory, then the actuality, of the phase ship. [pp. 39–40]

Of course, there is a catch in this, which is that the uncertainty principle really applies to quantum objects (such as the electron of the microworld) and not to macro-size objects like spaceships. But at least for the electron, when we completely know its velocity or momentum, the position cannot even be defined. You may argue that the electron must be somewhere—we just don't know where. This is not true; the electron's behavior is really close to mystical, as depicted in the following quote from the Hindu *Upanishads*:

> It is within all this
> And it is outside of all this.

ATOMS AND UNCERTAINTY

We now can explore some further differences between the atom and the solar system. The differences are brought about by the peculiarities of the motion of the electron as inherent in quantum mechanical uncertainty. The electrons are still supposed to orbit around the nucleus, but the orbits have to be fuzzy; this is the requirement of the uncertainty principle. A completely defined orbit would mean a perfect localization of the electron; furthermore, according to Newtonian mechanics, if we knew the orbits we could also tell the momenta of the orbiting electrons. However, this violates the uncertainty principle, according to which we can never describe both the position and the momentum of an electron simultaneously with arbitrary precision. Thus, we must conclude that the electronic orbits are fuzzy, imprecise, valid only in an average sense. And if the orbit is fuzzy, the momentum of an atomic electron cannot be determined with arbitrary precision, either. It turns out that when an electron is in one of these fuzzy orbits, the only thing we know precisely about it is its energy. For this reason the electronic orbital states are really energy levels.

The fact is that, when an electron is inside the atom, dancing in one of its fuzzy orbits, we cannot tell much about it. In the words of physicist Robert Oppenheimer:

If we ask, for instance, whether the position of the electron remains the same, we must say "no"; if we ask if the position of the electron changes with time, we must say "no"; if we ask whether the electron is at rest, we must say "no"; if we ask whether it is in motion, we must say "no." [*Science and Common Understanding*, p. 69]

Another quotation from the *Upanishads* sounds curiously similar to the dictum of Oppenheimer:

> It moves, it moves not;
> It is far and likewise near.

We cannot help but wonder if the sages of ancient India were describing an aspect of reality identical to that of the atomic electron.

But the mysticism can be postponed until later. The uncertainty principle enables us to understand the impossibility of something that SF writers have always wanted to do to the atom: squash it to smaller sizes. The argument goes like this. We know that the atomic nucleus is much smaller than the atom; there is a vast amount of empty space between the electrons and the nucleus, a space which has hardly any use. So why don't we reduce the size of the atom? A macroscopic object made of such reduced atoms would then be miniaturized. But we cannot do this because of the uncertainty principle. The size of the atom, the radius of the innermost fuzzy orbit of the electron, represents the uncertainty of the electron's distance from the nucleus. If we try to localize the electron any closer to the nucleus, making the atom smaller, the position uncertainty will decrease. This implies a corresponding increase of the uncertainty of the electron's momentum, according to the uncertainty relation—the position uncertainty is inversely proportional to the momentum uncertainty. If the former decreases, the latter must increase. And increase of the uncertainty of the electron's momentum means that it would be endowed with a huge, runaway velocity. Thus, such squashed atoms could not stay together.

In the book version of *Fantastic Voyage*, originally a movie, Isaac Asimov tries to give a rationale for miniaturization of objects, including human beings:

". . . Have you ever seen a photograph enlarged, . . . Or reduced to microfilm size? . . . the same process can be used on three-dimensional images manipulated from outside the universe of space-time." [p. 31]

Not a very useful analogy, is it? A photograph doesn't think, for example. Asimov himself knows this, of course. So when his character listening to the above comments retorts, "Now, teacher, those are just words," the "teacher" has only more words to offer. He says:

"Yes, but you don't want theory, do you? What physicists discovered ten years ago was the utilization of hyperspace; . . . The concept is beyond grasping . . ." [p. 32]

This is one of the few cases in which Asimov has violated his own basic principles of good science fiction. What he gives here is pure "scientific patter," to use H. G. Wells' language. But then again, I haven't seen anyone else do any better on miniaturization.

Actually, there are atoms that are smaller in size, made by the replacement of the electrons by other elementary particles known as mu-mesons. Mu-mesons, or muons, are particles that duplicate electrons in all particulars except that they are about 200 times more massive. Nobody quite knows why nature has this duplication, unless perhaps the mu-mesons in some fashion are higher-energy quantum states of the electrons. If that is the case, future technology might invent a way to convert, or rather excite, electrons into muons—and thus find a way to squash ordinary atoms into more compact muonic atoms. One problem: muons are short-lived, so we would need some kind of a speculative situation (call it a magic wand) to keep the muons from decaying.

ACCEPTING QUANTUM DUALITY

If you find it difficult to accept the idea of quantum duality, you may find it soothing to know that your difficulty is not unusual. To ascribe contrapuntal aspects like waveness and particleness to the same object is paradoxical, yet nature forces this paradox on us. I would like to make a couple of suggestions—as a "guide for the perplexed," to use E. F. Schumacher's words.

First, images like particles, as exemplified by billiard balls, and waves, such as water waves, originally were invented simply to describe the motions of billiard balls and water waves. Such language may be quite adequate for the macroworld of our everyday experience, but we have no right to expect the patterns of the microcosm to fit the same metaphor. Electrons and light are what they are; our consternation is due to our use of inadequate language which is just not applicable to this new domain.

Second, a picture from gestalt psychology may help. Look at the cartoon originally drawn by W. E. Hill and entitled "My Wife and My Mother-in-law" (Figure 46). What do you see? Initially, only the mother-in-law (or the wife). Only after a while do you see the other picture in the same lines. At some point your consciousness makes a jump and you discover the other picture, the wife if you started with the mother-in-law. The nose of the mother-in-law will transform into the wife's chin, the chin of the older woman will become the neckline of the younger woman, and so forth. Suddenly you discover a new way of looking at the picture; you have gained a new perspective. You still can look at only one of the two images at a time, but your awareness has enlarged to encompass duality.

This is the relationship of classical physics—in which waves are waves and particles are particles—and quantum duality. Physics before quantum mechanics looked at nature discretely as particles and waves. With quantum mechanics, we found both particle and wave in the same object—the electron—as its complementary aspects, just as you find both the mother-in-law

Figure 46. "My wife and my mother in law." *(Drawn after W. E. Hill, originally published in Puck, 1915)*

and the wife in the same picture in Hill's cartoon. The wave and particle aspects are complementary descriptions of the electron just as the wife and mother-in-law are complementary descriptions of the lines in Hill's drawing.

To understand the wavicle, to incorporate it into your personal philosophy, is a difficult quantum jump. So I will conclude this chapter with still another technique of dealing with the wavicle puzzle. Many people have commented that some of the concepts of quantum mechanics remind them of Zen practices. I find this Zen koan (paradox) illustrative in dealing with the problem of particle-wave complementarity:

> Zenmaster Joshu was asked: "Does a dog have Buddha nature or not?"
> To this Joshu replied, "Mu." (pronounced "moo")

What else could Joshu say? Because a yes or no answer is impossible. Everything has Buddha nature, according to Zen. But this simple truth is something that words cannot convey; the truth is experiential. So it is with the complementary nature of our wavicle. Is the electron a wave? Say "Mu." Is the electron a particle? Say "Mu" again. Go on answering "Mu" to such questions until you transcend the classical concepts of both particle and wave, until you understand the wavicle.

chapter sixteen

How to Bell Schrödinger's Cat

The quantum mechanical view of objects, with their wave-particle duality, is intuitively paradoxical. True, our puzzlement over how something can be both spatially extended as a wave and localized as a particle is mollified to a considerable extent by the notion of complementarity—the wave and particle aspects of the wavicle objects of quantum mechanics are complementary, and we can see only one aspect at a time—but doubts remain. To bring our uneasy feelings to the surface, let's consider a *gedanken* experiment.

Suppose we have an electron gun shooting electrons at a double-slit system, an opaque screen with two slits (as in Young's experiment in Chapter 6, except that now we use electrons instead of light) (Figure 47a). Because of their wave property, the electrons will pass through the slits and make secondary waves (as shown in the figure), which will interfere with each other. Now recall that when waves interfere in a region of space, they generate a characteristic interference pattern. At some points of space the waves will appear "in phase" with perfect timing and enhance each other; at other points the waves will arrive "out of phase," leading to a cancellation of their effects. This creates a typical interference pattern of alternate spots where the wave is particularly strong and spots where the wave has been virtually destroyed. If we let the electrons fall on a fluorescent screen after passing through the slits, this alternate reinforcement and cancellation shows up as bright and dark fringes on the screen (Figure 47b). Obviously, we are seeing the wave aspect of the electron's complementary character.

Now suppose the electron source is very weak, so weak that at any one time only one electron arrives at the slits. (It may be impossible to arrange this in practice, but remember that we are doing a *gedanken* experiment.) Will we still see the interference pattern? Does the probability-wave concept apply to even a single electron? We are not sure, but let's assume that it does. Now we can pose a paradox: how can one electron split up to pass through both slits? Without two beams of waves we cannot have interference, yet it is hard to imagine that one electron is at both places at the same time, half here and half there!

We can try to resolve the paradox in the following way. Suppose, as the electron passes through the screen containing the slits, we try to see whether it really splits up and passes through both slits at the same time. So we imagine that we have a flashlight, something to see the electron with. We turn it on, look for the electron passing through a slit or slits, and also look at what happens on the fluorescent screen. Unfortunately, as soon as we shine a

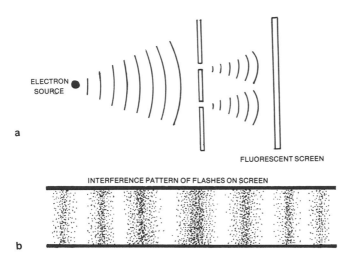

a

FLUORESCENT SCREEN

INTERFERENCE PATTERN OF FLASHES ON SCREEN

b

Figure 47. (a) The arrangement for an interference "double slit" experiment with electrons. (b) The electron interference pattern.

light on the electron, we are trying to ascertain its position; this increases the momentum uncertainty of the electron, which affects its wavelength through the de Broglie relation and destroys the wave behavior. In scientific terminology, the wave collapses. Correspondingly, we now see a flash on the screen behind only one of the slits; the interference pattern has disappeared. Obviously, we are now observing the particle, the localized characteristic of our electron wavicle—which is fine, except that we have failed to resolve the paradox.

Complementarity says that this is the way it must be—we see only one face of the electron at a time, never both faces; any attempt to see the other face destroys the face we begin with. We can reassert the view that in dealing with electron waves, we are better off always taking quite a few electrons into consideration, because electron waves are probability waves, and probability physics works better with greater numbers. But is this not tantamount to saying that quantum mechanics is an incomplete theory because of its probabilistic nature?

Perhaps at this point you are exasperated and scream against all these logical arguments back and forth: "The paradox cannot be resolved, and who cares if the electron is half here and half there?" True, electrons are too remote from your reality. So let's talk about a cat instead.

SCHRÖDINGER'S CAT

Schrödinger's cat is no ordinary cat—it was created and then at least half-killed by physicist Erwin Schrödinger, codiscoverer of quantum mechanics. You see, Schrödinger's cat is a paradox, or rather it is the instrument around which Mr. Schrödinger raises the paradoxical issue of the probabilistic nature of quantum mechanics.

Suppose we put the cat in a cage in which there is a single radioactive atom. There is also a Geiger counter, a device that will tick if the atom decays and emits radiation. Things are so arranged that the ticking of the Geiger counter breaks open a bottle of poison which kills the cat. The radioactive atom (which is a quantum object whose decay follows a probabilistic law) is chosen so that the chances are fifty-fifty that it will undergo the decay in an hour. So what happens after the hour?

Can quantum mechanics predict the state of the cat after the hour? If quantum mechanics were regarded as a causal theory, we would think so. But we must speak in terms of probabilities—quantum mechanics calculates only probabilities. After the hour, the probability that the cat is dead is fifty percent, as is the probability that the cat is alive. So the quantum mechanical state of the cat is a combination of these two states; we have a cat in a cage which, according to our theory, is half alive and half dead. This is what logic dictates. But nobody has ever seen a cat which is half dead and half alive! Indeed, if we open the cage we find either a dead cat or a live one, never a combination. What causes this development?

Clearly, there is something profoundly paradoxical about quantum mechanics. Are we ever to resolve the paradox? I will mention three ways: you can take your pick.

THE CONVENTIONALIST'S CANT VERSUS
HIDDEN VARIABLES

The conventional way to get out of the kind of predicament that Schrödinger's cat poses is to repeat that quantum mechanics is designed only to make predictions about processes involving a large number of objects. If there are 10^{23} cats, each in a separate cage, quantum mechanics can successfully predict that after an hour half of them will be dead and half alive. And quantum mechanics will be correct, as observations would surely verify. But if you ask the conventional physicist about the fate of a single cat, he will either be mum or give you a lecture using sophisticated ideas such as ensembles of cats. What he is telling you is that he isn't sure. Perhaps in his view quantum mechanics does not apply to a single cat; we never encounter this problem with electrons, he will say, there are always quite a few electrons. Nor does one ask such questions for electrons—are they alive or dead?—and quantum mechanics is designed for electrons, not for conscious objects like cats!

Does this kind of plea solve the paradox? It depends on whether you insist on having a theory that gives a complete description of reality. If you do, the paradox remains. Einstein was one such person who used to seek answers to such questions as, Who decides whether the cat is dead or alive after the hour is up? "God does not play dice" to decide such things, Einstein used to say. He felt there must be a causal way that the fate of the cat is determined; according to this view, some sort of ultimate theory—of which quantum mechanics is only a stopgap approximation—should be able to predict this.

When I was young, I loved to watch puppet shows. It surprised me no end that puppets could move, run, play. I didn't believe what I was told about the puppets being manipulated by hidden strings; the illusion was perfect to the eyes of a child.

Einstein maintained that the electrons—and quantum objects, in general—behave paradoxically because they too respond to hidden strings. He used the phrase "hidden variables" to speak of these hidden interactions. Einstein admitted that the success of quantum mechanics in predicting the physical reality in the micro-domain no doubt reinforces our illusion that quantum mechanics is the ultimate theory, incomplete (and imperfect) as it is, but he was convinced that eventually a deterministic theory will be found based on the idea of hidden variables.

THE CAT IN MANY WORLDS

In psychology there is a considerable documentation and study of people with schizophrenic personalities of many forms. The movies/books *Sybil* and *The Three Faces of Eve* portray multiple-personality individuals. For such individuals, physical reality must appear to be a conglomerate of many worlds in each of which they play a different character.

In science fiction, Philip K. Dick likes to write about many worlds. In his 1962 Hugo-winning novel, *The Man in the High Castle,* he created an unforgettable many-world reality. The book describes a post–World War II reality in which Japan and Germany have won the war and are occupying the United States except for a central buffer zone around the Rocky Mountains. An author in this buffer zone has written a book depicting a different reality in which the United States and its allies have won the war. The plot thickens when some of the characters of the story find themselves jumping in and out of both realities.

In 1957, Princeton physicists Hugh Everett and John Wheeler (read DeWitt, 1970, for a lucid exposition) suggested a resolution of the Schrödinger's cat paradox based on this fictional-sounding many-world idea. In this theory, both possibilities—live cat and dead cat—occur, but in different parallel realities, parallel universes. For every live cat we find in the cage, prototypes of us in a parallel universe open a prototype cage only to discover a prototype cat that is dead. The schizophrenia of the cat's wave function forces the universe itself to split into parallel branches. An infinite number of such parallel universes must exist, because infinite alternatives are acted out for all events that are open to a quantum system.

This is indeed a fascinating theory with many interesting implications, both philosophical and science-fictiony. Unfortunately, the parallel universes of this theory are completely decoupled from each other! Therefore, the authors maintain (copping out?), you can never verify the theory. Are there parallel universes? Might not a quantum object itself know when it's being schizophrenic? But, you object, quantum objects are not sentient, they cannot tell. But reserve judgment until you read the end of this book.

COLLAPSE AND CONSCIOUSNESS

Einstein once wrote (in *The Evolution of Physics,* written in collaboration with physicist Leopold Infeld) the following lines on the premise of science:

Without the belief that it is possible to grasp the reality with our theoretical constructions, without the belief in the inner harmony of our world, there could be no science. [p. 296]

If we believe that a complete understanding of reality is possible, we have no option but to reject the conventional neglect of the paradox of Schrödinger's cat, a neglect that occurs simply by insisting that quantum mechanics doesn't apply to a single cat in a lonely cage. And the imaginative idea of many worlds is just an escape unless we are prepared to face the consequences of coupling between all these worlds. What can we do to resolve the paradox without resorting to neglect or fantasy?

Let's recap the issues. There are two phases of the cat experiment. The first phase involves the time development of the quantum-mechanical state of the cat. Although difficult to reconcile, the time development of the system into a combination of live and dead cat is causal, the logic here unambiguously following from the equations of the theory. In the second phase, the observation stage, chance and probability and indeterminacy enter, because out of the two possible outcomes, only one materializes. The wave function collapses to only one of the possibilities, following the probabilistic rule dictated by theory. But for any one event, the outcome cannot be predicted with certainty. This is a basic acausal element in the theory.

So again, does God throw dice? Or are there hidden variables? Nobel Laureate physicist Eugene Wigner (1967) has introduced another interesting idea. He says that consciousness is the hidden-variable connection that determines the outcome of a quantum-mechanical collapse. The consciousness of the observer decides and triggers which of the possible outcomes will be manifested. And it has been recognized ever since Heisenberg enunciated his uncertainty principle that the division of the world into subjects and objects does not hold in the quantum domain: subjects can change the state of the objects they observe, via measurement. According to Wigner, probability and uncertainty enter through the intervention of this conscious observation in the problem.

Perhaps this is the clue. Whenever a conscious object interacts with a quantum system, we encounter such paradoxes as Schrödinger's cat. In order to understand where quantum mechanics takes us, we may have to involve ourselves with the science of consciousness—psychology—and combine it with physics, even if this takes us beyond the territory of both establishment physics and the Einsteinian school of thought.

It is not unforseen that a new paradigm that combines psychology and physics is called for; early in this century, psychologist Carl Jung predicted: "Sooner or later nuclear physics and the psychology of the unconscious will draw closer together as both of them, independently of one another and from opposite directions, push forward in transcendental territory. . . . " But there is a real surprise! With a more elaborate analysis of the situation we shall find that, while consciousness may very well be the solution to the paradox of quantum mechanics, we must be prepared to extend the notion of consciousness to a greatly expanded domain of reality.

BELL'S THEOREM AND THE ANSIBLE

Let's get back to the double-slit experiment with the electrons. Consider once again the passage of a single electron through the slits. One can pose a slightly different paradox than before. We know that with both slits open we must see the wave behavior of the electron, which produces an interference pattern. But with one slit closed, we must see a bright flash behind only the open slit—the electron now behaves like a particle, localized. Suppose while observing the single slit pattern, we suddenly open the other slit. According to quantum mechanics, the pattern must change immediately to the wave interference pattern. But how does the electron know at a distance about the other slit being open or closed? Nobody told the electron.

Of course, it is not ruled out that there is some sort of signals, through some hidden variables, that enable the electrons to do the right thing at the correct instant. The right thing also happens to be exactly what the probability rules of quantum mechanics demand, but with hidden variables we can describe reality better—all the way down to single electrons, for example. Most important, if we discovered what the hidden variables are, quantum mechanics could perhaps be reformulated into a completely deterministic theory without probabilities.

So hoped many physicists, including Einstein, who expressed his views in a paper written with two young collaborators, Boris Podolsky and Nathan Rosen. English physicist David Bohm later augmented these views. However, in 1965, physicist John Bell published research that shed new light on the entire subject. Bell's work shifted the question from the Einsteinian one—is the description of reality deterministic or probabilistic?—back to the paradoxical question which began this section: how does the electron know . . . ?

One of the attributes of the atomic electron is that its description needs a few "quantum numbers"—rather like identifying people with such symbols as social security numbers, telephone numbers, and so forth. The reason why a discrete numbering system should apply to submicroscopic reality has to do with the basic discrete nature of submicroscopic quantities, such as energy levels. In some sense, such eminent philosophers of the past as Pythagoras and Kepler already knew this—it was a conviction of both these men that certain discrete numbers are significant in the description of reality. Quantum numbers of the electrons are a vindication of their ideas.

For the electrons, the quantum numbers have physical significance. One of the quantum numbers that we shall be interested in can take only one of two values: $+\frac{1}{2}$ or $-\frac{1}{2}$; this two-valuedness relates to the spinning motion of the electrons. An electron can spin with its axis up (corresponding to the quantum number $+\frac{1}{2}$) or down (corresponding to the quantum number $-\frac{1}{2}$). If two electrons comprise a system with their spins in opposite directions (one $+\frac{1}{2}$, the other $-\frac{1}{2}$), their spins cancel out. Such a state of two electrons is called a singlet state.

If we arrange for two beams of electrons to collide with each other, it is possible to fix the conditions so that an electron from one beam will scatter from an electron of the other beam always in the singlet state; that is, the spins of the two electrons after the scattering will always be opposite to each other. Now suppose that after the electrons scatter, experimenters plan to detect them at two places separated by a large distance. One of the experimenters has a setup of magnets, called a Stern-Gerlach device, with which she can determine whether the electron went up or down with respect to some axis under her control. In other words, she has a window which only lets in an electron of the chosen kind of spin. Meanwhile, at the second distant place, another experimenter has set up his own Stern-Gerlach device at a known angle relative to the chosen axis of the first experimenter. The probability of what the second observer will detect, how many electrons pass through his window, is completely determined by quantum mechanical probability rules.

Next imagine that the first experimenter has changed her axis, the orientation of her window. Quantum mechanics quite unambiguously maintains that now the probability of detection of electrons by the second observer will change depending on the new relational angle between their two axes. But this raises the paradox again: how do the electrons know at a distance that the first axis was changed, so that they will behave accordingly to conform to the quantum-mechanical rules? Or perhaps the electrons do communicate via some sort of local hidden variables, via signals exchanged through space-time.

Bell was quite ingenious at this point. Assuming that such local hidden variables exist, he found a set of relationships among the expected results of observations carried out along three different axes at each of the experimental locations. These are the famous Bell Inequalities. Bell showed that if the hidden-variable interactions are local (and not "action at a distance") then his inequalities have to be satisfied. If the inequalities are found to be violated by the observational data, then locality of the hidden variables does not hold. Most important, Bell also found that it is a choice between probabilistic quantum mechanics or local hidden variables; if the inequalities turn out to be validated by experiment, then the probability rules must be modified, at least for the process under consideration. Thus, we can state Bell's theorem as follows: Hidden variables, in order to be compatible with probabilistic quantum mechanics, have to be nonlocal.

Over the years since Bell's work was published, seven experiments have been performed, five of which tell us that the Bell inequalities do not hold. The results of the other two are ambiguous. Local hidden variables are not a resolution for our paradoxes, and probabilistic quantum mechanics is right, after all!

However, the paradox, in the form that we posed it, still remains. How do the electrons know at a distance? Certainly not through any signals through space-time; this would mean local hidden-variable interaction of some kind—Bell's theorem rules that out. But then doesn't the paradox intensify? As Erwin Schrödinger wrote as early as 1935, "It is rather discomforting that the [quantum] theory should allow a system to be steered or piloted into one or the other type of state at the experimenter's mercy in spite of his having no access to it." Of course, conventional interpreters of quantum mechanics do not care; since they do not try to make a complete picture of what is happening, they unabashedly claim ignorance. So do we have to give up seeking a complete description of reality, yielding to the conventional view?

There is an alternative, although many physicists are appalled by its implications. Suppose it is possible for electrons to communicate at a distance instantaneously but without the intermediary of local hidden variables. The skeptic will respond that this negates relativity theory. But must we confine the needed superluminal (faster than light) information transfer to space-time? It is in ordinary space-time that relativity reigns supreme, and all signals are limited to the maximum speed of that of light. This is the reason that Einstein wanted his hidden variables to be local—strictly in accordance with the theory of relativity. Instead, suppose the hidden variables correspond to a dimension outside of space-time and that they give the electron some degree of freedom outside the domain of relativity. In the dimension that the hidden variables define, there is no space and no time; everything is already here because there is no there, and every time is now because there is no then. Such superluminal communication between electrons has been suggested by several physicists, among them Jack Sarfatti and Henry Stapp, as a resolution to the paradox posed in the beginning of this section. Henry Stapp (1977) of Lawrence Berkeley Laboratory writes:

The central mystery of quantum theory is "how does information get around so quick? How does the particle know that there are two slits? How does the information about what is happening everywhere else get collected to determine what is likely to happen here? How does the particle know that it was looked for in some far-away place and not found?" Quantum phenomena provide *prima facie* evidence that information gets around in ways that do not conform to classical ideas. Thus the idea that information is transferred superluminally is, *a priori,* not unreasonable.

Everything we know about nature is in accord with the idea that the fundamental process of nature lies outside space-time (surveys the space-time continuum globally), but generates events that can be located in space-time. [italics in the original]

Not surprisingly, SF writers have also caught on to the implications of quantum-mechanical indeterminacy—that it may free us from the bondage of the speed of light that relativity imposes. Especially, I want to quote here Ursula Le Guin, who wrote the following lines in her classic Hugo-winning novel, *The Dispossessed;* in these lines her physicist-hero, Shevek, in an alien world, is about to make a conceptual breakthrough as he ponders Einstein's plight in going beyond relativity:

Strangeness and familiarity: in every movement of the Terran's thought Shevek caught this combination, was constantly intrigued. And sympathetic: for Ainsetain [Einstein], too, had been after a unifying field theory. . . . He had not succeeded. Even during his lifetime, and for many decades after his death, the physicists of his own world had turned away from his effort and its failure, pursuing the magnificent incoherences of quantum theory with its high technological yields, at last concentrating on the technological mode so exclusively as to arrive at a dead end, a catastrophic failure of imagination. Yet their original intuition had been sound: at the point where they had been, progress had lain in the indeterminacy which old Ainsetain had refused to accept. [p. 224]

With this initial awakening of ideas, Shevek goes on to discover his equations that describe the new physics. The author describes the implication of Shevek's new physics in this conversation between Shevek and the ambassador from Terra:

He nodded. "What they want," he said, "is the instantaneous transferral of matter across space. Transilience. Space travel, you see, without traversal of space or lapse of time. They may arrive at it yet; not from my equations, I think. But they can make the ansible, with my equations, if they want it. Men cannot leap the great gaps, but ideas can."

"What is an ansible, Shevek?"

"An idea." He smiled without much humor. "It will be a device that will permit communication without any time interval between two points in space. The device will not transmit messages, of course; simultaneity is identity. But to our perceptions, that simultaneity will function as a transmission, a sending. So we will be able to use it to talk between worlds, without the long waiting for the message to go and the reply to return that electromagnetic impulses require." [p. 276]

It seems to me that, in inventing the ansible, Le Guin has come fairly close to the ideas described above. Particularly, the line "The device will not transmit messages, of course; simultaneity is identity" is highly suggestive of such an understanding of the implications of Bell's theorem.

The following quote points out where a physicist would differ with Le Guin, the science fiction writer, in the interpretation of the implication of Bell's theorem. French physicist Bernard d'Espagnat writes (1979):

It seems quite certain that these influences [through the "hidden" dimension] could not be employed to transmit any "useful" information, such as orders or instructions. No event that causes another event can be linked to it through this mechanism; the instantaneous influences can pass only between events that are related by a common cause.

This allowable information transfer takes the form of instant knowledge of what is "right," the true nature of things in a manner of coincidence. It is in the same category as the phenomenon of synchronicity, meaningful coincidences—those that, while not violating causality, transcend it—discussed by Carl Jung. Psychologist Jean Shinoda Bolen (1979) gives an example of synchronicity in *The Tao of Psychology*, which contains a delightful exposition of Jung's ideas:

I was in the kitchen in the midst of dinner preparation and mentioned to my husband Jim that I needed some flowers for the table. The children were playing outside, quite out of range of hearing. Moments later, Melody came in through the length of the house, a bouquet of pink geraniums in her hands, saying, "Here, Mommy." [p. 16]

Bell's theorem legitimizes similar kinds of communication.

If the above example seems trivial, neurophysiologist-author John C. Lilly describes a far more dramatic one which should intrigue even the skeptic. Lilly, who is famous for his experiments with dolphins, and his wife, Toni, spent the night in their motor home outside a friend's house on the Pacific coast:

In the morning they went into his house for breakfast. Burgess came out of his bedroom and said, "I have just had the damnedest dream. I dreamed that I was with my dog down under the house where it juts out over the beach. Suddenly a dolphin came swimming in on the waves and beached itself. My dog lay down by the dolphin in the shallow water. My wife and the neighborhood children came, turned the dolphin around, and pushed it back out to sea. It swam away."

The three of them, Toni, John, and Burgess, then speculated about this dream. The explanation for the dream was that it was a mental association of Burgess's, of the fact that the motor home had the license plate "Dolphin" on it and that John had worked with dolphins in the past.

While they were talking there was a sudden shout from below the house. Burgess and John went out on the porch and Toni and Burgess's wife went down to the beach. The two men looked over the balcony. There was a dolphin coming in on the waves, beaching itself. Toni and Burgess's wife and the neighborhood children pushed it back out to sea and it swam off. [*The Scientist*, p. 155]

Notice that in an incident like this there is no cause-effect connection between any of the knots of the total event, yet it makes sense that they are connected by a common cause. Lilly told me that this incident was instrumental in his establishment of "The Dolphin Foundation," dedicated to human-dolphin communication; is that too part of the synchronicity? Did some information transfer take place à la Bell's theorem that led to this intensification of the human-dolphin communication research?

Thus, if the above interpretation of Bell's theorem turns out to be right, and its psychological connection clearly established, then acausal phenomena such as "synchronous events" will find a definite place in the description of reality. It is especially interesting to note that in Jung's later years he attempted a collaboration with Wolfgang Pauli, one of the giants of quantum physics. Although not much is supposed to have come out of this collaboration, this may be a mistaken assumption. Jung and Pauli (1955) did agree upon a quaternio, a diagrammatic representation of the basic concepts needed to understand reality (Figure 48). And notice how these two scientists saw the complementary role that causality and synchronicity play in the shaping of our reality. So what came out of their collaboration may have been truly profound. Now, about twenty years later, Bell's theorem prompts us to accept a similar view.

Another important point. An inanimate object like the electron or a machine may receive "knowledge" through the dimension of hidden variables and may act accordingly. But it has no way to pass on that knowledge except through its actions. These actions are lawful by design in the statistical sense, and it is difficult, if not impossible, to reach any final conclusions about the existence of the hidden variables from these actions alone. In other words, even if the electron "knows" about the hidden connection, it cannot tell.

It is a long way from electrons to human beings, but suppose we ourselves

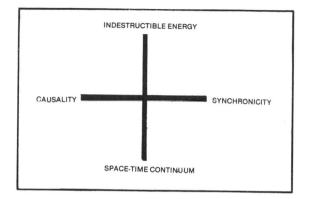

Figure 48. The Pauli-Jung quaternio.

were connected to the hidden variables. This would be the case if our mind-brain were a *macroscopic* quantum system and mind were a quantum-mechanical phenomenon, a model that will be discussed in more detail in the next chapter. With this assertion, we can easily understand "synchronicity events" involving us. In contrast to electrons, we possess awareness, mind. We can speculate that with proper attunement of our awareness we may be able not only to receive superluminal communication ourselves, but also to "tell" about it to other aware beings. If this view turns out to be correct, then we don't have far to look in search of Le Guin's ansibles, only at ourselves.

Finally, you are bound to ask sooner or later: what is the nature of these hidden variables? We can gain some insight into this question by pondering the implication of Bell's theorem on Wigner's suggestion that consciousness intervention is the key to the resolution of the Schrödinger's cat paradox. If Wigner's clue is correct and hidden variables have something to do with consciousness, then Bell's theorem says that this consciousness must be non-local, a dimension outside space-time. I shall have much more to say on this in a later chapter.

THE DANCING WU LI MASTERS

William Shakespeare wrote:

> All the world's a stage
> And all the men and women merely players

What is the play? This is our quest. The stage—the domain—is the universe of space-time, space and time together. The players are matter—men, women, dancing shoes—animate, inanimate. Watching the players on the stage do their thing gives us ideas of what the play is about. This is the purported purpose of science: to watch the play, to study the changes that matter undergoes, and to discover the plot of the play.

But there is a problem. You can watch a play with objectivity and believe that your watching doesn't interfere with the plot. Of course, most plays are so designed, with the audience separate from the players; the shadow universe of the theater is divided into players and watchers. But there is also another kind of show in which the audience participates in the play itself; there is no division between watchers and watchees.

Ultimately, the nature of the play determines what kind of watching is possible—an objective, unattached one or an involved, participatory one. Classical physicists, physicists before the advent of the twentieth century, believed the nature of the play to be independent of the players. Modern physicists, with quantum mechanics at hand, think otherwise.

Gary Zukav (1979) has written a book very appropriately named *The Dancing Wu Li Masters. Wu Li* in Chinese means physics. Thus, the book is about dancing physicists, if translated literally. Surprise! It's not about the dance, but the dancer. In classical physics, the dancer is irrelevant; only the dance—the play—counts. But not so in modern physics. Thus, the book is really about modern physics, where the difference between the dancer and the dance disappears. To talk about the dancers is to talk about the dance. So let's take time out to look at the style of the quantum *Wu Li* dancers, a few representative ones, at least. Fortunately for posterity, their lives are fairly well documented.

As a group these physicists displayed a variety of personality traits. Some of them were dreamers, others practical; some egotistic, others modest. Some were rather talkative, others extremely economic with words. Obviously, this is what you would expect to find among any group of talented people.

Take a dreamer—for example, Werner Heisenberg. He was a disciple of Neils Bohr from whom he very likely learned the art of creative dreaming. Niels Bohr himself reportedly made his most celebrated discoveries through the process of dreaming. So when young Heisenberg got stuck with the very difficult problem of figuring out the equations of the mechanics of the atom, what did he do? He ate a big dinner and went to sleep. And lo and behold, Heisenberg saw *the* dream. He dreamed of his physical quantities as represented by arrays of numbers. But these arrays of numbers were funny. Unlike ordinary numbers, they did not commutate with each other, which means $a \times b$ was not equal to $b \times a$, if a and b were two such arrays of numbers.

Now ordinarily one wouldn't think of representing physical quantities by noncommutating objects, especially if nobody had done it before. But in a dream everything is possible. What was so special about this dream is, of course, that this idea of representing physical quantities by noncommutating mathematical entities was the crucial piece of information that Heisenberg needed to write down his equation of quantum mechanics.

Does this mean that one has to be a dreamer in order to succeed in physics? By no means. One of Heisenberg's best friends, Wolfgang Pauli, was the complete antithesis of a dreamer. Pauli was a didactive logician of the highest caliber, but this did not keep him from discovering physical principles. In fact, Pauli's faculties in mathematical physics were so profound that one often wondered if nature could cope with them! Pauli's theories were so logical that if nature did not follow them (as was regrettably the case sometimes), it certainly was attributable to nature's irrationality.

Pauli's recognition as the outstanding theoretical physicist of his time was cemented when an experimentalist discovered the so-called Pauli effect. One day in a certain laboratory in Germany, an experimentalist had set up his apparatus and started to perform an experiment. All of a sudden the apparatus broke down for no reason at all. Nothing worked for a while. But after a time the experimental setup suddenly started working again all by itself. What happened? It turned out that Pauli was passing in a train by the town where the laboratory was. He was in the proximity of the laboratory during the exact period that the apparatus would not work. This was the Pauli effect: experiments did not work in Pauli's proximity.

Another attribute of Pauli was his outspokenness. He had a sharp tongue from which nobody was exempt. Even without provocation, Pauli could be very critical. Freeman Dyson, who conceived the Dyson sphere, tells of an incident. Dyson was invited to give a talk at a physical society meeting. He was passing by the hall when he noticed Pauli who, as usual, was surrounded by a few physicists. When one of them asked Pauli what he thought of Dyson's work, Pauli replied quite caustically in German (lest he be overheard). Unfortunately for Dyson, he knew German and was not at all happy with Pauli's rudeness.

But don't conclude that all physicists are so rude. Eugene Wigner, a physicist of the quantum era who is prominent today for his work on the role of consciousness in quantum mechanics, is renowned for his extreme politeness. Once Wigner had some problem in getting his car repaired; the repairman was procrastinating forever in finishing the job. When Wigner went back to the service shop for the third time and the car was still not ready, even he lost his patience and told the repairman, "Please, go to hell!" Now how many of us would say please in such a situation?

Some physicists are very talkative. The first prize in this department must go to Niels Bohr himself, the dean of the physicists of the quantum era. Just after Erwin Schrödinger discovered his famous equation, Bohr invited him to Copenhagen to discuss Schrödinger's work. Little did Schrödinger, who was not well acquainted with Bohr, know what he was in for! In the few days that Schrödinger was enveloped in the hospitality of the famous Bohr mansion, Bohr wore him out so completely with his constant barrage of questions, comments, and inquisitions that Schrödinger exclaimed in exasperation: "I would never have discovered my equation if I knew . . ."

But again, not all physicists are talkers. In fact, some of them are chary with words to a fault. Paul Dirac, who discovered the concept of antiparticle, is one such man. One time Dirac was giving a colloquium lecture. As the lecture ended, following the usual custom, the chairperson asked for questions from the audience. A person raised his hand and said, "Professor Dirac, I don't understand that equation of yours." Everybody was waiting to hear Dirac's explanation, but Dirac just sat there. Finally, the chairperson intervened: "Professor Dirac, aren't you going to answer the question?" Dirac responded, "That was a statement of fact, not a question."

The next story, about Einstein, perhaps reflects a most important and fairly common trait among truly great people. At the time of this incident, Einstein had already become a legend. It happened in the small university town of Princeton, New Jersey, where Einstein worked at the Institute for Advanced Studies. One day he and his assistant, Leopold Infeld, went to see a movie. When they found upon arriving at the theater that the movie would not start for fifteen minutes, Einstein expressed the desire to take a walk. But the gatekeeper had already taken their tickets, and Einstein became quite concerned about getting back in again. He insisted that the gatekeeper take a good look at their faces so that he would recognize them when they returned. The gatekeeper was quite amused. "Yes, Professor Einstein, I will recognize you," he assured him.

The final story was improvised to make a point; what point depends on your point of view. I heard it from an associate of Werner Heisenberg. The hero (?) of the story is Wolfgang Pauli, the master logician among the quantum dancers. The story begins when Pauli dies and goes to heaven, where presumably most physicists end up after they die. Pauli's friends who are already in heaven rejoice on this auspicious occasion and give him a hero's welcome, highlighted by an appointment with God Him/Her/Itself. When Pauli arrives in God's office, he finds God working away at a desk (don't be surprised that God works in an office at a desk—we all fashion God in our own image, even theoretical physicists). Without preamble, Pauli asks God the ultimate physical question, "Tell me, God, how did You do it? What's the ultimate mathematical equation that rules the workings of the universe?" God went to the blackboard (of course, God—the best mathematician around—has a blackboard!) and wrote down a very complicated equation. Pauli studied it for a few minutes before declaring, "I've tried it! It doesn't work!"

Pauli was well known for such judgments on other physicists' works, which reputation no doubt inspired the anonymous writer. However, I feel that the story symbolically expresses a view held by many physicists, that there is no "final" *mathematical* solution to the nature of reality. I suspect that any final answer must be subjective, to be found and reconciled in the domain of our consciousness; this is the lesson we can learn from quantum mechanics.

chapter seventeen

The Mind and the Quantum

One of the most profound influences of deterministic philosophy has occurred in the area of psychology. If the universe is deterministic, why should the behavior of human beings be different? One problem is that human beings seem to possess some unpredictable characteristics such as emotions, which do not appear to conform to the mold of determinism. But we can argue that emotions are part of our animal heritage; they are the nightmares of the "dragons of Eden" that still live within us in our hindbrain (the reptilian complex and the limbic brain), a remnant of our reptilian ancestry. This idea, originated by neurophysiologist Paul MacLean, has been promulgated by futurologist Carl Sagan (1977) in his book, *The Dragons of Eden*. A view is growing in which emotions are not an integral part of our truly human nature; to be truly human is to be essentially a logical being, with behavior much like a computer. A human *is* a computer, albeit a carbon unit. From a deterministic point of view, this is very satisfying, because we humans are then duplicating the machine universe. Much of behavioral psychology today is dedicated to bringing this machine self of ours to fruition.

If you are a *Star Trek* fan, you will recognize this emotion-versus-logic conflict as the perennial one between Dr. McCoy and Mr. Spock. And you also know which side the writers of *Star Trek* support. Much as Mr. Spock is admired, human emotions are recognized in these episodes as an essential and integral part of being human. And in *Star Trek,* the motion picture, we find that even Spock, given the chance to become completely logical, chooses not to.

Although science fiction in general has been quite supportive of determinism as far as the material universe is concerned, it is encouraging that when it comes to the human mind, it has steadfastly held on to such elements of indeterminacy as free will and emotions. You will see in this book that the SF writers' view is now being shared by an increasing number of physicists and psychologists; our mind is a key aspect of indeterminacy in the universe. However, let's first examine in a little more depth the position of the behavioral psychologists and the SF writers' responses to it.

PSYCHOLOGY AND SCIENCE FICTION

You undoubtedly know the story of Robert Louis Stevenson's nineteenth-century novel *The Strange Case of Dr. Jekyll and Mr. Hyde*. In this story, man's classic struggle between the "id" (our "evil" aspect) and the "superego" (our "good" aspect) is played out in the failed attempt of the good doctor to integrate his id with his superego personality. In the novel, a drug separates the id from the superego. But as the id is freed from the unconscious, it increasingly dominates the personality.

Freudian concepts such as id and superego are no less mysterious than the hyperspace of previous chapters. Understandably, psychologists with a more "scientific" bent would attempt to reformulate psychology without introducing such concepts, without the notion even of unconscious or the mind. Behaviorism sprang from such legitimate attempts by such men as John B. Watson and B. F. Skinner.

The experimental basis of the new theory was provided by Russian physiologist I. P. Pavlov, who discovered that reflexes—animal responses to stimuli—can be conditioned by simple association. In his classic dog and bell experiments, the dog could be conditioned to salivate at the ringing of a bell once it was trained to associate the ringing of the bell with the appearance of food. Eventually, this led to the idea that behavior, animal and human alike, is a result of a stimulus-response reinforcement mechanism acting throughout one's life. Behavior is deterministic.

With the advent of behaviorism, there was no more need for the concept of the mind and its even more esoteric sublayers such as the unconscious. Radical behaviorists assume that our perceptual apparatus, the brain, is a black box (you can't look inside it); they are not interested in the brain's internal mechanisms. They simply stimulate this black box and study its response. A number of such studies will determine what the average or reasonable response is. If an individual's response is not reasonable or "logical," then a behaviorist analyst will seek stimuli to modify the behavior of the "neurotic" black box. After a sufficient amount of this kind of therapy, all black boxes will behave deterministically.

Skinner, the guru of radical behaviorism, is so convinced of his deterministic model of the human psyche that in evangelistic fervor he wrote a utopian novel, *Walden II*. The novel is written more or less as a dialogue between a protagonist (Frazier) and an antagonist (Castle); the narrator-mediator is the author himself, lightly camouflaged by the name Burris (one of Skinner's initials stands for Burrhus). As Castle vigorously argues his case for liberalism, Burris retains a semblance of neutrality in the face of the obvious success of Frazier's ideas. The inhabitants of Walden II (with one of whom Castle converses in the following excerpt) undeniably have attained that ultimate of the American dream, a universally successful pursuit of happiness!

"What do you think of Walden?" she asked. . . .
"I think it's fine," I said. "A beautiful spot. And everyone so perfectly happy." My face burned with shame at this obvious maneuver.
"Happy?" she said with evident surprise.

I looked up. Perhaps I had struck something.

"Why, yes. You all seem very happy. Aren't you?"

"It's a funny thing," she said. "I haven't thought about that for a good many years. Why do you ask?"

"Why do I ask? Well, it seems to me it's a pretty important thing to know if you're going to size a place up."

"Why didn't you ask me if we were all well-fed? *There's* something I could of told you. Or whether we were healthy? Though it all comes to the same thing!"

"Why, I can see that you're well-fed and healthy," I said. "I don't need to ask."

"Don't we look happy?"

"But you can't always tell. . . . What sort of work do you do?" I said.

"Cook. Pastry. Couldn't you tell?"

"What labor-credits do they give you for that kind of work?"

"Oh, I don't know. I just get out the pies and cakes. . . ."

"How long do you work?"

"Oh, till I get the pies and cakes out. Mornings."

"Doesn't that give you a lot of time with nothing to do?"

"I almost never do nothing. I wasn't doing nothing when you came up. I was sort of resting."

"What else do you do with your time?"

"Oh, there's my daughters' children and their little friends. I spend a lot of time with them. I'm teaching them to cook . . . Then I have a flower garden this time of year. I love flowers. . . .

"What else do you do?"

"Well, there's our pinochle club. And sometimes, when we can't go out, we set up the tapestry frame. . . . We talk. There isn't much we don't know about. We get the news quicker than that little paper the young ones publish."

"Is that enough to keep you busy?"

"It doesn't keep me busy. I haven't been busy for years. I can come out here any time I like. It's a nice spot, isn't it?"

"It is," I said. "And you're one of the nicest things about it."

She smiled broadly. [italics in the original, pp. 218–220]

In *Walden II* as well as in his serious writings, Skinner makes a good case for behaviorism. In spite of this, many people—psychologists and SF writers included—see in behaviorism and conditioning the specter of mind control. Aldous Huxley's novel *Brave New World*, about pawns in a dictatorial system, tries to expose behaviorism in its threat to the human condition.

"A New Theory of Biology" was the title of the paper which Mustapha Mond had just finished reading. He sat for some time, meditatively frowning, then picked up his pen and wrote across the title-page: "The author's mathematical treatment of the conception of purpose is novel and highly ingenious, but heretical and, so far as the present social order is concerned, dangerous and potentially subversive. <u>Not to be published!</u>" He underlined the words. "The author will be kept under supervision. His transference to the Marine Biological Station of St. Helena may become necessary." A pity, he thought, as he signed his name. It was a masterly piece of work. But once you began admitting explanations in terms of purpose—well, you didn't know what the result might be. It was the sort of idea that might easily decondition the more unsettled minds among the higher castes—make them lose their faith in happiness as the Sovereign Good and take to believing, instead, that the goal was somewhere beyond, somewhere outside the present human sphere; that the purpose of life was not the maintenance of well-being, but some intensification of knowledge. Which was, the Controller reflected, quite possibly true. But not, in the present circumstance, admissible. He picked up his pen again, and under the words "Not to be published" drew a second line, thicker and blacker than the first; then sighed. "What fun it would be," he thought, "if one didn't have to think about happiness!" [p. 119]

Clearly, what suffers most under an authoritarian regime with the fixed goal of achieving happiness for its subjects is, as Huxley suggests, the idea that the purpose of life could be anything but the pursuit of happiness: that the enlargement of knowledge, creativity, and spirituality must also have a place in the human psyche.

Huxley's position is well taken. However, behaviorism cannot be ignored totally in favor of humanistic aspirations, because it embodies some truth. Anthony Burgess, in his novel *A Clockwork Orange,* points this out beautifully. In this story, Alex is a juvenile delinquent who is conditioned by the authorities to become incapable of violence, even in self-defense. But now Alex, a victim of conditioning, is not able to care for himself. Politicians create an uproar about this inhumane treatment of Alex, and eventually the government is forced to decondition him into his old violent self. The novel ends with Alex fantasizing renewed acts of violence, but ironically, his violent mentality now is a product of social conditioning itself. Are we, who supposedly grow up "normally" in our society, clockwork oranges? Clearly, socialization is conditioning; without some conditioning, survival is impossible. But how far should the conditioning extend?

A new twist in deterministic psychology is based principally on the idea that the human brain acts like a computer. Psychobiologist Steven Rose (1976) has called this idea "machinomorphia," but the idea has some, if only partial, validity. Computers (the phrase "artificial intelligence" is perhaps more appropriate here) have been improved to such an extent as already to have passed the criterion of being intelligent, according to many researchers. No doubt, many future innovations will be made in this field until artificial intelligence becomes an accepted reality. When we are forced to deal with such a reality, it certainly will not be by such arbitrary rules as Asimov's "laws of robotics," which clearly assert man's supremacy over machines.

That is, if human brains are simply computers, who is to say which computer is superior? Science fiction's response to this kind of question is interesting, aside from philosophical considerations, and will be discussed later.

THE SCHISM AND THE NEW PHYSICS

Upon the success of his book on celestial mechanics, mathematician Pierre Simon de Laplace became famous—so famous that one day the Emperor Napoleon himself summoned him. When Laplace appeared before Napoleon, the Emperor asked, "Monsieur Laplace, you have not mentioned the name of God in your book. Why?" (In those days it was customary to refer to God a few times in any book of knowledge. So Napoleon was curious. Who was this Laplace that he dared not to mention God in his book?) Laplace is supposed to have replied: "Your Majesty, I have not needed that particular hypothesis." With determinism, God is not necessary.

The romantic poets of the eighteenth century reacted unfavorably to such godless adherence to mechanical laws. William Wordsworth, England's poet laureate for a long time, had this to say, in "Cave of Staffa":

> Thanks for the lessons of this spot-fit school
> For the presumptuous thoughts that would assign
> Mechanical laws to agency divine;
> And, measuring heaven by earth, would overrule infinite power.

And another poet of that time, Thomas Campbell, wrote, in "To the Rainbow":

> When science from creation's face
> Enchantment's veil withdraws
> What lovely visions yield their place
> To cold material laws.

The only way poets could arrest the intrusion of science into their vision of reality was to hold on to poetic truth as a separate reality where science doesn't apply. This is the same schism that we observed in the last section, the schism between behaviorism and humanistic psychology, or deterministic science and spirituality. The machine way of looking at the world has created this schism. The division that we see today between scientists and nonscientists is another facet of this schism. And science fiction is right smack in the middle, in the twilight zone between science and the arts; can it do anything to bridge the schism?

Surprisingly, physics itself in its most recent twist, quantum mechanics (originally intended for submicroscopic particles, but now also applied to macroscopic systems such as superconductors), may have given us material with which to find the much-needed bridge that closes the gap—to soften the dichotomy between our truths, the schism between science and our values, between determinism and free will. How this integration will come about is not yet clear, but some of the pieces of the puzzle are falling in place. The major theme of the new physics, as we have seen in Chapter 15, is a picture of matter in the atomic scale that suggests an unsuspected aspect of reality, as cogently stated by one of the architects of quantum mechanics, Werner Heisenberg:

Atoms are not things. The electrons which form an atom's shells are no longer things in the same sense as classical physics, things which could be unambiguously described by concepts like location, velocity, energy, size. When we get down to the atomic level, the objective world in space and time no longer exists, and the mathematical symbols of theoretical physics refer merely to possibilities, not to facts.

If electrons are not things in the classical sense, what are they? Quantum mechanics says that they are wavicles, both waves and particles, both localized and dispersed, as the occasion demands. It is this wave nature of matter—matter waves—that makes quantum mechanics revolutionary. Loosely speaking, if matter is dispersed all over, then reality is not as materially diverse, separate, as it looks; there may very well be an underlying spiritual oneness. Also, if matter is dispersed, then strict causality, the absolute relationship between cause and effect on which determinism is based, does not hold. In that gap of acausality, there is room for free will.

THE MIND AND THE QUANTUM

In the novel *I Will Fear No Evil*, SF writer Robert Heinlein makes a surgical brain transplant the starting point of his story. A wise and canny old man's brain is transplanted into a beautiful young woman's body. And when the brain is transplanted, according to Heinlein, the old man's mind is transplanted with it. Today few readers would question this; backed by a majority of scientists, most of us accept a basically monistic view of the mind-brain—that mind is a property of the brain, not a separate entity. This prevalent monistic view has led to the identity theory—that mind can be defined as the total of brain activity at any given time.

Yet not too long ago philosopher René Descartes was sold on the idea of duality, that mind and body (brain) are separate dual entities: transplanting one would not guarantee the transfer of the other, according to this notion. From today's neurophysiological perspective such a dualistic notion may seem superfluous and mystical, but there are some deep questions here that have to be dealt with.

According to neurophysiology, it is the electrical activities of the nerve cells (neurons) that determine the state and functions of the brain. And the prevalent wisdom has it that the neurons are much like the elements of a computer. As one of the characters of Poul Anderson's novel *Brain Wave* puts it:

"You know how a neurone works? Like a digital computer. It's stimulated by a—a stimulus, fires a signal, and is thereafter inactive for a short time. The next neurone in the nerve [system] gets the signal, fires, and is also briefly inactivated." [p. 13]

And later in the same novel, we find the following comment: "The minute electrical impulses . . . represented neural functioning—sense awareness, motor reaction, thought itself . . . "

But there is a real paradox here. Nobel Laureate physiologist Sir John Eccles, who supports the notion of a modified Cartesian dualism of the mind-brain, expresses the paradox succinctly: "Why do we have to be conscious at all? We can, in principle, explain all our input-output performance in terms of the activities of the neuronal circuits; and consequently consciousness seems to be absolutely unnecessary." What Eccles is saying is that if neuronal circuits act like computer circuits and the brain's behavior is given by a computer-behavioristic model of input-output performance, then why do we seem to possess a very developed mental world? Why do we have mental experiences when there is no need for them? To Eccles, this can only mean that mental experiences such as free will belong to a separate world, outside the physical world, existing independently from it.

Thus, according to Eccles, the way to counter the extreme behaviorist position that the mind-brain acts like a machine and that the mind is an illusion is to postulate a separate mental world. Fortunately, there is another way to "save the mind." A new model of the mind-brain based on quantum mechanics is now being developed by some scientists. The basic idea of this model is a generalized identity postulate: the state of the brain at any given time is the mind, but it is a quantum-mechanical state, mind you—a macroscopic quantum-mechanical state. I am not speaking about the quantum mechanics of the underlying submicroscopic electrons and atoms of the brain—the "normal" quantum behavior in the microstructure does not persist all the way to the macrostructure. Instead, what is being postulated here is a quantum-mechanical order at the macrolevel itself. Strangely, a quantum-mechanical mind-brain admits of both determined behavior *and* free will, but without having to postulate a separate mental entity.

A quantum-mechanical state changes in two ways. One change is a continuous time development of the state in accordance with its equation of motion, the Schrödinger equation. The other is a discontinuous change brought about by measurement, previously referred to as the collapse of the wave function that describes the state. It is this latter type of change that introduces probability and chance in quantum systems. You have seen an example of this in Schrödinger's cat. The state of the cat after the hour, its wave function, is a causal state determined by the dynamics of the system—whether the atom will decay, for which there is a 50 percent probability; thus, the state is an equal fifty-fifty admixture of live cat and dead cat. As absurd as it sounds, this is perfectly causal and determined; no paradox yet. But when we look, we find the cat either dead or alive; only one of the two possibilities materializes at any one time. This materialization of one of several possibilities (each with a definite probability dictated by the dynamics of the system) when we perform an observation on a quantum-mechanical state is what is referred to as the state's collapse. The outcome of the collapse can be predicted only probabilistically. And now paradoxes can occur, because we can ask: who chooses the outcome in an individual case? As you can see, words like "choose" naturally enter. This is the key to finding a quantum-mechanical explanation of mentation based on free will and choice.

Classical identity theorists make one unnecessary and unfounded assumption—that the brain has only one machinery, the classical neural machinery. Recently, a biologist-physicist group at the University of Alberta, Canada—C. I. J. M. Stuart, Y. Takahashi, and H. Umezawa (1979)—has questioned this assumption. These scientists propose that there exists in the brain, apart from the classical neural machinery, another set of elementary modes—they call these corticons—the interaction among which determines the quantum-mechanical state of the brain. They find experimental evidence of this quantum-mechanical nature of the overall brain state in the brain-wave research of neurophysiologist E. Roy John and his collaborators.

You may have read Michael Crichton's SF novel *The Terminal Man*, or seen the movie based on this story. A man (who happened to be a computer specialist) suffered from blackouts due to extensive brain damage caused by an accident. As no conventional cure was possible, neurologists inserted into the "pleasure center" of his brain a number of electrodes that could be activated by a tiny computer implanted in the patient's shoulder. The computer was programmed to activate the electrodes whenever convulsion of the shoulder muscles started. However, the brain liked the pleasure of stimulation so much that it began to induce blackouts at an ever increasing rate. The idea of the novel is based on experiments carried out mostly on rats that suggest the existence of such centers in the brain; rats would sometimes choose the "pleasurable" electrical stimulation in preference to food.

E. Roy John, in his work, also inserts electrodes into the brain, usually a cat's brain. But instead of using the electrodes to stimulate the brain, he uses them to record the mass activity—technically called the evoked potential—of the neurons. And lo! John has discovered that the significance of the mass activity extends well beyond that of the component neurons and parts. John refers to this mass activity of the brain as belonging to the "hyperneuron";

says he: "the content of subjective experience *is* the momentary contour of the hyperneuron." [Restak, 1979]

Stuart *et al.* assume that what John calls the hyperneuron is the overall quantum state that they postulate. In addition, let's assume that the elements of the classical neural machinery act as "detectors" of the quantum-mechanical state of the brain; they are the precipitators of its collapse. If there is a previous memory of an external stimulus and learned behavior corresponding to it, the memory of the learning exists as a quantum state of the brain. Usually, there will be several such memory states, each corresponding to a different learned behavior response related to the same stimulus. Now when an identical stimulus is presented once again, the state of the brain will develop into a combination of these remembered states. The classical neural machinery now precipitates a collapse of this combination quantum state, actualizing only one of the memory states, according to the probability rules dictated by the dynamics of a given situation. The evidence seems to suggest that the collapse triggers a recognition followed by a set of behaviors. This behavior set is deterministic and classical. It is as if a memory record, an "engram," is activated and played back by the recognition. This classical engram has been known to neurophysiologists for some time; only the evidence of the quantum aspects of the brain is new.

In one class of experiments, John (1976) trained cats with two different types of simple stimuli to perform two different behaviors. When a cat was presented with an ambiguous stimulus, it would seem to recognize the new stimulus; the neural pattern corresponding during the learning with one or the other of the conditioned stimuli would "light up," and each recognition would usually be followed by the corresponding learned behavior. Once the recognition occurred, the behavior could be predicted. At the same time, the recognition itself was found to be probabilistic, predictable only in a statistical sense.

This kind of data leads me to believe that there are two complementary machineries in the brain. One is quantum mechanical and corresponds to the overall state of the brain at any given time. The other is classical and corresponds to deterministic behavior after the wave function collapses. The collapse itself is brought about by the interaction of the classical machinery with the quantum-mechanical system, an interaction we normally refer to as a measurement process or detection.

The entire situation resembles the discovery of quantum mechanics for the atom. Initially, any discussion of the internal structure of the atom was considered mystical, as Freeman Dyson (1958) has pointed out; so today is the discussion of the mind considered mystical by staunch behaviorists. The classical approach to the atom was very much like the stimulus-response deterministic approach to the mind-brain, in which the mind-brain is treated as a "black box." Just as, with the development of quantum mechanics, the internal states of the atom could be dealt with, so with the advent of the quantum-mechanical model of the mind-brain, we now can understand the "internal" aspects of the mind-brain, mentation.

If our brain consisted solely of the classical neural machinery with no quantum modality, then clearly the brain's action would be totally deterministic, as the behaviorists contend. Thus, behaviorism corresponds to the classical theory of the brain. The quantum theory suggests a humanistic mind with both free will and determinism. Like the quantum theory in physics, it encompasses classical behaviorism as a limiting case. Consciousness arises because of the interaction of the quantum-mechanical brain states with the classical machinery. The quantum-mechanical, probabilistic nature of brain processes also ensures free will for single events. For a large number of responses to the same stimulus, we might even be able to calculate detailed probabilities for the possible responses, if ever the mechanics were fully uncovered. Also, in specific situations, if the probability is overwhelming for the brain state to develop into one particular learned state, the behavior would appear deterministic.

Let's illustrate once more, through an example from atomic physics, how quantum-mechanical probability implies free will for single events. Imagine an atom in one of its excited states; one of the electrons of the atom is in a higher energy level and now can jump to any of the available lower levels. The quantum mechanics of the atom enables us to calculate the probability of the transition to each of the lower levels for this electron. But it cannot tell us to which one a particular electron will jump, or when. This uncertainty implies that an individual electron has a choice to jump and a choice of any of the lower levels, subject only to overall constraints. The presence of quantum states in the brain implies free will in the same sense. The difference between the electrons and the brain is, of course, the neural machinery. In the case of the electron, there is free will but there is no awareness of it; the electron does not have anything like our classical neural machinery.

The ideas presented here, while providing a model for the mind, make it amply clear that the ego, the mind's "I-ness," depends crucially on the behavioristic component of the brain—the neurophysiology of the neural memory pathways, the engrams. Thus, a baby with only a few engrams inherited from the genes has hardly any ego-awareness. The ego slowly develops (emerges is perhaps a better word) as the neural machinery makes more and more engrams. So from starting this chapter with a debate between humanistic psychology behaviorism, we arrive finally at a solution which acknowledges the validity of both.

Brain transplants in the future? Who knows? Concerning transplanting the mind with the brain, we can say for sure that all the learned engrams and the quantum machinery will go with the brain, and with them all the play of probabilities that we refer to as the mind.

But there is still more to the quantum-mechanical picture. The classical neurophysiologist looks at the mind as a closed entity—mind is "contained," in their contention. On the other hand, as a quantum-mechanical state in the nonlocal hidden-variable interpretation I favor, the mind is open; it is connected to the nonlocal reality of the hidden variables. If you are receptive to this openness of your brain-mind, many science-fictiony phenomena, such as telepathy, become tractable, as discussed in the next chapter.

I am reminded of a couple of cartoons (Shapiro, 1975). In one, a student asks a science professor, "Professor, how do you know so much?" The professor answers, "I open my eyes." This is the way of the scientist, who studies the external reality. But the other cartoon shows a Zen master and his disciple. The disciple asks, "Master, how do you know so much?" The Zen master replies, "I close my eyes." Is it possible to "know" with closed eyes? It is, if the mind doesn't close with the eyes. John Lilly (1977) has documented many experiences in his "isolation tank" (a shelter which filters out most external sensory stimulations) that indicate that our mind is not a closed entity—it's not strictly contained within the skull. On the other hand, Lilly's and others' experiences in the isolation tank are quite commensurate with the quantum-mechanical openness and hidden connection that I believe the mind to have.

chapter eighteen

The Paranormal and Time Travel Stories

What do time travel stories have to do with paranormal phenomena? Well, that depends. From an entirely objective point of view, one can imagine time travel to occur only through some sort of new and unusual physical situation which admits of closed time loops—geodesics in space-time of material particles that close on themselves. Poul Anderson's T-machine (in *The Avatar*) utilizes such an idea, based on the recent work of physicist F. J. Tipler, who showed that a closed time loop can indeed occur in the field of a superfast rotating cylinder. As Tipler is well aware, however, the conditions of such high-speed rotation are impossible to achieve in practice. Another objective idea of time travel involves passing through a rotating black hole, an equally "impossible" idea.

At their root, time travel stories depend on one thing: that past, present, and future times have some sort of "simultaneous" existence. This view of time, called nonlinear time in philosophy, provides the conceptual basis for an alternative perspective for time travel stories. In physics, time is linear, and deviations can occur only through very special situations like those mentioned above. The nonlinearity of time, on the other hand, has a psychological reality. In our psyche, past, present, and future do exist simultaneously, it's as simple as that. Can this form the basis for time travel in the future? I don't know the answer. However, the understanding of parapsychological phenomena such as precognition in terms of Bell's theorem and the quantum picture of the mind-brain is perhaps giving us some hints. There is nothing definite, but rather a glimpse at something that could have much potential. Read on.

TELEPATHY

Mind-to-mind communication between humans is very common in science fiction and usually goes under the name of telepathy. Most SF writers—Asimov, Heinlein, Herbert, Silverberg, van Vogt, Wilhelm, to mention a few—have used the telepathic capabilities of characters to enhance their story lines. The word "esper" is now sometimes found in the SF literature—it denotes people with telepathy and other ESP (extrasensory perception) attributes.

But rarely does an SF writer care (or should I say dare) to offer a "scientific" explanation for the phenomenon of telepathy. One of those rare exceptions, in the novel *Pebbles in the Sky*, is Isaac Asimov. Here is his brainchild:

With the lowering of brain cell resistance, the brain may be able to pick up the magnetic fields induced by the microcurrents of the other's thoughts and reconvert it into similar vibrations in itself. It's the same principle as that of any ordinary recorder. It would be telepathy in every sense of the word—. [p. 304]

The picture of telepathy here is one of creation of an electromagnetic signal in space generated by the "microcurrents of one's thoughts," and the reception and recording of these waves in the telepath's brain. It is the sort of explanation that a scientist would conjure up—telepathy must consist of some kind of electromagnetic wave transmission, if it exists at all; and not coincidentally, Asimov is an accredited scientist. Such a model, however, does have the advantage that it can be tested; we can search for the electromagnetic waves supposedly involved in telepathy with modern technology's supersensitive detectors. Every once in a while, you will find a declaration in the newspaper by some group of scientists that telepathy doesn't exist. If you read their claims carefully, you will discover that what they really are saying is that they have been unable to detect any electromagnetic signals between the subjects that were supposed to have communicated telepathically. But if you point out to these researchers that telepathy may not involve electromagnetic waves, good luck! Should we bother even to research this question unless there is hard scientific evidence for the phenomenon itself? Fortunately, there is a large group of scientists who have been studying the phenomenon itself without preconceived opinions of how it takes place. Let's briefly look at their findings.

First, there are card-reading experiments in which someone reads cards physically in a room while another person reads the same cards telepathically from another room. The results are then compared with results that could be obtained by chance guessing. Many statistically significant data have been found, especially recently with the use of computer programs.

Another set of experiments carried out at Maimonides Medical Center in New York City can properly be called telepathic dream experiments. The telepathic subjects were monitored for electroencephalogram readings and rapid eye movement (which indicates dream sleep) by a technician who awakened them after each period of dream sleep and recorded their dream recollections. While the subjects slept, senders in a distant room viewed randomly selected targets (such as a painting) and attempted to relay telepathically the images of the targets to the sleeping telepaths. Except for normal dream distortions, the subjects' dreams were indeed found to contain images telepathically communicated to them. These experiments have been described in detail in the book *Dream Telepathy* by Ullman, Krippner, and Vaughn (1973), the researchers who took part in the experiments.

Finally, there are the famous distance-viewing experiments performed at the Stanford Research Institute by physicists Russell Targ and Harold Puthoff. One experimenter leaves the laboratory for a previously undisclosed site, signaling his arrival via walkie-talkie; at the same time another experimenter, who stays behind with the telepathic subject, asks the subject to describe and draw a picture of the site being visited. The correlation between the resulting description, especially the drawings, and the visited site has been reported to be unusually high for both "psychic" and ordinary subjects. Targ and Puthoff's (1977) work is described in their book *Mind-Reach*.

In my judgment, these and other experiments now being carried out have scientific credibility. Perhaps they are not definitive yet, but they are indicative—at least to the extent that we should examine whether room exists for such a phenomenon within science. I will offer the following comments from this point of view.

Most interestingly, some of the successful telepathic experiments show that the telepathic ability of people seems to be unhindered by distance. If telepathy were a space-time phenomenon involving signals such as electromagnetic waves, there would have to be some attenuation of the waves with distance, the usual inverse-square-law attenuation being the most likely. No wonder scientists have been unable to detect electromagnetic signals in connection with telepathy; it seems that telepathy doesn't involve such signals.

How does telepathy occur then, if it does? Bell's theorem, with its implied superluminal communication through the dimensions defined by the hidden variables, gives us a possible basis for understanding telepathy. The question Bell's theorem enables us to ask is: if electrons can communicate at a distance without a space-time signal, can we?

In the last chapter, I suggested that our mind-brain operates as a macroscopic quantum-mechanical system. According to hidden-variable theorists, all mind-brains must be connected via the hidden variables, which operate in a nonlocal fashion and show no attenuation with distance. In *Childhood's End*, Arthur C. Clarke speaks of a mind-linkage which is reminiscent of the present picture:

Imagine that every man's mind is an island, surrounded by ocean. Each seems isolated, yet in reality all are linked by the bedrock from which they spring. If the ocean were to vanish, that would be the end of the islands. They would all be part of one continent, but their individuality would have gone.

Telepathy, as you have called it, is something like this. In suitable circumstances minds can merge and share each other's contents, and carry back memories of the experience when they are isolated once more. [p. 176]

I wouldn't describe the quantum-mechanical picture in quite the same way; on the other hand, I don't know quite how to describe it. So instead of trying to describe it any further, let me discuss some aspects of the experimental findings about telepathy that, in fact, support the quantum picture.

Indeed, the quantum basis of telepathy may solve one riddle that has puzzled many researchers in this area for a long time. No telepath ever has been found to be successful all the time, even statistically speaking. Often they have a dry run, in which their ability of mind reading is nonexistent, their successful predictions matching those by chance of any other individual. In the quantum view, with the acausal nature of the phenomenon, such a failure is inherent; since you are not causing telepathy, if it happens, it happens. Just as it is impossible to foresee when a particular electron will make a quantum jump, so it is impossible to foresee when a particular telepath will successfully receive telepathic communication.

It is also to be noticed that none of the scientifically controlled telepathic experiments deals with transfer of specific instructions; instead, they are the instantaneous conveyance of available knowledge from one point of space to another. Although acausal, phenomena perceived this way are not in direct conflict with the causality principle.

Obviously, the present picture makes telepathy a much less spectacular experience than many SF writers would have bargained for. It is surely a far cry from the telepathic scenario envisioned by Joanna Russ in her novel *And Chaos Died,* in which an entire culture is based on a people's ability to read minds. Yet, if the ideas presented here turn out to be correct and there is a "scientific" explanation of telepathy after all, then all of us should be grateful to science fiction for keeping telepathy in public view through a time when there was very little evidence and lots of mistrust for it. The most credit for this respectful attitude goes to John W. Campbell, the late editor of *Analog,* who always gave his wholehearted support to the idea of such extrasensory perceptions as telepathy.

COMPLEMENTARITY, MIND, AND TIME: THE CONCEPTUAL BASIS OF TIME TRAVEL STORIES

While giving a lecture on time to college freshmen, I mentioned that time is a one-way street, always going from the past to the future. One student in the front row was visibly perturbed by what I said. "What about the time tunnel?" he blurted out.

This was back in 1967, when there was a television show by the name of, you guessed it, *The Time Tunnel.* The opening scene of the show had a picture of a tunnel that connected our present with the past. The show was about a couple of astronauts, used as human guinea pigs to experiment with time travel to the past, who got stuck; they could go from one time in the past to another, but could not come back to the present. The producers must have done a fairly good job, since at least one person was convinced by the show that time travel to the past was possible.

But most time travel stories in science fiction use the idea that it is possible to travel in time to both the past and the future. To be sure, different sounding concepts are used; for example, the television show *Star Trek* employs "time warps" to get to the past. However, the underlying assumption—the basic philosophy—behind all this is the idea that past, present, and future all coexist simultaneously.

In one of Isaac Asimov's novels, *The End of Eternity,* 150,000 years of human history are imagined to coexist simultaneously while they are connected by and controlled from a "corridor." Within the closed corridor, an elite group, the "eternals," travels freely between times and makes "reality changes" as it sees fit. The purpose of the changes is to maintain the power of the elite group itself by preserving the status quo. Clearly, there are three somewhat independent ideas here: (1) past, present, and future realities all coexist, (2) there exists a corridor, presumably outside space-time, that connects all these different time realities, and (3) it is possible to travel the corridor between the various time levels and even to interfere in a particular time reality.

Present-day science insists that time is linear—that is, that the course of time is represented by a line, with the successive instants of time taking the shape of points on the line. However, in philosophy (particularly in Eastern thinking) the notion of nonlinear time has persisted. What is nonlinear time? Perhaps I can illustrate with an episode from the *Bhagavad-Gita,* a classic of Indian philosophy. A fierce battle is about to begin between two blood-related factions of the country's ruling elite, a battle to establish the "right," of course. Before the battle begins, Arjuna, the leader of the "right" faction, loses his appetite for battle. He doesn't want to kill his relatives, he says. Now Krishna, the spiritual advisor of the "right" group, must justify all this killing that is about to occur; otherwise, Arjuna won't fight. So Krishna begins to argue his case. At the peak of the argument, he says, "The enemy has already been slain, O Arjuna. I urge you to carry out the causal connection." He then shows Arjuna a glimpse of the future: array after array of the enemy soldiers, dead.

Thus, in the nonlinear view, the future, like the past, has already happened. There is no difference between past and future. SF writers tend to take the same view of time. In *The Dispossessed,* Ursula Le Guin's hero Shevek explains nonlinear time:

"Well, we think that time 'passes,' flows past us, but what if it is we who move forward, from past to future, always discovering the new? It would be a little like reading a book, you see. The book is all there, all at once, between its covers. But if you want to read the story and understand it, you must begin with the first page, and go forward, always in order." [p. 178]

Is there any evidence for nonlinear time? I respectfully submit that there is. But first it is necessary to understand the nature of the evidence in favor of the linear view of time. The basis of the linear view is provided by the arrow of time: the idea that time is a one-way street, the arrow always pointing to the future. Physicists have tried to understand time's arrow through the physics of thermodynamics, cosmology, and electromagnetic wave propagation. However, many insiders feel that the issue is not as settled as it seems from the outside. For example, many physicists question if an arrow of time can be justified on the basis of considerations of entropy or thermodynamics.

The entropy arrow of time is based on the second law of thermodynamics—that entropy always increases; thus, a later time of evolution of the universe is distinguished in principle from an earlier time because the corresponding entropy is greater. Unfortunately, there are some uncertainties regarding the validity of the entropy law in such global matters. Similarly, because the universe expands with time, we can fix time's arrow by looking at the galactic separation, which should increase with time. But this arrow of time is also suspect because there is as yet no universally accepted cosmological theory which allows us to define a "cosmic time" free of any assumption. And even if such a cosmic arrow of time existed, what would its relation be to the entropy arrow of time? Questions like this continue to baffle physicists. Only the electromagnetic arrow of time seems devoid of criticism.

The electromagnetic arrow of time is really a causal arrow of time, grounded in the principle of causality—the idea that cause always precedes effect. In the causal view, the electromagnetic waves that propagate signals through space are always outgoing waves diverging from a source; they are called "retarded" waves. However, mathematically, the equations of physics permit waves that converge onto a source. Such "advanced" waves are not exactly unknown to SF writers, as previously mentioned, since they were used as a rocket propellant in the fantasy novel *A Voyage to Arcturus* by David Lindsay. Lindsay imagines that his voyagers are able to travel to the fantasy planet "Tormance" of the Arcturus star system by using a bottle of advanced waves—where light waves, instead of traveling out, continuously travel in—thus providing new momentum and acceleration for the spaceship. Unfortunately, Lindsay notwithstanding, nobody actually has ever seen a situation where waves converge onto a source, its cause. Obviously, the causal view prevails in our universe, giving us an arrow of time. If we accept causality, we must accept its arrow of time and the linear view of time with it.

SF writers as a group would love to see this lock of causality broken. Instead of cause producing effect, the time travel stories of SF writers often feature effects that bring about a cause. Asimov has used this theme not only in *End of Eternity,* but also in several other stories, in one of which, "The Last Question," mankind develops an effect—a grand computer—that becomes the cause of its own creation.

In connection with causality, the time travel stories that make the most profound impression on readers are the "closed loop" ones employing a cause-effect-cause circle. The masterpiece of such stories is Robert Heinlein's "All You Zombies" (Gunn, 1979). The story line goes like this: a young girl is impregnated by a man who disappears in a hurry. The young woman gives birth to a child by Caesarean section. During the operation, the attending physicians notice that she is a hermaphrodite and are compelled to change her sex: she becomes a he. And in her new identity, she (he) continues to look for the man who impregnated her until she (he) discovers that he was really she (or rather the man that she became) coming from another time frame. There is a little inconsistency here because sex-changed people are sterile. But never mind. We have our first causal circle. Heinlein makes it even more intriguing with yet another twist. The child is born and then is taken twenty years back in the past and left near a foundling home. So the child is the mother is the father. A person has given birth to him/herself. And when that happens, where is the meaning of causality or cause-effect sequence? Here we are faced with the age-old philosophical question: which comes first, the chicken or the egg? A closed loop has no end and no beginning, so who can tell?

One thing is clear. Time travel, if allowed to occur both ways, contradicts causality. The question can be asked: is causality really supreme, or is there a way to circumvent it? Although objects basically are affected only by signals coming from their past, there are, in the submicroscopic domain of nature, the antiparticles (for example, positrons) which travel time in a perverse way, from the future into the past. According to Nobel Laureate physicist Richard Feynman, an electron not only interacts with electrons coming from its past but also with electrons coming from its future (which are designated as positrons). Thus, if there were antimatter galaxies in the universe, we too—like the electron—would be faced with the prospect of communicating with worlds which have a time arrow directed opposite to ours. Then, of course, there are the hypothetical tachyons, faster-than-light particles, which add further to the confusion surrounding causality. These issues are far from being settled in a completely satisfactory fashion. However, nobody has seen either antimatter galaxies or tachyons; and even if such things exist, many physicists believe that it is still possible to save causality. We seem to be stuck with the fact that our physical reality obeys causality.

Where then are the evidences I promised for nonlinear time? Actually, the evidence is right here, within us, in our own minds. The evidence is psychological. In psychology, do we not routinely live in the past when we visualize and reactivate a memory? And do we not also become momentary visitors to our future when we project ourselves forward through our hopes and visions? And if these examples seem too trivial, consider the experiments of neurosurgeon Wilder Penfield (1975) who, during the course of treatment of epileptic patients, applied electrical stimulations via electrodes to various parts of patients' brains. The patients often reported the conscious re-experiencing of vivid memories, auditory sequences, visual images, or both. Penfield and his associate Perrot wrote about these experiences of their patients: "[the] vividness or wealth of detail and the sense of immediacy that goes with them serves to set them apart from the ordinary process of recollection which rarely displays such qualities."

Thus, we have to face a paradox: the objective reality requires that time be linear, but this is not the case with our subjective reality, which admits a certain amount of nonlinearity or the simultaneous existence of past, present, and future. One way to solve the paradox is to assert that time is both linear and nonlinear—that the perceptions are complementary. Ursula Le Guin seems to have reached a similar conclusion in *The Dispossessed*. Her hero, Shevek, talks about two ways to approach time. One is to experience it as a succession, a flow: he calls it the sequential approach. But there is also his simultaneity theory in which there is no past, present, or future—everything is always now. Le Guin's hero also sees the two aspects of time as complementary and attempts to combine them into a theory of "chronosophy."

The complementarity of time can be compared with the two faces of a coin, except that the coin seems to be a Susan B. Anthony dollar and the lookers seem to be male chauvinists. Whenever we are looking at reality through the space-time universe, only one face habitually appears—only the eagle face, only the linear aspect. We can ask: Why? The answer, or at least a clue, comes from physicists Richard Feynman and John Wheeler, as mentioned before. They examined the issue of the electrodynamic arrow of time and pondered over the question of why advanced waves are not manifest in physical reality, although the mathematical equations of electromagnetism do not preclude them. Their conclusion was strange: in every case of wave emission from a source, there are both retarded and advanced waves as the equations of physics demand, but the advanced waves are cancelled by advanced waves sent forth by the universe itself. It is a universal conspiracy that signals never travel backward in time, that effects don't produce causes, and causality veils our perception.

So, if we are to see the other aspect of time, the nonlinearity, we have to look beyond the material universe. In previous chapters, we spoke of hidden variables, a dimension of reality outside physical space-time-matter-motion reality. Perhaps this is where the psychological evidence for nonlinearity originates, because only through ourselves are we connected to this hidden dimension.

In this hidden complementary reality, there is no there, and telepathy—instant signalless communication across space—is possible. Similarly, there is no then, and communication across time is possible—precognition. Precognition means knowing in advance. People who do research on telepathy are naturally curious about precognition. The same Russell Targ and Harold Puthoff, previously mentioned for their distance-viewing experiments that suggest the possibility of telepathy, have found evidence supporting precognition. The evidence is not conclusive but highly suggestive. Again we must warn the reader that precognitive knowledge that is transferable through hidden variables is not a message in the usual sense, it is not causative. It is the conveyance of a knowledge to be experienced and is acausal.

If these views are correct, then the nature of time is one of the issues in which SF writers have made a genuine contribution in insisting on physically weird things like time travel, and playing their elusive games with causality.

So where are we on the three attributes of time travel that Asimov contemplates in *The End of Eternity?* On the first two, the preceding discussion implies a resounding agreement. Yes, Dr. Asimov, past, present, and future do exist simultaneously, in a domain of reality that quantum physicists have called hidden variables and we are accepting as a complementary reality. You can call it a corridor through time, but I don't know if that makes much sense, because, the way I see it, the hidden reality is really timeless. And as for the third item concerning time that you and others want for your story lines—that it is possible to travel physically through this corridor between times—I have misgivings. Because you see, what you want will also mess up causality in the physical universe. I don't think that the universe permits it. It seems to me that all paranormal phenomena must be acausal, without contradicting causality of the physical universe. Still, you score two out of three. Not bad at all!

chapter nineteen

Mysticism in Science Fiction and the New Physics

The last few chapters have made it amply clear that quantum mechanics promises to expand our reality beyond the most daring imaginings of some of us. But the imagination of the SF writer demands more. Some aspects of the SF writer's reality customarily are labeled as mysticism. Does quantum mechanics have anything to say about mysticism? The answer must be affirmative, if only because the acknowledgment is unavoidable that quantum mechanics is itself a bit mystical in places; to understand the quantum-mechanical wavicle, for example, the concept of "transcendence," with its mystical connotation, enters naturally.

But is this relationship with mysticism significant? If you are prepared to accept the hidden variable interpretation of quantum mechanics, the answer is obvious. Because hidden variables are *beyond* the material universe, they are mystical almost by definition. You may argue from history that so was the inside of the atom at one time! But there is a difference in this case. Atoms can be studied by material means, while definitionally this hidden dimension of reality cannot. As explained earlier, Bell's theorem shows that the hidden variables are nonlocal; they belong to dimensions outside of our space-time.

There is hope against this inaccessibility, however, if you consider speculative ideas about such a possible quantum-mechanical theory of mind-brain as that put forth in Chapter 17. If *we* are quantum-mechanical entities, Bell's nonlocality also applies to us; the local confinement of our brain-minds inside our skulls is only an apparent confinement and not absolute. In other words, mystical transcendence becomes a possibility if nonlocality is correct.

Is it useful to consider ideas that rest so much on speculative substrata? Transcendental experiences are inherently subjective experiences, and as such are never the same; they can never be exactly replicated. How can we connect science with mysticism if there is no shared experience in the latter? Isn't it true that the power of science derives from the commonality of its ideas, the reproducibility of its experiments?

To respond to such questions, I think, we must first develop a conceptual basis for describing mystical experiences. Without such a basis, all subjective experiences seem different; but with one, some common ground emerges. Thus, it is advantageous to consider *even* half-baked ideas with the possibility that the process may develop some meaningful base for the discussion of mystical phenomena. I admire science fiction because it is so inclusive of different ideas. And I would like science to operate with similar receptivity.

THE JOY OF ALL THINGS

Roger Zelazny's *Lord of Light* is an SF novel set in a mystical framework. In one episode, the novel's main character pretends to be the enlightened Buddha; however, a disciple of this fake Buddha describes an authentic experience:

"Illustrious One," he [the disciple Sugata] said to him [the fake Buddha] one day, "my life was empty until you revealed to me the True Path. When you received your enlightenment, before you began your teaching, was it like a rush of fire and the roaring of water and you everywhere and a part of everything—the clouds and the trees, the animals in the forest, all people, the snow on the mountaintop and the bones in the field?"
"Yes," said Tathagata [another name of Buddha].
"I, also, know the joy of all things," said Sugata. [p. 111]

The experience of oneness, Sugata's "joy of all things," is what mystics variously have termed enlightenment, satori, samadhi, or moksha. In modern psychology, Abraham Maslow called this state of awareness the "peak" experience, or the longer duration "plateau" experience. It is the experience of a unitive consciousness that underlies all things, according to mystical thought. Thomas Merton used the phrase "transcendental consciousness" to describe this unitive consciousness; Franklin Merrell-Wolff calls it "consciousness without an object"; and in Taoism it is known as the "absolute Tao." To Quakers, it is the "inner light." Carl Jung described the experience of "individuation" as the moment when the finite mind realizes that it is rooted in the "infinite." And Arthur C. Clarke's mysterious "Overmind," in his SF novel *Childhood's End,* is suggestive of this unitive consciousness.

There are many names for both this unitive entity and the experience of that entity. We must recognize that while their meanings vary from tradition to tradition, all cultures seem to agree that the experience represents (1) the highest state of consciousness; (2) transformation of the self, a perception of union with the infinite; and (3) a transcendence, an experienced reality which transcends time and space (White, 1972). Do these ideas have any validity as ideas for scientific investigation? Physicist Fritjof Capra, in *The Tao of Physics,* has explored the parallels of mystical thought and modern scientific thought. Perhaps the reason these parallels have sparked the interest of so many people today is that our present evolution of knowledge and awareness has prepared us for the timely question: are scientists and mystics, working from different perspectives and using different methods of investigation, speaking of the same underlying reality? Are the hidden variables of quantum physics and the unitive consciousness of mysticism equivalent?

Physicists generally have chosen to ignore Capra's message and the thorny questions it arouses. The admission of such questions would be tantamount to the statement that the presently accepted laws of physics (which act as parameters of scientific activity) are limiting laws, similar to the laws of classical mechanics which exclude the consideration of the submicroscopic reality of atoms. If such an admission were made, it would be difficult to continue business-as-usual, present-day physics. Thus, there is a lot of inertia against a change in our underlying metaphysics. Furthermore, modern science thrived by refuting magic and the miraculous; to examine the mystical idea of the oneness of all things, scientists would have to overcome the tried-and-true impulse to reject such notions out of hand. And no slight deterrent to the pursuit of such mystical ideas is the desperate need of the individual ego for the experience of separateness and uniqueness. (If "I" merge into the unitive consciousness, what remains of "me"?)

But these reactions and feelings notwithstanding, something inherent in quantum mechanics suggests an ultimate oneness of all things. According to quantum ideas, not only is matter composed of patterns of probability waves, but these patterns themselves are not isolated. As Ian Watson describes it in his SF novel *Miracle Visitors*:

> When you investigate something, you change the nature of what you investigate. Impossible to intervene without altering reality. Physicists knew that well enough; they called it indeterminacy. [p. 281]

It is the consequence of the uncertainty principle—the principle of indeterminacy—that the subject, while it investigates the object, changes reality, changes the state of the object. And no change in nature is ever one-sided; the subject also changes in the process. It is impossible to consider the subject and the object as separate systems; they are interconnected. Thus, when you acknowledge indeterminacy, you implicitly acknowledge the unitary consciousness, the proposition that all things are part of a web of interconnectedness:

> All things by almighty power
> Hiddenly
> To each other linked are,
> That thou cans't not stir a flower
> Without troubling of a star.
>
> [Francis Thomson,
> "The Mistress of Vision"]

English physicist David Bohm, who took to heart the Einsteinian tradition of discontent with the traditional (not surprisingly, since he was a student of

Einstein), understands and expresses the message of quantum mechanics perfectly (Bohm and Hiley, 1975):

One is led to a new notion of unbroken wholeness which denies the classical idea of analyzability of the world into separately and independently existing parts. We have reversed the usual classical notion that the independent "elementary parts" of the world are the fundamental reality, and the various systems are merely particular contingent forms and arrangements of these parts. Rather, we say that inseparable quantum interconnectedness of the whole universe is the fundamental reality, and that relatively independently behaving parts are merely particular and contingent forms within this whole.

As English physicist James Jeans had said earlier, "The universe looks more like a great thought than a great machine." He too heeded the message of the new physics.

And now with Bell's theorem firmly established to guide us, we have begun to see more clearly into the nature of this "unbroken wholeness" and this "great thought." The wholeness exists as a hidden reality, it is the conglomerate of the hidden variables that, according to Bell's theorem, operate in a dimension outside space-time. The hidden variables which guide the electron's overt statistical behavior and perhaps are responsible too for the statistical response of the mind-brain, giving it a semblance of free will, are like a unitive consciousness. Erwin Schrödinger (1967) knew about this when he wrote:

Consciousness is a singular of which the plural is unknown, and what seems to be a plurality is merely a series of different aspects of this one thing, produced by a deception (the Indian Maya); the same illusion is produced by a gallery of mirrors. [p. 90]

Thus, there seems to be a convergence of the thinking of mystics and physicists, and of psychologists and paranormal researchers, who all seem to assert as a result of their experience that there is an underlying reality that exists beyond the diversity of the material universe. It is exciting to me to find that this same unitive description of reality has made a grand entry in science fiction; the following insight flashed into the mind of Miracle Visitors' protagonist, John Deacon, a psychologist researching the nature of consciousness:

Really, all the "separate" entities and objects in the world were more like amplitude peaks along a continuous line of being. And so the world was dual: it was continuous—yet full of separate objects, too. . . .
Nor was the consciousness that resided in all these separate points of view quite so myriad and separate as it seemed. Rather, it was all one and continuous—yet with innumerable local amplitude peaks, resonances of individual be-

ings each possessing its own unique energy signature, its own signature of personal awareness. [Watson, p. 299]

Sri Aurovinda of India described this unity in diversity as "all in each and each in all." And neurophysiologist Karl Pribram discovered a cogent metaphor from physics to describe it, the metaphor of the hologram.

THE HOLOGRAPHIC MODEL OF REALITY

In ordinary photography, a lens is used to create an image of an object on the film in the camera. In holography, or holistic photography, coherent light (coherent because all its waves dance in step) is used to record the image of an object in the form of an interference pattern called the hologram. The hologram, when viewed with coherent light passing through it, reproduces a three-dimensional image of the original object.

Figure 49a shows the arrangement for making a hologram of an object. The usual source of coherent light is the laser. The beam from a laser is split into two parts. One part of the beam is reflected by the object and subsequently allowed to interfere with the other part (called the reference beam) on a photographic plate. Figure 49b shows a typical interference pattern recorded on a hologram: as you see, there is no resemblance to the original object; by looking at the lines, one cannot guess what object produced such diverse lines. Yet when seen through laser light via the arrangement shown in Figure 49c, the hologram reproduces a three-dimensional image of the original whole.

One fascinating aspect of the hologram is that *every* little part of it has all the information necessary to construct the whole picture. This is because every part of the film received a piece of the light coming from the object, recording its interference with the reference beam. True, if you take a very small piece of the hologram, some of the detail will be lost and the resolution of the picture will not be very good; but even so, you will be able to make out the original object to a surprising extent. Who says a part is not the whole? It is with a hologram.

Since the hologram has this incredibly unique property that every part of it contains all the information to construct the whole, albeit with reduced resolution, neurophysiologist Karl Pribram has introduced the idea of a holographic universe as a metaphor to describe the unity in diversity that we spoke of in the last section. When we look at a hologram with coherent light, we see the whole; but without the benefit of coherent light, there is no whole, there is only a diverse pattern of interference lines. Mathematically, the interference lines represent the unitive reality in the frequency domain, one divided into many. But even so, the pattern is such that every part of it has encoded in it all that is in the whole. Thus, according to Pribram, the material universe

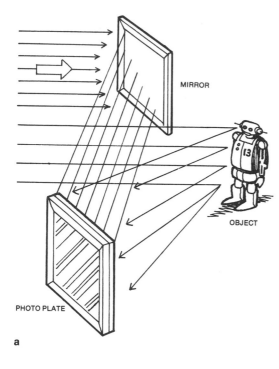

MIRROR

OBJECT

PHOTO PLATE

a

b

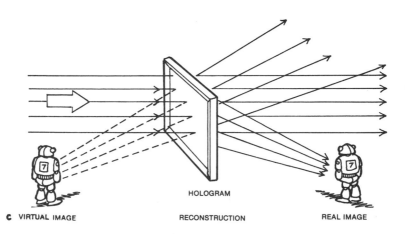

c VIRTUAL IMAGE   HOLOGRAM   RECONSTRUCTION   REAL IMAGE

Figure 49. (a) The making of a hologram. (b) The interference pattern of swirls on a prepared hologram *(artist's concept).* (c) The reconstruction of the image of a hologram.

with all its diversity represents reality in the frequency domain, hiding the unitive reality underneath.

Physicist David Bohm (1977) sees reality likewise as unfolded and enfolded. The unfolded reality is the material universe that we directly experience, it is the "explicate" order of things. But beyond, there is an "implicate" reality, Bohm maintains. The implicate order is enfolded within the explicate order, as similarly, the interference lines of the hologram enfold the image of the whole.

But where is the evidence of this unitive consciousness, this enfolded order of things, this underlying reality? Bell's theorem is suggestive of it, but is not a proof. The quantum wavicles of the submicroscopic world cannot tell us any more about this unitive reality than the mere hint via Bell's theorem. Analogies and metaphors such as the Pribram-Bohm model described above are helpful in making a picture, but a metaphor isn't enough. To see beyond the metaphor, we have to discover the metaphorical coherent light. Where is that coherent light? The alchemical touchstone that transforms ordinary explicate reality into its essential unity?

BEYOND THE STARGATE

Science fiction writers rarely speak of hidden variables or unitive consciousness; instead, they speak of hyperspace. But it has been clear all along to some SF writers that the concept of hyperspace is no different from those other two. In his novel *Star Maker,* Olaf Stapledon talks about "the center of a four dimensional sphere whose curved surface is the three dimensional cosmos." Sounds like a fairly ordinary description of hyperspace, right? But listen to Stapledon when he comes to the description of the Star Maker:

> The star of stars, this star that was indeed the Star Maker, was perceived by me, its cosmical creature, for one moment before its splendour seared my vision. And in that moment I knew that I had indeed seen the very source of all cosmical light and life and mind; and of how much else besides that I had as yet no knowledge. [chap. 13]

What SF writers were really saying became clear to me when I saw/read the classic movie/novel *2001: A Space Odyssey* by Stanley Kubric/Arthur C. Clarke. This story is about an extraordinary journey through a stargate into a tunnel (you could call it the hyperspatial tunnel). But astronaut Bowman, who makes the journey, emerges in a strange world where he is reborn to become the starchild. This is very close to the mystical concept of spiritual rebirth following transcendence to the dimension of the unitive consciousness, or hidden variables, if you prefer. Thus, crossing the stargate is the science fiction metaphor for transcendence.

The important question is: can we transcend at all? Artificial intelligence researcher Doug Hofstadter, in his book (1979) *Gödel, Escher, Bach: An Eternal Golden Braid,* recognizes that whether we can distinguish between artificial and human intelligence perhaps depends ultimately on whether humans can transcend, because machines probably cannot. And Hofstadter, as a behaviorist-rationalist in his point of view, denies the idea that humans can transcend. He thinks that transcendence is a delusion; he cites the example of the dragon in one of Escher's pictures (Figure 50). The dragon believes that it has gone through a hole in the paper and reemerged through another hole, yet anybody outside the space of the dragon can readily see that it is quite hopelessly confined in the plane of the paper—it hasn't *really* gone outside its two-dimensional universe. Perceiving transcendence as such a delusion, Hofstadter sees no deterrent for artificial intelligence of the future to be as potent as human intelligence (and even more so, because of its unlimited potential for doing what it already does better than humans).

Many SF writers are intrigued by this idea that machines will emerge one day as a superior intelligence, one which may perhaps take over the world from us. If you are thinking that this is absurd because "we can always pull the plug," think again. Computers of the future need not depend on us for their power supply; they could be equipped with solar cells and with enough storage capacity to survive without our assistance. However, is it probable that artificial intelligence will one day try to dominate us? Such domination would necessitate a sense of purpose; if somehow such a purpose were programmed into the computer, who knows?

From where I stand, from the point of view of the mind-brain model developed earlier, a computer's intelligence, arising *in toto* from its classical silicon machinery, is totally determined and devoid of real freedom—the connection to cosmic unity. Gregory Benford, in his SF novel *In the Ocean of Night,* puts this succinctly when a member of a machine-intelligence civilization says: "Organic forms are in the universe of things and also reside in the universe of essences. There we cannot go." Benford clearly believes that human beings can transcend, as implied when the same computer character points out to his human audience: "You are a spontaneous product of the universe of things. We are not. This seems to give you . . . windows." Stargate, windows—transcendence again.

So, over Hofstadter's objections, let's assume that we can transcend. The ultimate question that must be asked then is: how do we transcend? How do we find the stargate and pass through it?

TRANSCENDENCE IN SCIENCE FICTION

If you think I am about to provide recipes for transcendence, I must disappoint you. Transcendence is a difficult thing to talk about. Robert A. Hein-

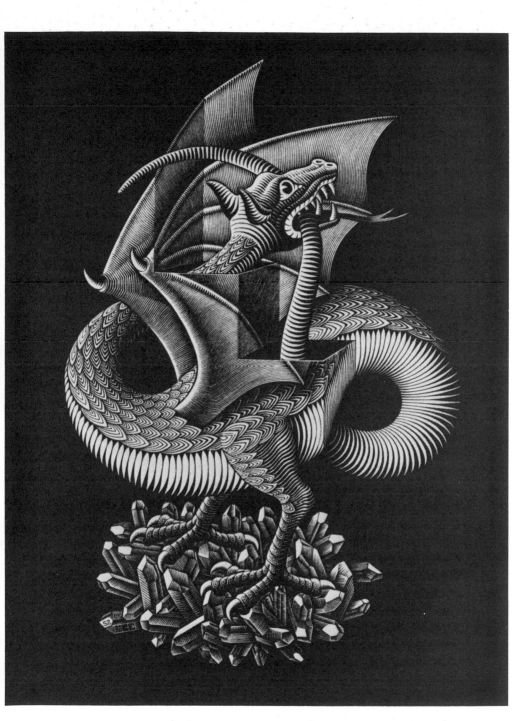

Figure 50. Escher's dragon. Is the attempt to transcend as futile as his attempt to get out of the paper? *(M. C. Escher, Dragon, © Beeldrecht, Amsterdam/V.A.G.A. and Vorpal Gallery, Haags Gemeentemuseum—The Hague, 1981)*

lein, who must be a closet mystic behind his pragmatism, coined the now popular word *grok* to describe the situation. Transcendence is something to experience, to grok, to share. And for this reason, it is very hard to be specific. Yet I promised earlier to try to develop a scientific basis to deal with transcendental phenomena, to attempt to look for commonalities. I believe in keeping promises. So here goes.

One way to handle the whole issue of transcendence is to invoke "outside" intervention. Sri Aurovinda among others conceived the idea of the descent of divinity. In science fiction, Arthur Clarke has used this idea forcefully in his classic novel *Childhood's End.* Clarke imagines a scenario of collective transcendence. In *Childhood's End,* the cosmic power that Clarke calls the Overmind, having selected humanity to become part of itself, sends to earth a group called the Overlords. They eliminate violent conflict between peoples, acting as caretakers of humanity until an entire generation of humans is born with awesome powers that emerge from a bond of universal awareness. Eventually, after the parent generation dies, the new breed destroys the earth as they flex their new powers before joining the Overmind. The display of power in this merger with the Overmind is not only awesome, but to many readers very depressing.

Thus, Clarke looks upon transcendence as a "scientific" phenomenon, objective and deterministic, as a step in the evolution of the intelligent races of the universe. But is it perhaps too objective? Just as electricity is enjoyed by everyone, so is this collective unification of the chosen race. There are no questions to ask, no quest to be made, and no individual choice by the participants. At least electricity one can refuse, but not Nirvana à la Clarke.

Could transcendence be an aspect of evolution generated by collective forces operating on a cosmic scale? Yes, it could, but I feel uneasy about this model. So, while acknowledging the power and logic of such an idea, let me develop an alternative model of transcendence, a model in which transcendence is seen as the outcome of individual choice. This model also can be viewed as "scientific," but only if you allow your definition of science to expand enough to embrace subjective values.

Remember Jerry Cornelius, Michael Moorcock's existentialist antihero who searches for victory in the war of entropy? Jerry doesn't win his battles, Moorcock seems to say in his books, because he himself is the source of entropy. And this indeed is true of most of us; our actions occur along the path of maximum probability, wherever entropy leads us. To win the entropy battle, we have to give up the path that maximizes entropy, the probable path which is mapped by the behavior and beliefs we fashion from our past experiences. English poet Percy Bysshe Shelley put it aptly, in "To the Skylark":

> We live before and after
> And pine for what is not.

If, instead, we start living moment to moment, in the here-now, we can arrest the progress of entropy in our lives. This is the beginning of the path of transcendence, or what anthropologist-philosopher Carlos Castaneda calls the "path of the heart."

As a human born and educated on Mars by the Martian "old ones," Michael is the "stranger" to earth in Robert Heinlein's best-selling novel, *Stranger in a Strange Land*. He is naturally popular with women. One of his girlfriends ("water brothers") responds to a query from her boss, Jubal Hershaw, Michael's eighty-year-old mentor, with this explanation:

"Anne? What's so special about the way that lad kisses?"

Anne looked dreamy, then dimpled. "You should have tried it."

"I'm too old to change. But I'm interested in everything about the boy. Is this something different?"

Anne pondered it. "Yes."

"How?"

"Mike gives a kiss his whole attention."

"Oh, rats! I do myself. Or did."

Anne shook her head. "No, I've been kissed by men who did a very good job. But they don't give kissing their whole attention. They *can't*. No matter how hard they try parts of their minds are on something else. Missing the last bus—or their chances of making the gal—or their own techniques in kissing—or maybe worry about jobs, or money, or will husband or papa or the neighbors catch on—Mike doesn't have technique . . . but when Mike kisses you he isn't doing *anything* else. You're his whole universe . . . and the moment is eternal because he doesn't have any plans and isn't going anywhere. Just kissing you." She shivered. "It's overwhelming." [italics in the original, p. 175]

Contrast that description with a *Playboy* cartoon in which a man, lying beside his nude and obviously amorous girl, is reading *The Joy of Sex* and scolding, "Cut it out. Can't you see I'm reading?" To this guy and millions like him, sex has become cerebral, planned, anything but spontaneous. Like Moorcock's poor Jerry Cornelius, they are lost in their search for the utopia of negentropyland, perfection in sex. But their very acts keep producing more and more entropy, engulfing them in the existential unhappiness of disorder.

However, it would be unfair not to acknowledge that the concept of here-now is experiential and very difficult to grasp intellectually. I remember once giving a physics-and-philosophy lecture on nonlinear time after which a student asked me the meaning of here-now. How I tried to give a satisfactory answer! I referred to relativity, I quoted from Nietzsche's *Vision and Enigma*—but I was unable to satisfy the student. Finally, in exasperation, I said to him, "Maybe you should ask this question of Ram Dass, who wrote a book named

Be Here Now. He seems to *know* what he is writing about." At that moment, it became clear to me that I didn't.

But since we are engaged in an intellectual exercise with the definite purpose of finding a conceptual basis for transcendence, let's detour into the theory of relativity. In relativity, the history of objects (humans included) is pictured in terms of so-called "world lines," lines that signify the object's trajectory in a space-time diagram. A space-time diagram is a graph obtained by plotting time (actually, the speed of light times time) along the vertical axis and spatial distance along the horizontal axis. Now suppose we take an origin and draw the time and space axes through it (Figure 51). By construction, lines at 45° to either axis are the world lines of light, the paths along which light travels. Since material particles travel at a speed slower than light, by construction their world lines are confined within the cone (in three dimensions) defined by the light lines; this cone is called the light cone.

The origin *O* is an observer's here-now point. Just hers, nobody else's— very personal. The part of the light cone behind her is her past light cone; the part before her is her future light cone. All events in the past can affect her when she is at her here-now point, and her actions now will affect her future; but the vast areas of space-time marked no-signals region cannot affect her at her here-now: it does not exist for her—her world is just the area inside the cone. Or is it? Since her past events exist only in her memory, they are a phantom reality. The future exists for her only if she creates it (When's the chapter going to end? Maybe the tea water is ready). Thus, nothing else is real when she is at her here-now point, she is all there is. When Erwin Schrö-dinger said, "I am this whole world," was he speaking from this here-now point? At this point, we are at the edge of our reality, and at the edge of transcendence. And a jump can happen.

Carl Jung sees this jump as the moment of individuation, the moment of ultimate truth, when the ego-self dissolves and the individual psyche discovers its root. Kate Wilhelm has written a unique psychological SF novel, *Margaret and I,* which is really a *gedanken* experiment in Jungian psychology. This is a story of two simultaneous realities, that of the material universe in tandem with that of the unitive consciousness. By telling the story from the viewpoint of heroine Margaret Oliver's unconscious, Wilhelm accomplishes the fantasy touch, that twilight frame of reference which is effective in telling a story that shifts back and forth between two alternate realities. The story then depicts situations that exemplify the *weltanschauung* of Carl Jung, his ideas of personal (the diversity) and collective (the unity) unconscious, synchronicity (the causal, connecting principle which acted as the precursor of the quantum-mechanical view of acausal phenomena adopted in this book), and the "big dreams" that lead to Margaret's experience of the collective unconscious. Wilhelm's story ends with a powerful description of the beginning of the process of individuation, when Margaret and "I" become one:

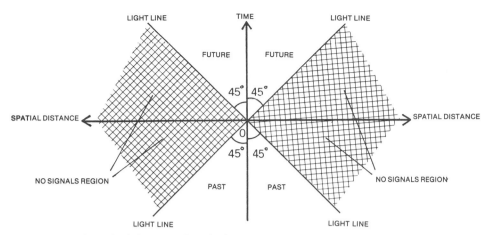

Figure 51. The light cone. O is the here-now point.

Margaret stopped at the doorway and looked at them. It was as if they were behind a transparent substance that she could walk through or not, but they didn't know existed. She-I could see the whole of it from a place that was at once inside the room, and was at a distance from it, so that all of it was visible simultaneously. . . . I looked once at the people behind me, dolls, playing at being alive, and then slipped out to the streak of light, and let myself go up to it, higher and higher. I wove around it, in and out of the cool light that bathed me and purified me and made me tingle with my own aliveness. . . . Margaret turned from the window and for a moment saw the others as I did, frozen in attitudes of laughing and talking, cups and glasses stopped. . . . She smiled inwardly, and she/I left the house, taking nothing from it, needing nothing from anyone there. [pp. 246–247]

But Margaret was fortunate, because circumstances led her to reexamine her own life. For most of us the delusion of one reality continues. Philosopher Ken Wilbur (1980) calls this self-protection of the personal ego "the Atman project." He says that at *every* instant we stand at the crossroads between polarities—life and death, Eros and Thanatos. Thanatos, the archetype of death, drives us toward the cosmic unity by sacrificing the ego. But our ego-self is clever, it perverts the drive into a false one, the ego-death wish becomes a sacrificial ritual, wishing the death of others, or even carrying it through literally. It is not a coincidence that Moorcock's antihero Jerry Cornelius is an assassin.

But so far we are speaking in generalities; are there any specifics? Recent research is making it quite plausible that what most of us experience during creative and meditative moments are milestones in our journey along two complementary paths to transcendence. Psychologist Roland Fischer portrays these complementary pathways in the form of a diagram (Figure 52). Recent understanding of the brain's neurochemistry has helped considerably in clarifying Fischer's idea. For example, it is now widely believed that during meditation, parts of the brain have a relatively high amount of the neurochemical serotonin, which has the effect of slowing down the brain's neural activity (as in sleep). A similar effect occurs in the isolation tank experiences pioneered by John Lilly (1977). In contrast, the presence of anxiety in the creative state is now well documented. Creative anxiety may be the result of overproduction of an excitatory neurochemical such as acetylcholine. This predominance of one type of chemical over another produces the difference in sensations between the two pathways to transcendence, between the creative experiences of the physicist or science fiction writer, on the one hand, and the meditative experiences of the mystic on the other. The excitatory pathway works by jamming the brain with too much activity; in the inhibitory pathway, too little activity or sensory isolation seems to be the key. Hence, the difference in the experiences. But ultimately, according to Fischer, both pathways can lead to the same transcendental state, and as indicated in the bottom of Figure 52, Fischer even theorizes that one may be able to cross over from one side to the other, from samadhi to rapture, and vice versa.

Psychologist Charles Tart of the University of California speaks of state-dependent psychologies, because, with the kind of altered states of consciousness that we are dealing with in creativity or meditation, the view of reality clearly differs in these different states. In *Miracle Visitors,* SF novelist Ian Watson puts it this way:

Each altered state of consciousness possessed its own internal logic, different to a greater or lesser extent from the logic of ordinary baseline consciousness.

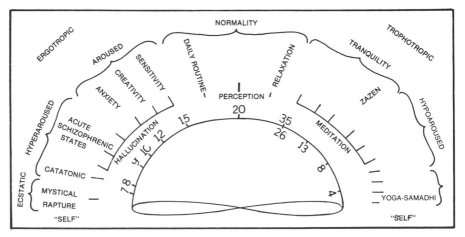

Figure 52. Neurochemistry and Nirvana according to Roland Fischer. *(After Roland Fischer)*

Each altered state had a rationality that was perfectly coherent, yet could be wholly alien to everyday reason. This was why it was so difficult for the traditionally 'objective' scientist to study these states. [p. 26]

To make inroads of understanding in this new domain of reality, the explorer must expand the traditional view of his laboratory as being separate from himself; he must agree to regard himself as part of the experiment. Like the scientist-hero Deacon of *Miracle Visitors*, the explorer must allow himself to experience the altered states and must extend his science from the merely experimental to include the experiential as well.

In the model that we have for the mind-brain, the free will of the mind comes from the quantum nature of the system of which it is part. But when we accept nonlocal hidden variables à la Bell's theorem, the mind-brain is recognized to have the hidden connection. I have discussed before how these connections may be our vital instruments for paranormal ability. But ultimately, the most astounding aspect of these hidden variables is that once we admit them, there is no more free will. The hidden variables determine what we, at the level of material reality, interpret as free will. Thus, the ultimate choice of an explorer experimenting with transcendence is this: he can stay with the space-time-matter-motion reality and feel gratified that he has free will and ego-self; alternatively, he can declare all this to be maya (illusion), give up the ego, and seek to relate to the cosmic self. It's the passage from knowing to being. In this passage, science and religion, physics and mysticism, tend to merge.

One of the key concepts in the path of transcendence has always been the surrendering of the ego. This is why there is so much stress in mystical practices on faith, gurus, guides, or khidr (in Sufism). Ian Watson describes the final surrender of John Deacon to his khidr thus:

"Where is this place?" he asked, touching the map.
"Right here, John," smiled the stranger. "Right now! You can enter it anywhere. Only you can't return again—except extraordinarily."
The map was a one-way membrane leading to another state. . . .
"You too can lose your name now, if you wish." The stranger took him by the arm.
"I wish it," said the one who had been called John Deacon.
The map stretched vastly now, becoming in reality what it had only hitherto been the emblem of. As it became fully real to him, he stepped inside it with the stranger—who was no longer strange at all. . . . [p. 334]

Ultimately, transcendence is a decision to join the dance, a very special dance, because there is no stage, there is no audience, nobody is watching—or perhaps everybody is watching—and there is only the dance:

Neither from nor towards; at the still point
There the dance is.
But neither arrest nor movement. And do not call it fixity.
Where past and future are gathered . . .
Except for the point, the still point,
There would be no dance, and there is only the dance.

[T. S. Eliot, "Burnt Norton")

Bibliography

Alexander, Thea. *2150 A.D.* New York: Warner, 1976.

Anderson, Poul. *The Avatar.* New York: Berkley, 1978.

————. *Brain Wave.* New York: Ballantine, 1954.

————. *Ensign Flandry.* New York: Ace, 1966.

————. *Tau Zero.* New York: Berkley, 1970.

Anthony, Piers. *Battle Circle.* New York: Avon, 1978.

————. *Macroscope.* New York: Avon, 1969.

Asimov, Isaac. *End of Eternity.* Greenwich, Conn.: Fawcett Crest, 1955.

————. *Fantastic Voyage.* New York: Bantam, 1966.

————. *Foundation Trilogy.* New York: Avon, 1974.

————. *The Gods Themselves.* Greenwich, Conn.: Fawcett Crest, 1972.

————. *Pebbles in the Sky.* In the collection *Triangle.* Garden City, N.Y.: Doubleday, 1951.

————. *The Stars, Like Dust.* In the collection *Triangle.* Garden City, N.Y: Doubleday, 1951.

Bell, John S. "On the Einstein Podolsky Rosen Paradox." *Physics 1* (1965): 195–200.

Benford, Gregory. *In the Ocean of Night.* New York: Dell, 1978.

Berry, Adrian. *The Iron Sun.* New York: Warner, 1977.

Bester, Alfred. *The Stars My Destination.* New York: Berkley, 1975.

Blish, James. *Spock Must Die.* New York: Bantam, 1975.

————. *The Triumph of Time.* In the collection *Cities in Flight.* Garden City, N.Y.: Doubleday, 1970.

————. *The Best of James Blish.* New York: Ballantine, 1979.

Bohm, David. *Fragmentation and Wholeness.* Atlantic Highlands, N.J.: Humanities Press, 1977.

Bohm, D., and Hiley, B. "On the Intuitive Understanding of Nonlocality as Implied by Quantum Theory." *Foundations of Physics* 5 (1975): 93–109.

Bolen, Jean Shinoda. *The Tao of Psychology.* New York: Harper & Row, 1979.

Bova, Ben, ed. *The Science Fiction Hall of Fame*, 2A. New York: Garden City, N.Y.: 1973.

Bradbury, Ray. *Fahrenheit 451.* New York: Ballantine, 1973.

Brown, Fred. *What Mad Universe?* London: Pennyfarthing, 1978.

Brunner, John. *The Sheep Look Up.* New York: Ballantine, 1972.

Burger, Dionys. *Sphereland.* New York: Crowell, 1969.

Burgess, Anthony. *A Clockwork Orange.* New York: Ballantine, 1972.

Cameron, A. G. W., ed. *Interstellar Communication*. New York: W. A. Benjamin, 1963.

Campbell, John W. *Who Goes There?* In the collection *The Best of John W. Campbell*. Garden City, N.Y.: Doubleday, 1976.

Capra, Fritjof. *The Tao of Physics*. Berkeley: Shambhala, 1975.

Clarke, Arthur C. *Childhood's End*. New York: Ballantine, 1974.

————. *The Fountains of Paradise*. New York: Harcourt Brace Jovanovich, 1979.

————. *Imperial Earth*. New York: Harcourt Brace Jovanovich, 1976.

————. *Profiles of the Future*. New York: Bantam, 1972.

————. *Rendezvous with Rama*. New York: Ballantine, 1974.

————. *Tales from the White Hart*. New York: Ballantine, 1967.

————. *2001: A Space Odyssey*. New York: New American Library, 1968.

————. *The Wind from the Sun: Stories of the Space Age*. New York: New American Library, 1973.

Clement, Hal. *Mission of Gravity*. New York: Ballantine, 1978.

Cournos, John, ed. *American Short Stories of the Nineteenth Century*. New York: Dutton, 1967.

Crichton, Michael. *The Terminal Man*. New York: Bantam, 1974.

D'Espagnat, B. "The Quantum Theory and Reality." *Scientific American*, November 1979, p. 158.

DeWitt, B. S. "Quantum Mechanics and Reality." *Physics Today* 23 (1970): 30.

Dick, Philip K. *The Man in the High Castle*. New York: Berkley, 1974.

————. *Do Androids Dream of Electric Sheep?* Garden City, N.Y.: Doubleday, 1968.

Dickson, Gordon. *Mission to Universe*. New York: Ballantine, 1977.

Dyson, Freeman J. "Innovations in Physics." *Scientific American* 199 (September 1958): 74–84.

————. "Time Without End: Physics and Biology in an Open Universe." *Reviews of Modern Physics* 51 (1979): 447.

Eccles, Sir John. *Brain and Conscious Experience*. New York: Springer, 1966.

Einstein, A., and Infeld, L. *The Evolution of Physics*. New York: Simon & Schuster, 1960.

Eliot, T. S. *Four Quartets*. New York: Harcourt Brace Jovanovich, 1943.

Feynman, R. P., Leighton, R. B., and Sands, M. *The Feynman Lectures on Physics*. Reading, Mass.: Addison Wesley, 1964.

Glut, Donald F. *The Empire Strikes Back*. New York: Ballantine, 1980.

Gunn, James E. *The Listeners*. New York: Signet, 1974.

————, ed. *The Road to Science Fiction #3*. New York: New American Library, 1979.

Haldeman, Joe. *The Forever War*. New York: St. Martin's Press, 1974.

Harness, Charles L. *Firebird*. New York: Pocket Books, 1981.

Heinlein, Robert A. *I Will Fear No Evil*. New York: Berkley, 1970.

————. *The Moon Is a Harsh Mistress*. New York: Berkley, 1968.

————. *Space Cadet*. New York: Scribner's, 1950.

————. *Stranger in a Strange Land*. New York: Berkley, 1968.

————. *Time for the Stars*. New York: Ace, 1965.

Herbert, Frank. *Dune*. New York: Chilton, 1965.

Hofstadter, D. J. *Gödel, Escher, Bach: An Eternal Golden Braid*. New York: Basic, 1979.

Hogan, J. P. *The Genesis Machine*. New York: Ballantine, 1978.

————. *Inherit the Stars*. New York: Ballantine, 1977.

Hoyle, Fred. *The Black Cloud*. New York: New American Library, 1973.

Hoyle, Fred, and Elliot, John. *A for Andromeda*. Greenwich, Conn: Fawcett Crest, 1964.

Hoyle, Fred, and Wickramsinghe, Chandra. *Lifecloud*. New York: Harper & Row, 1979.

Huxley, Aldous. *Brave New World*. New York: Harper & Row, 1969.

John, E. Roy. "How the Brain Works—A New Theory." *Psychology Today*, May 1976.

Jung, C. G. Aion. *Collected Works*, 9. Princeton, N.J.: Princeton University Press, 1951.

Jung, C. G., and Pauli, W. *The Interpretation and Nature of the Psyche*. New York: Pantheon, 1955.

Knight, Damon. *Beyond the Barrier*. Garden City, N.Y.: Doubleday, 1964.

————. *In Search of Wonder*. Chicago: Advent, 1967.

————, ed. *Turning Points*. New York: Harper & Row, 1977.

Le Guin, Ursula. *The Dispossessed*. New York: Avon, 1974.

Lilly, John. *The Deep Self*. New York: Warner, 1977.

————. *The Scientist*. New York: Lippincott, 1978.

Lindsay, David. *A Voyage to Arcturus*. New York: Ballantine, 1974.

Maslow, Abraham. *The Psychology of Science*. New York: Harper & Row, 1966.

Matheson, Richard. *The Shrinking Man*. New York: Bantam, 1969.

Miller, Walter. *A Canticle for Liebowitz*. New York: Bantam, 1961.

Minkowski, H.; Einstein, A.; Lorentz, H. A.; and Weil, H. *The Principle of Relativity*. New York: Dover, 1923.

Moffit, Donald. *The Jupiter Theft*. New York: Ballantine, 1977.

Moorcock, Michael. *The Cornelius Chronicles*. New York: Avon, 1977.

————. *The Final Programme*. New York: Avon, 1968.

Nikhilananda, Swami. *The Upanishads*. New York: Harper & Row, 1964.

Niven, Larry. *All the Myriad Ways*. New York: Ballantine, 1971.

————. *Neutron Star*. New York: Ballantine, 1968.

————. *Ringworld*. New York: Ballantine, 1981.

————. *A World out of Time*. New York: Ballantine, 1977.

Niven, Larry, and Pournelle, Jerry. *Lucifer's Hammer*. Greenwich, Conn.: Fawcett Crest, 1977.

————. *The Mote in God's Eye*. New York: Pocket Books, 1974.

O'Neill, Gerard K. *The High Frontier*. New York: Bantam, 1978.

Oppenheimer, J. R. *Science and the Common Understanding*. New York: Simon & Schuster, 1954.

Penfield, Wilder, et al. *The Mystery of the Mind: A Critical Study of Consciousness and the Human Brain*. Princeton, N.J.: Princeton University Press, 1975.

Pohl, Frederik. *Gateway*. New York: Ballantine, 1978.

Radhakrishnan, S. *The Bhagavad-Gita*. New York: Harper & Row, 1973.

Restak, R. M. *The Brain: The Last Frontier*. Garden City, N.Y.: Doubleday, 1979.

Robinson, Jeanne and Spider. *Stardance*. New York: Dell, 1980.

Roddenbury, Gene. *Star Trek, the Motion Picture*. New York: Pocket Books, 1979.

Rose, Steven. *The Conscious Brain*. New York: Random House, 1976.

Russ, Joanna. *And Chaos Died*. New York: Berkley, 1979.

Sagan, Carl, ed. *Communication with Extraterrestrial Intelligence*. Cambridge, Mass.: M.I.T. Press, 1973.

————. *The Dragons of Eden*. New York: Random House, 1977.

Scholes, Robert, and Rabkin, Eric. *Science Fiction*. New York: Oxford, 1977.

Schreiber, Flora R. *Sybil*. New York: Warner Books, 1974.

Schrödinger, Erwin. *What Is Life?* Cambridge: Cambridge University Press, 1967.

Serviss, Garrett P. *A Columbus of Space*. Westport, Conn.: Hyperion, 1973.

Shapiro, Deane H., Jr. *Precision Nirvana*. Englewood Cliffs, N.J.: Prentice-Hall, 1978.

Shaw, Bob. *Orbitsville*. New York: Ace, 1982.

————. *Other Days, Other Eyes*. New York: Ace, 1972.

Shea, Robert J., and Wilson, Robert Anton. *Illuminatus*. New York: Dell, 1975.

Silverberg, Robert. *To Open the Sky*. New York: Berkley, 1978.

Simak, Clifford D. *Way Station*. New York: Ballantine, 1980.

Skinner, B. F. *Walden Two*. New York: Macmillan, 1962.

Spinrad, Norman. *Agents of Chaos*. New York: Popular Library, 1978.

Stapledon, Olaf. *Star Maker*. Middlesex: Penguin, 1937.

Stapp, Henry. "Are Superluminal Connections Necessary?" *Nuovo Cimento* 408 (1977): 191.

Stevenson, R. L. *The Strange Case of Dr. Jekyll and Mr. Hyde*. New York: Penguin, 1980.

Stuart, C. I. J. M.; Takahashi, Y.; and Umezawa, H. "Mixed System Brain Dynamics: Neural Memory as a Macroscopic Ordered State." *Foundations of Physics* 9 (1979): 301–327.

Targ, Russell, and Puthoff, Harold. *Mind-Reach*. New York: Delta, 1977.

Thigpen, Corbett H., and Cleckley, Hervey M. *Three Faces of Eve*. New York: Popular Library, 1974.

Ullman, M.; Krippner, S.; and Vaughn, A. *Dream Telepathy*. New York: Macmillan, 1973.

van Vogt, A. E. *Slan*. New York: Berkley, 1975.

Varley, John. *The Ophiuchi Hotline*. New York: Dial Press, 1977.

Verne, Jules. *Journey to the Moon (De la Terre à la Lune)*. New York: Airmont, 1964.

—————. *Round the Moon*. New York: Airmont, 1968.

—————. *Twenty Thousand Leagues Under the Sea*. New York: New American Library, 1969.

Vonnegut, Kurt, Jr. *God Bless You, Mr. Rosewater*. New York: Dell, 1974.

—————. *Sirens of Titan*. New York: Dell, 1971.

Watson, Ian. *Miracle Visitors*. New York: Ace, 1978.

Wells, H. G. *Experiment in Autobiography*. New York: Macmillan, 1934.

—————. *The First Men in the Moon*. New York: Lancer, 1968.

—————. *The Invisible Man*. New York: Bentley, 1980.

—————. *The Time Machine*. New York: Oxford, 1977.

—————. *War of the Worlds*. New York: Airmont, 1964.

White, John, ed. *The Highest State of Consciousness*. Garden City, N.Y.: Doubleday, 1972.

Wigner, Eugene. *Symmetries and Reflections*. Bloomington, Ind.: Indiana University Press, 1967.

Wilbur, Ken. *The Atman Project*. Wheaton, Ill.: Theosophical Publishing House, 1980.

Wilhelm, Kate. *Margaret and I*. New York: Pocket Books, 1980.

—————. *Where Late the Sweet Birds Sang*. New York: Pocket Books, 1977.

Zelazny, Roger. *Lord of Light*. New York: Avon, 1967.

Zukav, Gary. *The Dancing Wu Li Masters*. New York: Morrow, 1979.

Index

Permissions Acknowledgments

Grateful acknowledgment is made for permission to reprint:

Figure 39 (*Circle Limit III*) and Figure 50 (*Dragon*): Copyright © Beeldrecht. Amsterdam/ V.A.G.A., New York, Collection Haags Gemeentemuseum, The Hague, 1981; photographs courtesy of Vorpal Gallery.

"The Tuning Fork," by Louise McNeill from the *Christian Science Monitor:* Copyright © 1977 The Christian Science Publishing Society. All rights reserved. Reprinted by permission.

Excerpt from "Common Time" in *The Best of James Blish*, by James Blish, edited by Lester del Rey: Copyright © 1979 by Random House, Inc. Excerpt from *The Jupiter Theft,* by Donald Moffitt: Copyright © 1977 by Donald Moffitt. Excerpt from *Brain Wave*, by Poul Anderson: Copyright 1954 by Poul Anderson. Excerpt from *A World Out of Time*, by Larry Niven: Copyright © 1976 by Larry Niven. Excerpt from *Nerves*, by Lester del Rey: Copyright © 1956, 1976 by Lester del Rey. Excerpt from *Gateway*, by Frederik Pohl: Copyright © 1976, 1977 by Frederik Pohl. Reprinted by permission of Ballantine Books, a Division of Random House, Inc.

Excerpt from *The Gods Themselves*, by Isaac Asimov: Copyright © 1972 by Isaac Asimov. Excerpt from *Tau Zero*, by Poul Anderson: Copyright © 1967 by Galaxy Publishing Co., copyright © 1970 by Poul Anderson. Excerpt from *Pebbles in the Sky*, by Isaac Asimov: Copyright 1950 by Isaac Asimov; and excerpts from *The Stars, Like Dust*, by Isaac Asimov: Copyright 1951 by Isaac Asimov. Reprinted by permission of Doubleday & Company, Inc.

Excerpt from *Walden Two*, by B. F. Skinner: Copyright 1948, renewed 1976 by B. F. Skinner. Reprinted by permission of Macmillan Publishing Company.

Excerpts from *The Fountains of Paradise*, by Arthur C. Clarke; excerpts from *Imperial Earth*, by Arthur C. Clarke: Copyright © 1976 by Arthur C. Clarke. Excerpts from *Rendezvous with Rama*, by Arthur C. Clarke: Copyright © 1973 by Arthur C. Clarke. Excerpt from "Burnt Norton," in *Four Quartets*, by T. S. Eliot. Reprinted by permission of Harcourt Brace Jovanovich, Inc.

Excerpt from *Deadline*, by Cleve Cartmill: Copyright 1944 by The Condé Nast Publications, Inc., renewed 1972 by The Condé Nast Publications, Inc. Reprinted by permission of Davis Publications, Inc.

Excerpt from *A Canticle for Liebowitz*, by Walter Miller: Copyright © 1955 by Walter Miller. Reprinted by permission of the Harold Matson Company, Inc.

Excerpt from *2150 A.D.*, by Thea Alexander: Copyright © 1972, 1976 by Thea Alexander. Reprinted by permission of Warner Books/New York.

Excerpt from *Brave New World*, by Aldous Huxley: Copyright 1932, 1960 by Aldous Huxley. Excerpt from *The Scientist*, by John Lilly (J. B. Lippincott, Publishers): Copyright © 1978 by Human Software, Inc. Excerpt from *The Dispossessed*, by Ursula K. Le Guin: Copyright © 1974 by Ursula K. Le Guin. Excerpts from *The Black Cloud*, by Fred Hoyle: Copyright © 1957 by Fred Hoyle. Reprinted by permission of Harper & Row, Publishers, Inc.

Figures 25 and 32 from *The Concepts of Physics*, by Amit Goswami: Reprinted by permission of D. C. Heath and Company, Lexington, Mass., 1979.

Excerpts from *Mission to Universe*, by Gordon R. Dickson: Copyright © 1965, 1977 by Gordon R. Dickson. Reprinted by permission of the author.

Excerpt from *The Stars My Destination*, by Alfred Bester: Copyright © 1956 by Alfred Bester. Excerpt from *Avatar*, by Poul Anderson: Copyright © 1978 by Poul Anderson. Reprinted by permission of Berkley Publishing Corporation, 200 Madison Avenue, New York, N.Y. 10016.

Excerpt from *Firebird*, by Charles Harness: Copyright © 1981 by Charles L. Harness. Reprinted by permission of Pocket Books, Inc., a Division of Simon & Schuster, Inc.

Excerpt from *The Forever War*, by Joe W. Haldeman: Copyright © 1974 by Joe W. Haldeman. Reprinted by permission of St. Martin's Press, Inc.

Excerpt from *The Sirens of Titan*, by Kurt Vonnegut, Jr: Copyright © 1959 by Kurt Vonnegut, Jr. Reprinted by permission of Delacorte Press/Seymour Lawrence.

Excerpts from *Stardance,* by Spider and Jeanne Robinson: Copyright © 1977, 1978, 1979 by Spider Robinson and Jeanne Robinson. Reprinted by permission of The Dial Press.

Excerpt from *Dune,* by Frank Herbert: Copyright © 1965 by Frank Herbert. Reprinted by permission of Chilton Book Company, Radnor, PA.

Excerpt from *Ensign Flandry,* by Poul Anderson: Copyright © 1966 by Poul Anderson. Excerpt from *Orbitsville,* by Bob Shaw: Copyright © 1975 by Bob Shaw. Excerpt from *Miracle Visitors,* by Ian Watson: Copyright © 1978 by Ian Watson. Reprinted by permission of Ace Books, a Division of Charter Communications, Inc.

Excerpt from *2001: A Space Odyssey,* by Arthur C. Clarke: Copyright © 1968 by Arthur C. Clarke and Polaris Productions. Reprinted by permission of The New American Library, Inc.

Excerpts from *Neutron Star,* by Larry Niven: Reprinted by permission of the author.

Excerpt from *Lucifer's Hammer,* by Larry Niven and Jerry Pournelle (Fawcett Crest): Copyright © 1977 by Larry Niven and Jerry Pournelle. Reprinted by permission of Jerry Pournelle.

Excerpt from *The Invisible Man,* by H. G. Wells: Reprinted by permission of the author's estate.

Excerpt from *Do Androids Dream of Electric Sheep?,* by Philip K. Dick: Copyright © 1968 by Philip K. Dick. Used by permission of the author's estate and its agents, Scott Meredith Literary Agency, Inc., 845 Third Avenue, New York, N.Y. 10022.

Excerpt from "Kyrie," by Poul Anderson, from *Black Holes,* edited by Jerry Pournelle (Fawcett Crest): Reprinted by permission of Poul Anderson.

Excerpt from "Thunder and Roses," by Theodore Sturgeon from *Astounding Analog Reader,* edited by Harry Hanson and Brian W. Aldis (Doubleday): Reprinted by permission of Theodore Sturgeon.

Excerpt from *Spock Must Die,* by James Blish: Copyright © 1970 by Bantam Books, Inc., copyright © 1970 by Paramount Corporation. Reprinted by permission of Bantam Books, Inc.

Excerpt from *Silence, Please,* by Arthur C. Clarke: Copyright 1954 by Popular Publications, Inc. Reprinted by permission of the author and the author's agents, Scott Meredith Literary Agency, Inc., 845 Third Avenue, New York, N.Y. 10022.

Excerpt from *To Open the Sky,* by Robert Silverberg: Reprinted by permission of the author and the author's agent, Kirby McCauley Limited.

Excerpts from *Space Cadet,* by Robert A. Heinlein: Copyright 1948 by Robert A. Heinlein, copyright renewed. Reprinted by permission of Charles Scribner's Sons.